EDUCATIONAL TRENDS IN THE 1970s

A Quantitative Analysis

ORGANISATION FOR ECONOMIC CO-OPERATION AND DEVELOPMENT

Pursuant to article 1 of the Convention signed in Paris on 14th December, 1960, and which came into force on 30th September, 1961, the Organisation for Economic Co-operation and Development (OECD) shall promote policies designed:

- to achieve the highest sustainable economic growth and employment and a rising standard of living in Member countries, while maintaining financial stability, and thus to contribute to the development of the world economy;
- to contribute to sound economic expansion in Member as well as non-member countries in the process of economic development; and
- to contribute to the expansion of world trade on a multilateral, non-discriminatory basis in accordance with international obligations.

The Signatories of the Convention on the OECD are Austria, Belgium, Canada, Denmark, France, the Federal Republic of Germany, Greece, Iceland, Ireland, Italy, Luxembourg, the Netherlands, Norway, Portugal, Spain, Sweden, Switzerland, Turkey, the United Kingdom and the United States. The following countries acceded subsequently to this Convention (the dates are those on which the instruments of accession were deposited): Japan (28th April, 1964), Finland (28th January, 1969), Australia (7th June, 1971) and New Zealand (29th May, 1973).

The Socialist Federal Republic of Yugoslavia takes part in certain work of the OECD (agreement of 28th October, 1961).

Publié en français sous le titre :

TENDANCES DE L'ENSEIGNEMENT
DANS LES ANNÉES 70

Une analyse quantitative

This report, which has been prepared by the Secretariat under the programme of work of the Education Committee, reviews the main quantitative trends in educational development in Member countries during the 1970s. The data underlying the analysis of significant changes in education during this period are set out in the annex.

The report is published on the responsibility of the Secretary-General and does not necessarily reflect the views of Member governments.

Also available

POLICIES FOR HIGHER EDUCATION IN THE 1980s. Intergovernmental Conference OECD, 12th-14th October, 1981 (July 1983)
(91 83 03 1) ISBN 92-64-12448-9 234 pages £9.50 US$19.00 F95.00

EDUCATION AND WORK: THE VIEWS OF THE YOUNG (July 1983)
(96 83 02 1) ISBN 92-64-12464-0 122 pages £4.80 US$9.75 F48.00

COMPULSORY SCHOOLING IN A CHANGING WORLD (April 1983)
(91 83 02 1) ISBN 92-64-12430-6 150 pages £8.50 US$17.00 F85.00

THE FUTURE OF VOCATIONAL EDUCATION AND TRAINING. "Document" Series (March 1983)
(91 83 01 1) ISBN 91-64-12425-X 70 pages £3.30 US$6.50 F33.00

EDUCATIONAL STATISTICS IN OECD COUNTRIES. "Document" Series (February 1981) bilingual
(91 81 04 3) ISBN 92-64-02119-1 232 pages £4.80 US$12.00 F48.00

Prices charged at the OECD Publications Office.

THE OECD CATALOGUE OF PUBLICATIONS and supplements will be sent free of charge on request addressed either to OECD Publications Office, 2, rue André-Pascal, 75775 PARIS CEDEX 16, or to the OECD Sales Agent in your country.

TABLE OF CONTENTS

INTRODUCTION

This report presents statistics on the development of education in OECD countries during the seventies -- a period marked by a dramatic change in the position of education, from one of growth at the beginning of the decade in the wake of the massive expansion of the sixties, to one of stagnation and then of contraction as the decade advanced. Behind this change lie broader economic, social and demographic factors, the impact of which will be apparent in the analytical commentary which precedes the statistical data.

The data in this report refer to sixteen (1) of the OECD countries. These constitute 90 per cent of the population of the whole area and therefore are sufficiently representative of all countries. These data have been put together from national publications at the disposal of the Secretariat and then reviewed and completed by the countries concerned. Because of the length of time taken by the processing, analysis and publication of national educational statistics, none of those provided is more recent than 1981. They have been chosen and presented with a view to illustrating the contrasts and similarities that exist between countries in specific areas rather than establishing international comparisons as such.

The analytical commentary has been organised around a number of themes designed to throw light on major trends in education which are significant to policy formulations. These are:

i) The demographic factor;

ii) Participation at the different levels of education;

iii) Participation of women;

iv) Socio-economic inequalities in educational participation;

v) The relationship between educational levels of the population and employment opportunities;

vi) Teaching and financial resources.

A summary of the main trends under each of these themes is presented below.

I. THE DEMOGRAPHIC FACTOR

Analysis of the demographic data (see Graphs 1) shows that during the period 1970-75 the size of the pre-school age group decreased in 14 of the

16 countries, the two exceptions being Australia and Japan. Between 1975 and 1980 the decrease affected all countries, except Spain and Yugoslavia. For the whole period 1970-80 it was particularly marked, amounting to 25 per cent or more in Austria, Denmark, Germany, the Netherlands and the United Kingdom.

A decline of between 1 per cent to 6 per cent in the population of primary school age for the period 1970-75 was experienced by Finland, France, Germany and the United Kingdom. For Canada and the United States it was over 10 per cent. During the period after 1975 the decline became general except for Australia and Japan, where the age group increased, and for France and Spain where it remained static. For the period 1970-80 the decline was particularly pronounced in Germany: 35 per cent.

During the period 1970-75 the population of lower secondary age increased in all countries except Finland, Greece, Sweden and Yugoslavia. Between 1975 and 1980 that population began to decrease in more than half the countries reviewed.

The population of upper secondary age increased between 1970 and 1980 except in Finland, Japan and Yugoslavia. In Germany, it increased by 29 per cent.

The situation with regard to higher education is less clear, particularly since it is much more difficult to define the age group corresponding to this level. If one takes the age group corresponding annually to higher education attendance in different countries (as is shown in the graphs) the population increased in half the countries between 1970 and 1975 and in nine of them between 1975 and 1980. In Japan it decreased by 29 per cent between 1970 and 1980.

The almost universal decline in the population of primary school age, which has already begun to affect the lower secondary age population, will in due course affect the upper secondary age and subsequently the post-secondary age population.

In Canada, Finland, Spain, the United States and Canada there has been a reversal in the downward trend of the birthrate. In spite of the uncertainties of any demographic projections, this reversal is likely to affect all countries (see Table below) so that there will be increased enrolments in both pre-primary and primary education in most countries by the late eighties and in nearly all countries by the early nineties (2).

Few OECD countries are now immune to the problem of coping with a fall in the size of the age groups at the lower levels of the education system and a rise in those at the higher levels, while at the same time taking account of the fact that the latter will also decrease in the medium or long term according to the country. This phenomenon of fluctuating school populations poses difficult problems for educational planning, particularly for the allocation of financial resources and the supply of teachers and the use of building stock.

Graph 1

TRENDS IN POPULATION OF AGE GROUPS CORRESPONDING TO THE DIFFERENT LEVELS OF EDUCATION

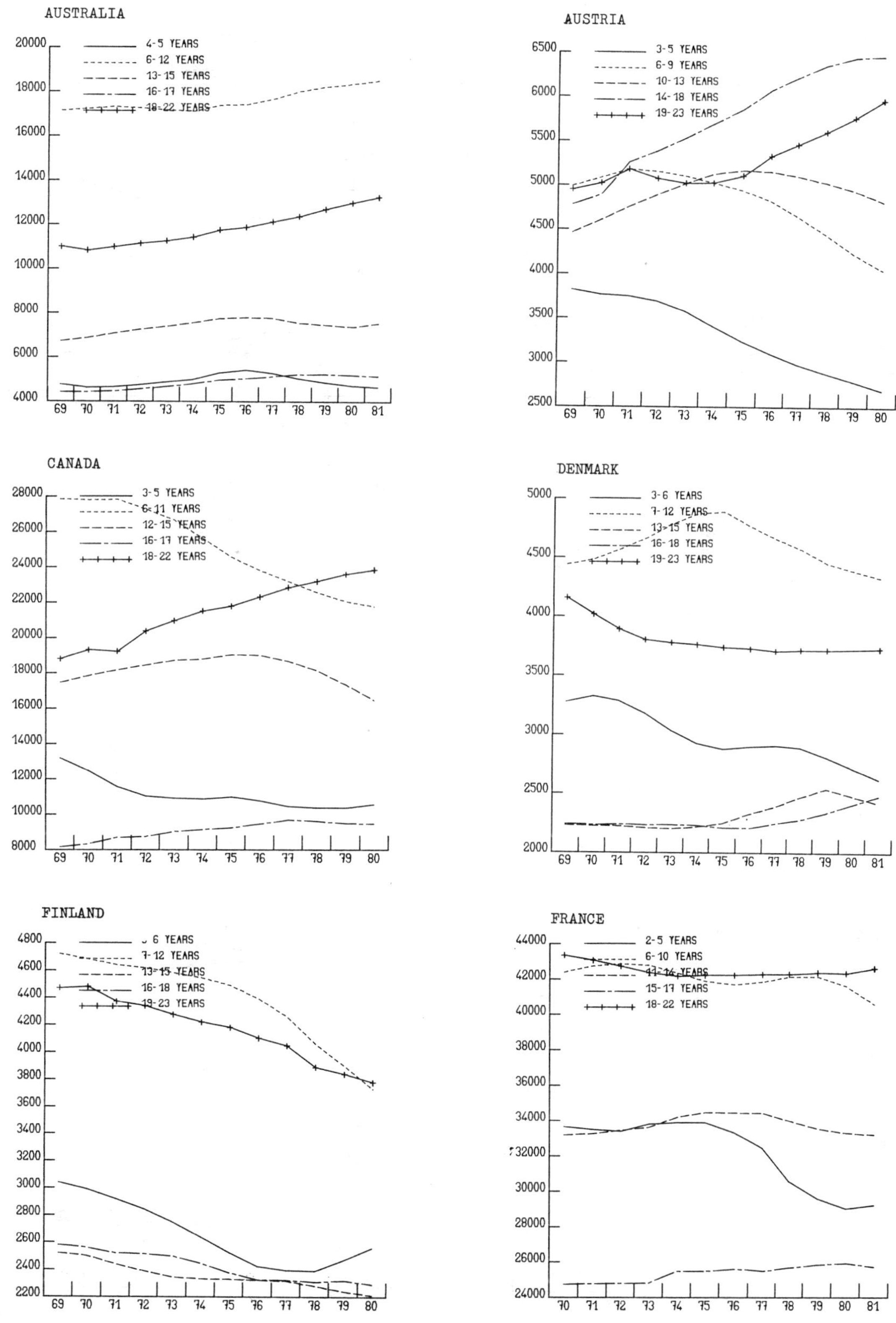

Graph 1 (cont'd)

TRENDS IN POPULATION OF AGE GROUPS CORRESPONDING TO THE DIFFERENT LEVELS OF EDUCATION

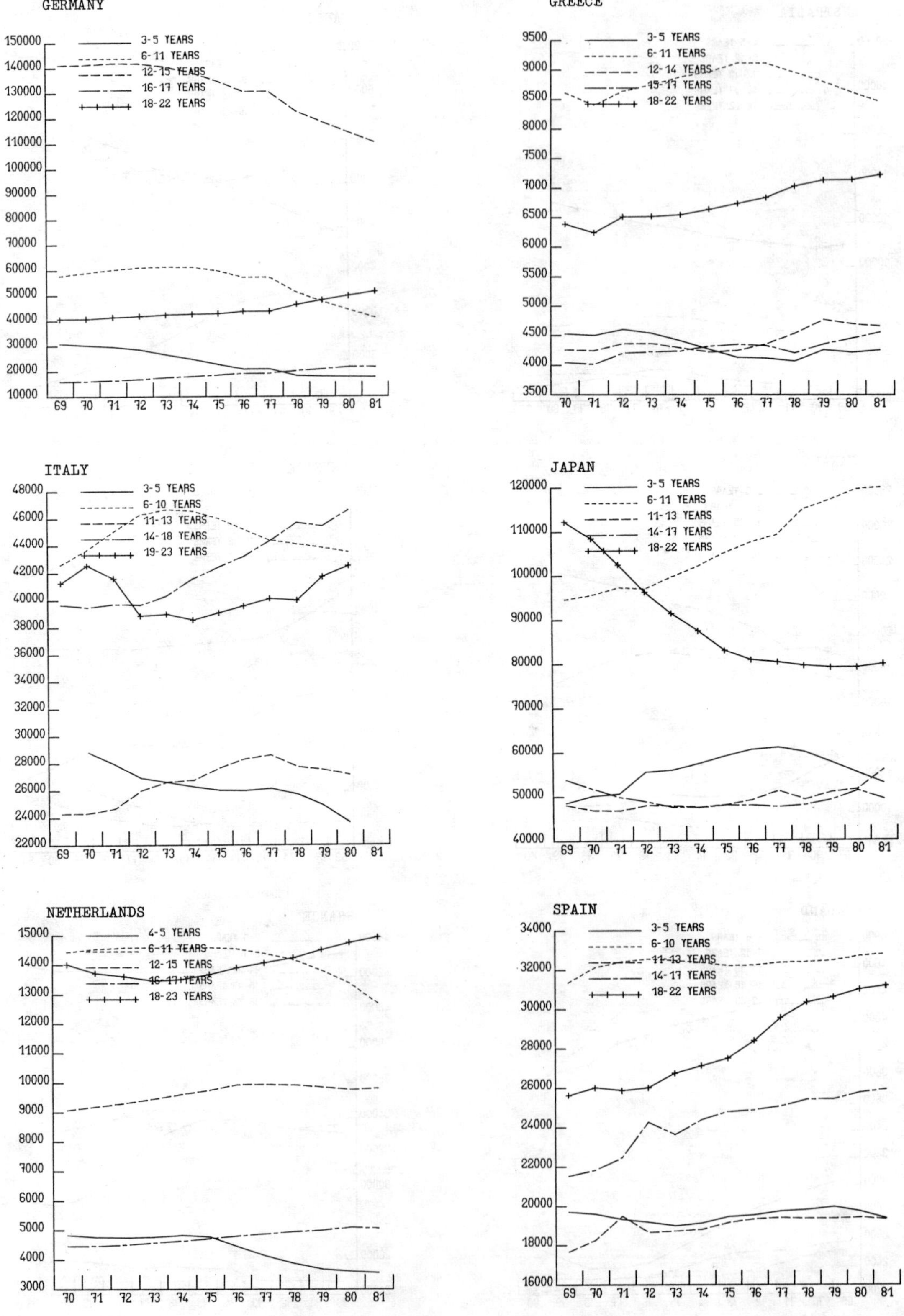

Graph 1 (end)

TRENDS IN POPULATION OF AGE GROUPS CORRESPONDING
TO THE DIFFERENT LEVELS OF EDUCATION

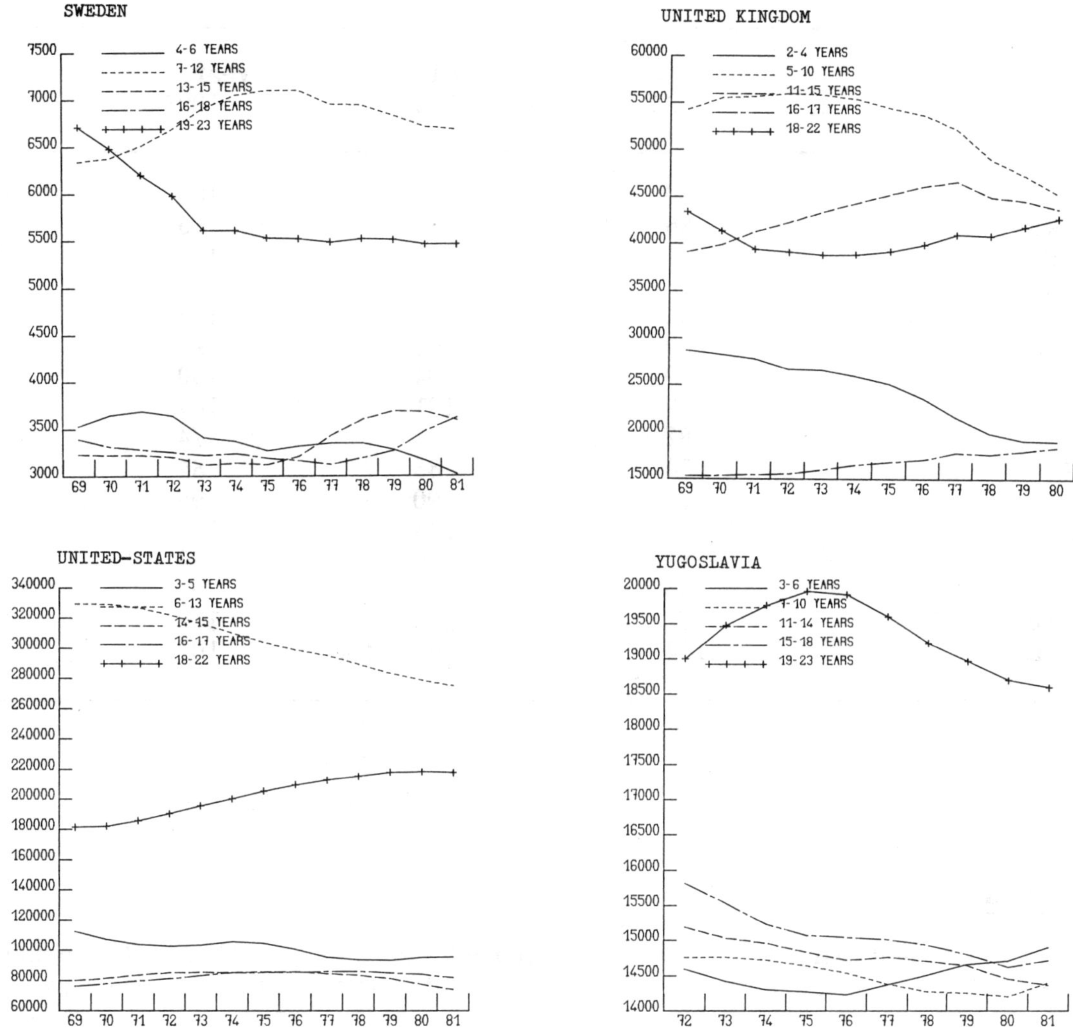

Population in hundreds of thousands
Date of reference :
30 june except Austria, Denmark (1978-1980), France, Germany, Greece (1978-1979), Italy, Netherlands (1977-80), Spain, Sweden (1976-1980), United Kingdom (1978-1980) at 31 december and Japan at 31 october.

INDEX OF GROWTH OF POPULATION AGED 5 TO 9
(Projections) 1980 = 100

	Middle of the year			
	1985	1990	1995	2000
AUSTRALIA	90	97	101	103
AUSTRIA	86	84	86	81
CANADA	104	111	111	105
DENMARK	88	91	96	96
FINLAND	106	110	107	99
FRANCE	89	90	90	88
GERMANY	89	94	100	96
GREECE	99	101	104	108
ITALY	82	72	74	75
JAPAN	94	83	84	90
NETHERLANDS	86	90	95	98
SPAIN	101	105	103	
SWEDEN	87	90	92	93
UNITED KINGDOM	83	83	91	96
UNITED STATES	101	118	122	118
YUGOSLAVIA	104	103	101	97

II. PARTICIPATION AT DIFFERENT LEVELS OF EDUCATION

Pre-Primary

The pre-primary sector has experienced vigorous growth in all countries since 1965, partly as a result of demographic growth but also pressure from working parents and views about the educational and social value of pre-schooling, particularly for children from disadvantaged backgrounds. Between that date and around 1980 the participation rate of children aged three to five doubled, or more than doubled, in Canada, Denmark, Germany and the United Kingdom. It almost doubled in Japan and the United States.

However, the scale of participation varies considerably from country to country (even though it is not always clear whether national data concern only children in pre-primary schools or also those in public or private day nurseries). In France, virtually all three- to five-year-olds and a third of two-year-olds attend a pre-primary school. In Germany, more than 75 per cent attend, and in the Netherlands two-thirds of the children aged from four to six. The participation rate is 50 per cent or more in Italy, Spain, the United States, and Denmark, where three- to four-year-olds attend kindergarten. In Japan, the rate is just above and in Canada below 40 per cent. In the United Kingdom, compulsory schooling begins at the age of 5, so the rates are not comparable with those of other countries.

The expansion of pre-primary schooling will no doubt continue in countries where the participation rate of three- to five-year-olds is relatively low, although, in view of the economic situation, some countries may decide to slow down the expansion of this sector, particularly if there is an increase in the population of the age groups concerned. However, where the rate is very high there will be a fall in enrolments as a consequence of falling birthrates. Even in countries where there is an increase in the participation rate, total enrolments may fall for the same reason (see Graphs 2).

Compulsory Schooling

Given that OECD has just published an in-depth survey of this sector (3) it will suffice here to present the essential facts. During the period 1970-80, total enrolments in primary and first cycle secondary education (which are the levels, in the majority of countries, which correspond to compulsory schooling) decreased in all the countries studied, except in Austria, Norway, Spain and Japan; in this latter country, there is an actual increase of the order of 23 per cent. The decrease has been entirely due to the demographic factor, the only one that affects the school population at this level since the compulsory schooling obligation is respected almost 100 per cent in all Member countries.

However, it is important to note that this overall decrease conceals important differences in the evolution of the two levels of compulsory schooling. This is best illustrated by the example of Germany, which also applies to many other Member countries: the drop in total enrolments between 1971 and 1980 amounted to 6 per cent; in the same period, however, enrolments in primary school decreased by 32 per cent while those in first cycle secondary education increased by 18 per cent.

The duration of full-time compulsory schooling now varies from 8 to 11 years and few countries appear likely to prolong it. The critical importance of compulsory schooling is reflected in the fact that in most countries, in spite of a decrease linked to demographic trends, it still accounts for two-thirds or more of the total enrolments in all levels of education. In some countries (e.g. Germany), full-time schooling is followed by compulsory part-time schooling. Without making this type of education compulsory, many countries have taken steps to enable all young people leaving after their compulsory schooling (or certain categories of them, particularly those who do not find jobs) to receive training -- whether inside or outside the school system -- that will help them acquire or improve their occupational skills.

During the last fifteen years there has been a steady reduction in the size of classes. This now varies from 20 pupils in Denmark, Italy and Sweden to 33 in Japan and is paralleled, at least during the primary cycle -- although the number of pupils per class and that per teacher do not always coincide -- by an improvement in teacher/pupil ratios, which is particularly striking in the Scandinavian countries as far as the early years of schooling are concerned. The percentage of very small schools, which varies considerably from country to country, is tending to decline. This tendency is likely to become more marked because of the fall in numbers, itself a result of demographic changes -- at any rate in countries that have not wished or not

Graph 2

COMPARISON OF CHANGES IN THE RATE OF PARTICIPATION IN PRE-PRIMARY EDUCATION AND THE POPULATION IN THE CORRESPONDING AGE GROUP (1)

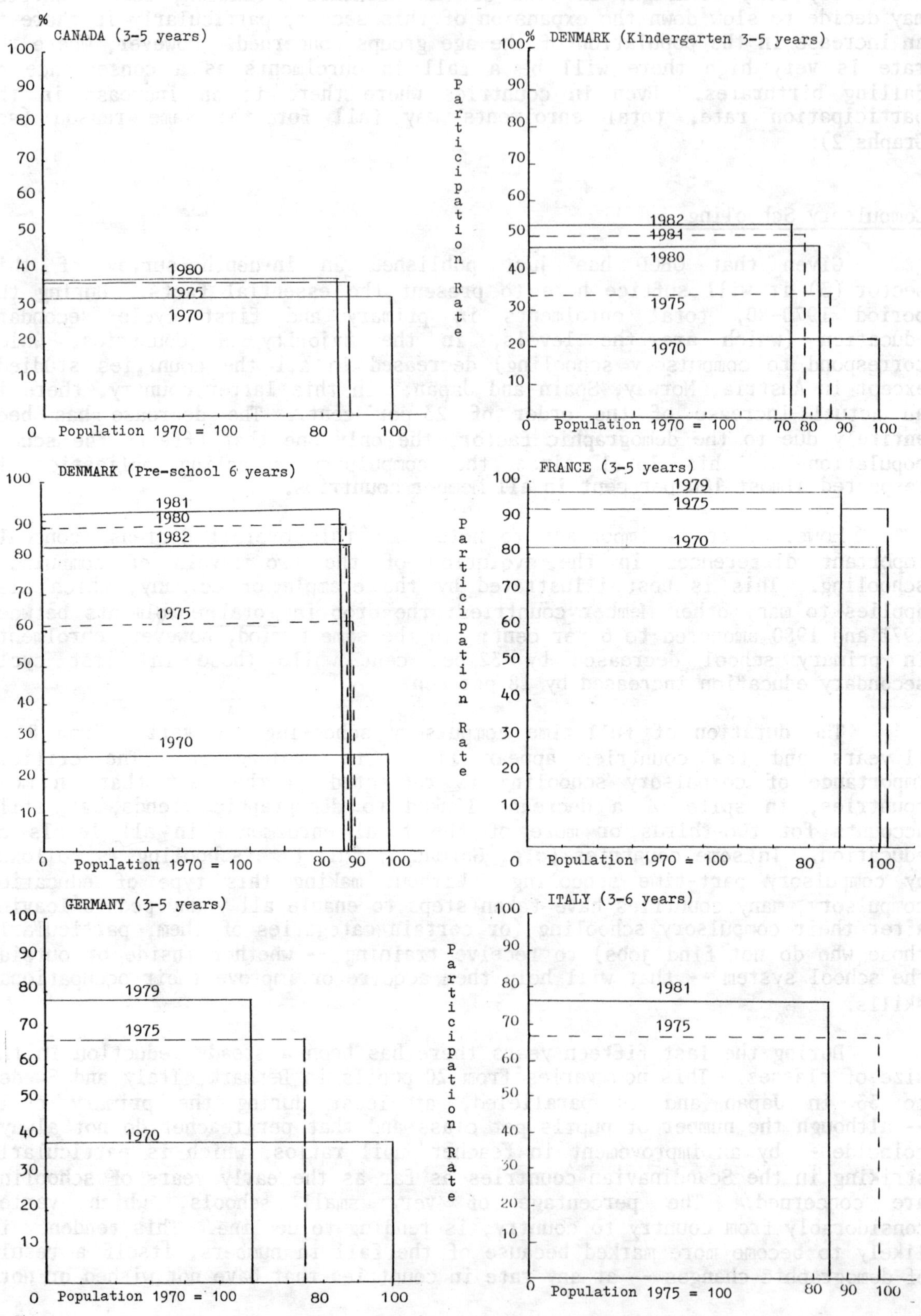

Graph 2 (end)

COMPARISON OF CHANGES IN THE RATE OF PARTICIPATION IN PRE-PRIMARY EDUCATION AND THE POPULATION IN THE CORRESPONDING AGE GROUP (1)

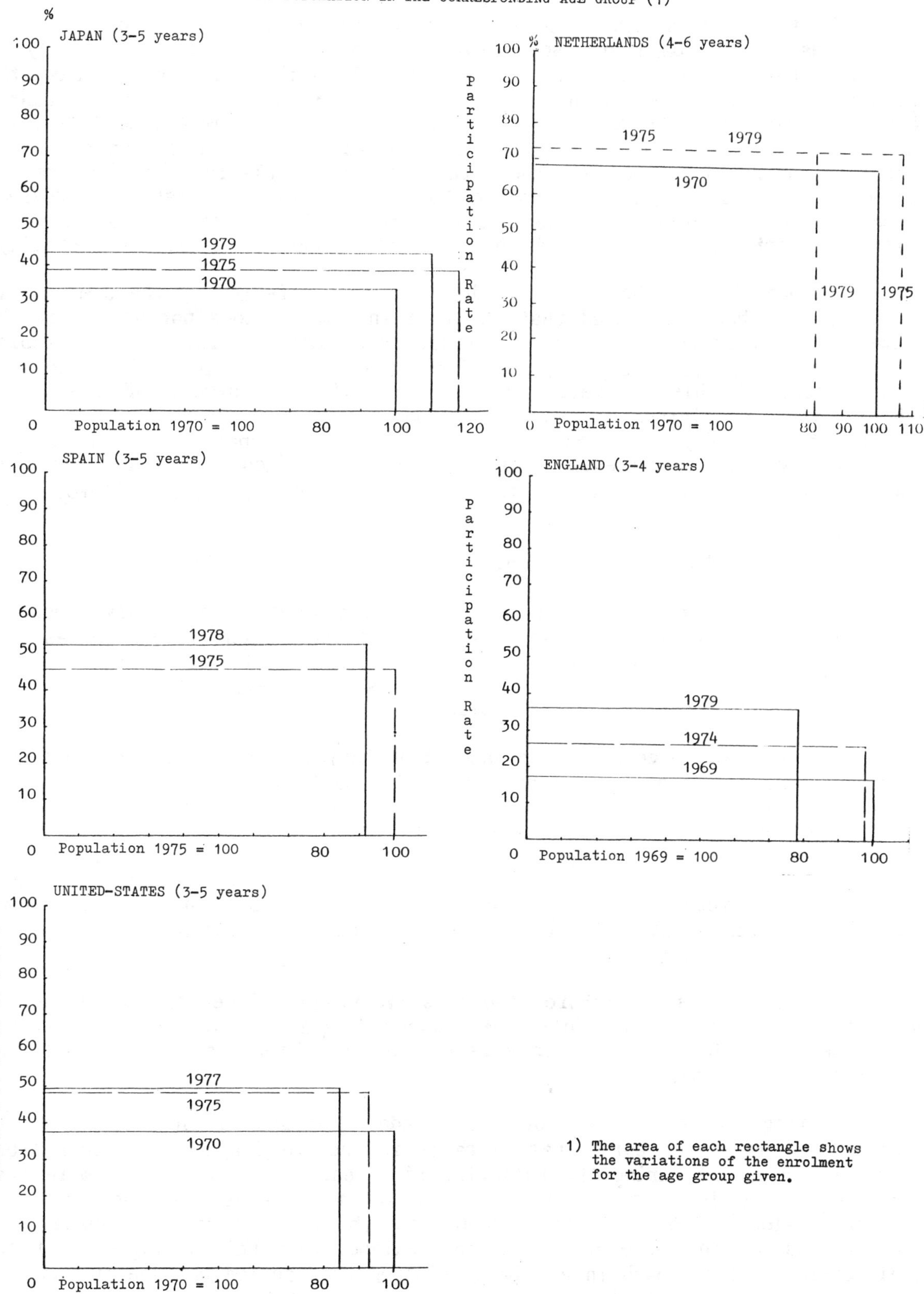

1) The area of each rectangle shows the variations of the enrolment for the age group given.

been able to take measures to prevent the closure of such schools, particularly in small rural communities.

Most countries would appear to have completed their reforms of the structures of the compulsory school by the end of the 1970s. A majority of countries has now established the common school as the only, or at least the predominant type, covering both cycles, i.e. primary and lower secondary. Several countries still retain a parallel system at the lower secondary level and show no signs of departing from it. In this sense, OECD countries have probably entered a period when the structures of compulsory schooling are not likely to undergo significant change for some time. It must be stressed, however, that there are considerable differences both between countries and within countries in the way in which the common school is organised internally.

Though this is the level of education most affected by the demographic downturn, it should be noted that the fall in numbers does not happen at the same time in primary schools and in lower secondary schools. A main problem facing most countries today is, therefore, that of foreseeing and coping with the effects of this asymmetry on the use and redeployment of resources, whether these be financial, material (school buildings) or human (teachers and other school staff). At the same time, the major debate about quality in education which is currently going on in Member countries relates with particular acuity to educational standards at the compulsory school level.

Upper Secondary Education and Training

Since 1975, the number of pupils enrolled in upper secondary education has steadily risen, except in Canada and the United States. The rise has been less pronounced than for the period 1970-1975, except for Denmark, Spain, Japan, Yugoslavia and, above all, Sweden, where a major reorganisation of upper secondary education has taken place.

Except for Greece, Japan and Yugoslavia, enrolments in full-time technical and vocational education have continued to increase and usually at a faster rate than in general aducation (Germany being one exception, and France another where short vocational courses are concerned). Part-time vocational education and apprenticeship, which had experienced declining enrolments between 1970 and 1975 (Denmark, France, Germany and the Netherlands), have attracted more young people but their growth rate has been generally lower than in full-time technical and vocational education -- except in Finland and France (see Table 1) (4).

In most cases, therefore, the relative weight of general education has diminished, while that of full-time technical and vocational education has increased -- as has to a lesser extent that of apprenticeship and part-time vocational education.

During the first part of the decade, the growth in enrolments was accompanied by rising participation rates in the 16-19 age group. This trend was also borne out during the following five-year period in rather more than half the countries considered, although in most cases the pace of this increase slowed. In the other countries though (Australia, Canada, the Netherlands in the case of boys, New Zealand, the United Kingdom and the United States) the growth in enrolments during this period was due in the main to the increase in the 16-19 age group. Participation rates in this age group have in fact remained very much the same or have diminished, but there does seem to have been an upturn in some countries since 1980.

These overall figures actually conceal considerable differences with regard to the trend of enrolment by single year of age (see Graphs 3 and Tables 2 to 5). At 16, the rate of enrolment generally shows an increase, mainly due to higher participation in part-time courses (except in Germany, where the rate is falling). The rate can rise to or exceed 85 per cent in countries with a strong tradition of part-time education (Austria, Germany, Switzerland and, to a much lesser extent, France), in countries where a large proportion of 16-year-olds are still in the first cycle of secondary education (Denmark, the Netherlands) and, lastly, in those where attendance at a comprehensive secondary education establishement is almost the rule at that age (Canada, United States, Japan -- although data by age are not available for this latter country).

Although less clear-cut the same trend is apparent for 17-year-olds, but rates of enrolment for this age are declining sharply compared with those at 16. In other words, many young people tend to prolong their studies one year after the end of their compulsory schooling, but no longer. This is not unrelated to the present employment difficulties for school graduates, many of whom prefer to undergo additional training, in order to improve their chances in the labour market, rather than leave school and join the ranks of the unemployed.

With regard to the situation at 18 years of age, a distinction must be made between the countries in which secondary education has not yet been completed and those where a high proportion of 18-year-olds have already left school, either permanently or temporarily, having finished that part of their education. Whereas in the former, the rates of enrolment are still relatively high, in the latter they are markedly lower than those at 17.

By 19 years of age, secondary education has generally been completed and the rates of enrolment are generally much lower than for the previous age groups: relatively less so, however, in countries where there is a strong part-time sector. At this age, and in some countries, there is a fall in the rate of enrolment of males in higher education, particularly in full-time university courses (which also applies to the 18-year rate in countries where secondary education has ended by that age). This may be due to the fact that a growing number of students tend to delay entry into higher education, and also to the diminished demand for teachers, which traditionally provided a main motivation for students to embark on higher education studies.

However, these rates, whether overall or by single age, refer only to formal education, and they would certainly be considerably higher if they included the various types of training that have become available outside the normal system in most Member countries, particularly in recent years.

Transfers within differentiated upper secondary systems continue to be made almost exclusively from general education to full-time vocational education or from the latter to apprenticeships or part-time education. Moreover, early exits from the system occur most frequently in the least prestigious branches (see Table 6).

Graph 3

TRENDS IN PARTICIPATION RATES OF POPULATION AGED 16 TO 19

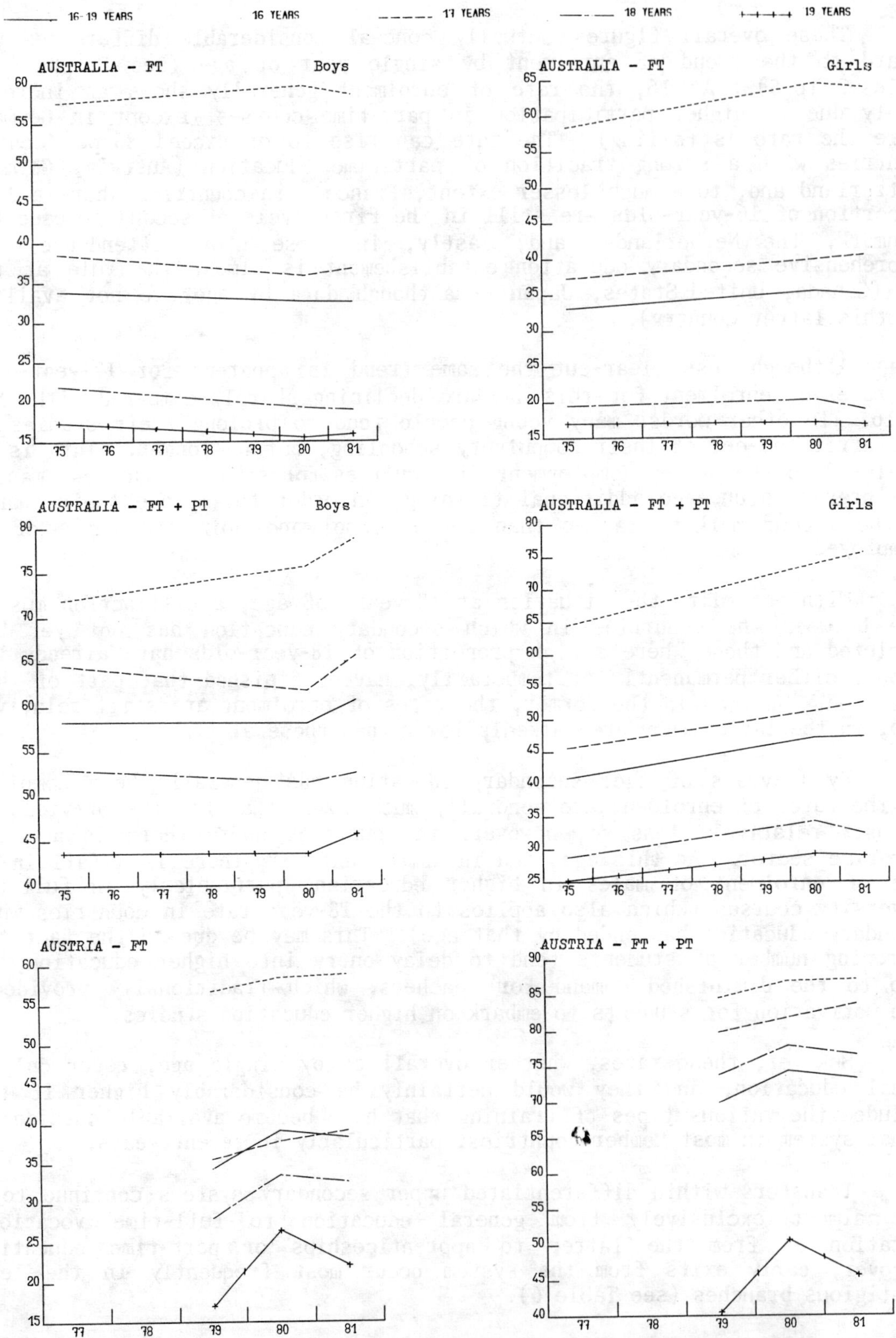

Graph 3 (cont'd)

TRENDS IN PARTICIPATION RATES OF POPULATION AGED 16 TO 19

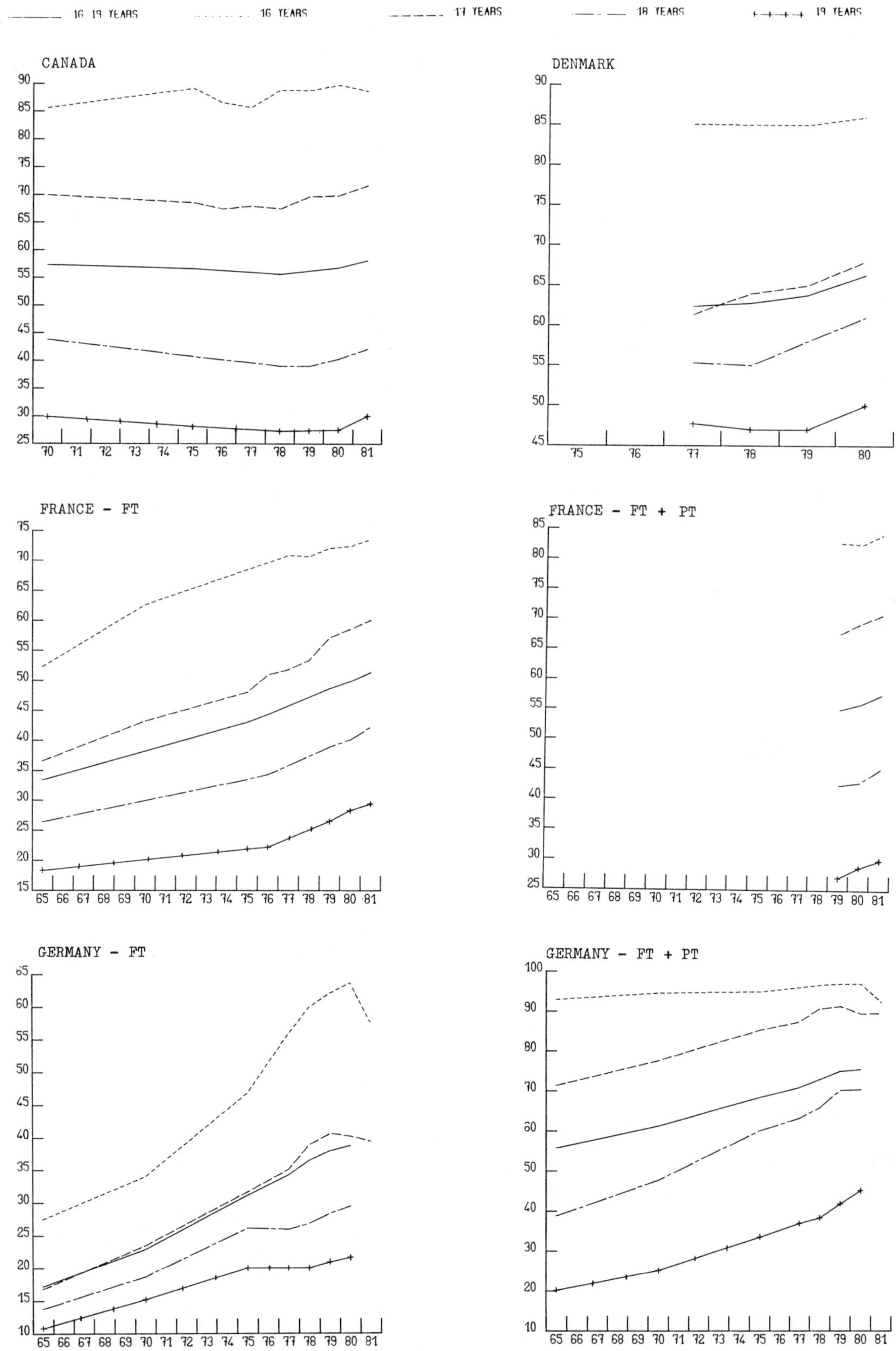

Graph 3 (cont'd)

TRENDS IN PARTICIPATION RATES OF POPULATION AGED 16 TO 19

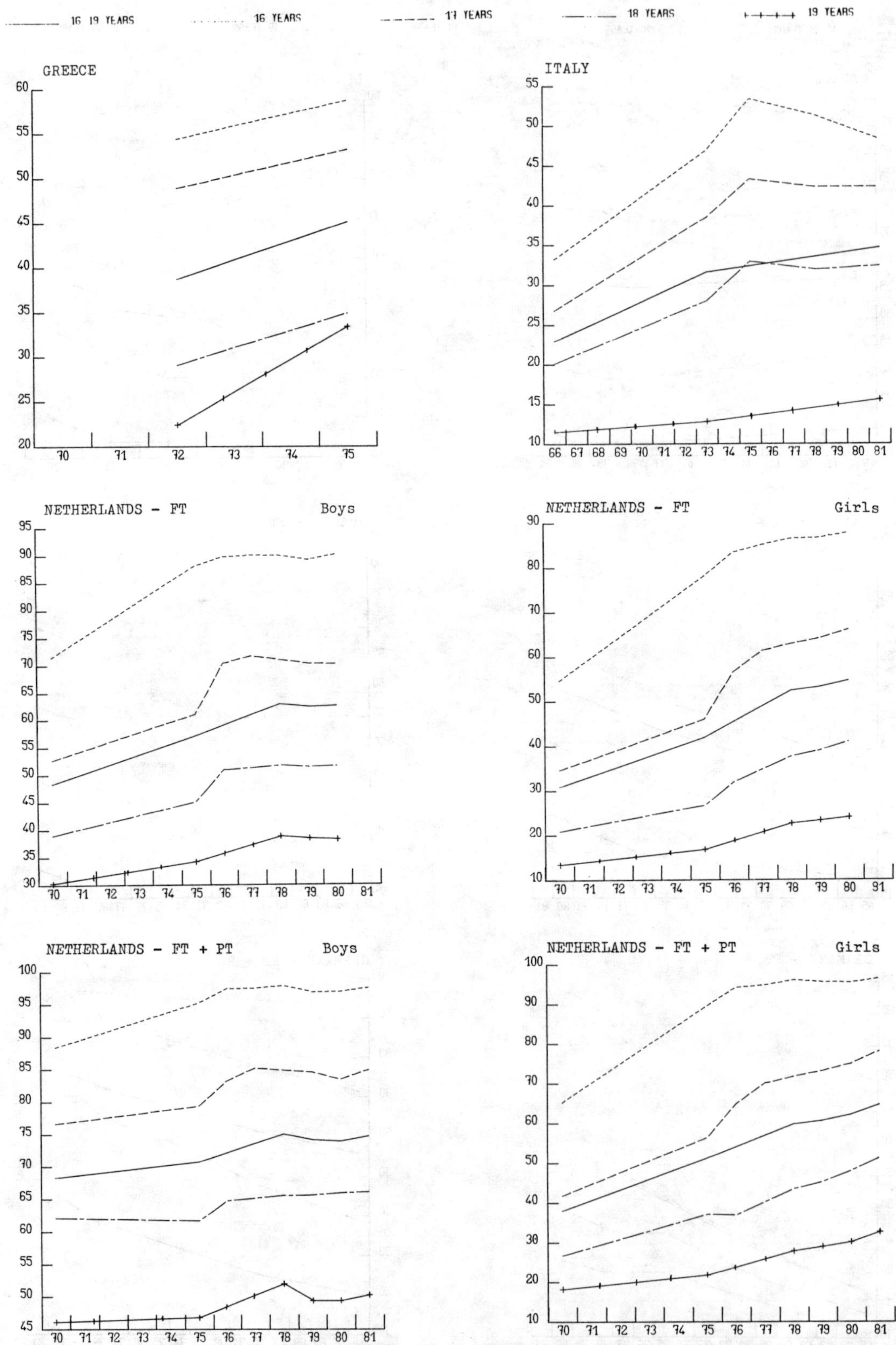

Graph 3 (cont'd)

TRENDS IN PARTICIPATION RATES OF POPULATION AGED 16 TO 19

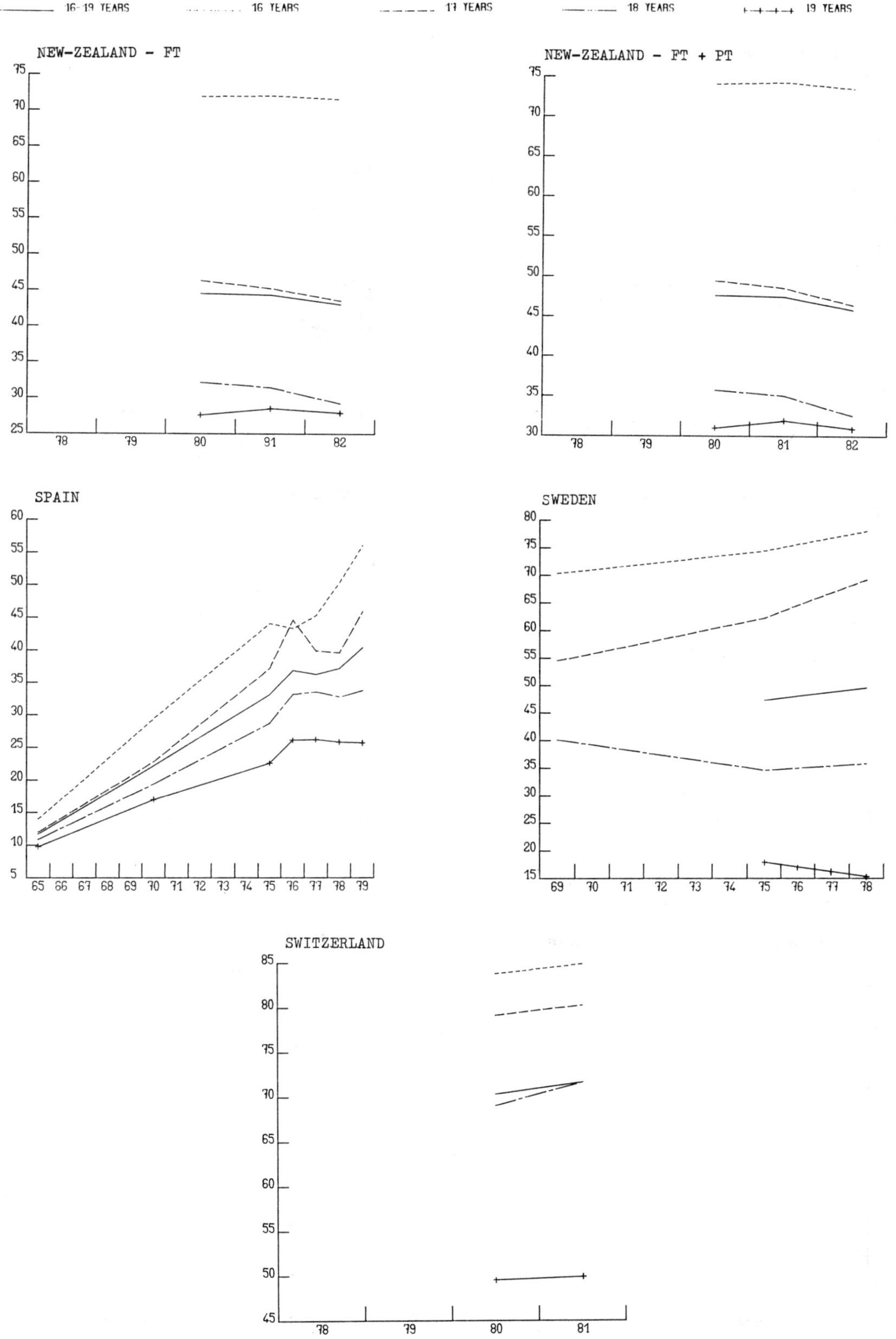

Graph 3 (cont'd)

TRENDS IN PARTICIPATION RATES OF POPULATION AGED 16 TO 19

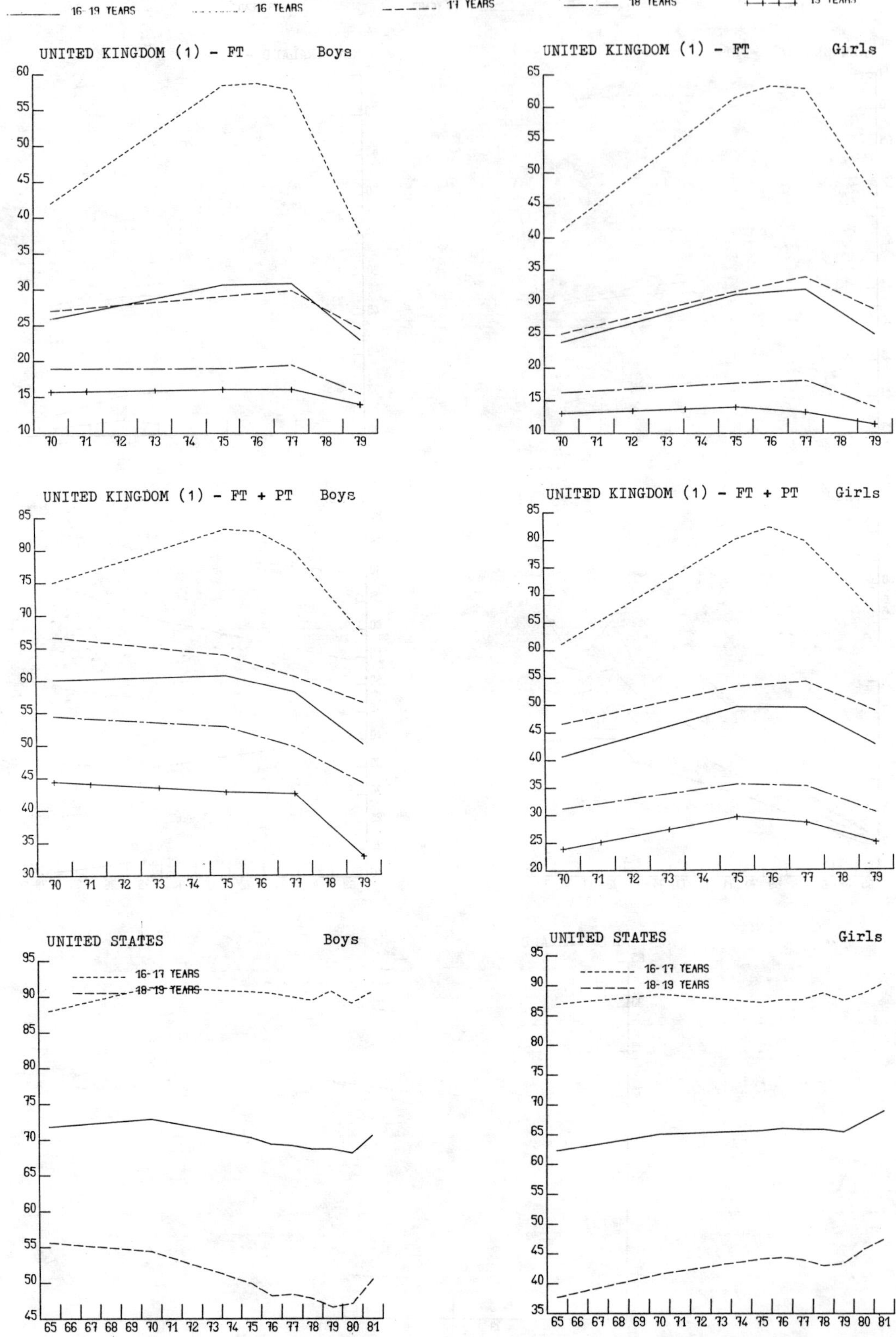

Graph 3 (end)

TRENDS IN PARTICIPATION RATES OF POPULATION AGED 16 TO 19

16-19 YEARS 16 YEARS 17 YEARS 18 YEARS 19 YEARS

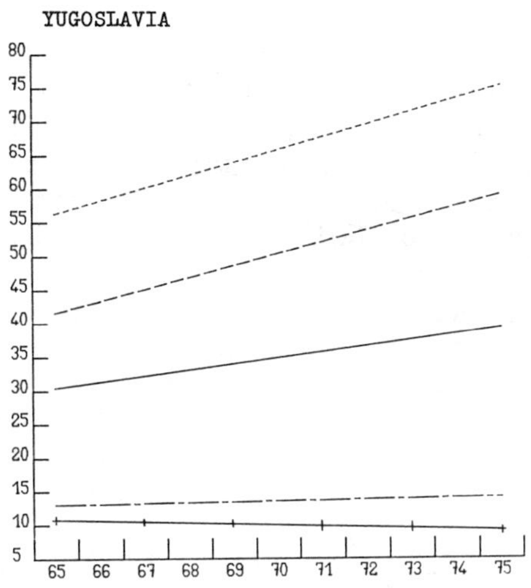

FT = Full time PT = Part time

1) In 1979, age at 31st August i.e at beginning of academic year and not at 31st December as for the previous years. This explains, totally or partially, the decrease of the enrolment rates, particularly at the age of 16 and 17.

The likelihood of a pupil completing the upper secondary cycle varies considerably from country to country. In Canada, Japan and the United States, between 70 and 90 per cent of the age cohort remain until the last year or obtain a leaving certificate. By contrast, the percentage is 35 in Australia. In France, only 24 per cent of 18-year-olds remain in the system (see Table 7).

The number of upper secondary leaving certificates awarded to pupils completing general studies (except for men in Finland and the United States), has continued to increase since 1975 but at a slower rate than in previous years. As regards technical and vocational education, it is necessary to distinguish between countries where the number has increased (Finland, France short vocational, Spain) and countries where it has only slightly increased (France long technical, Italy, the Netherlands) (see Table 8).

In some countries it would appear that within the last few years the percentage of the age groups obtaining a qualification leading to post-secondary studies (Japan, the United States for all forms of post-secondary education, the Netherlands for university entrance) has diminished. That percentage varies enormously, from 88 in Japan and 74 in the United States to less than 25 in Austria, Denmark, Germany and Spain (see Table 9). It should be remembered, however, that educational systems in the various countries differ widely, particularly with regard to methods of selection and the aims pursued. However, this fall covers too few years to confirm whether we are witnessing a positive downward trend or merely a temporary variation -- particularly since the figures have risen to a certain extent in some countries since 1980.

The relative or absolute decline of the age cohort qualified for entry into higher education will be reinforced by a decline in the size of the age group that has already begun in some countries and will become generalised in the near future. In many countries, this will bring a fall in the number of enrolments in upper secondary education, even if the rate of enrolments begins to increase. The same problems with regard to the use of resources will then arise at this level as are now being experienced in the primary and lower secondary sectors. To these will be added the problem of the number of options open to pupils, which will in some cases have to be reduced, for lack of sufficient candidates, unless secondary schools are reorganised and regrouped in a new way.

Post-Secondary Education

The rate of transfers from secondary to post-secondary education is notably higher in countries with a selective upper secondary system, where only a minority of an age cohort qualifies for higher education, than in countries where the great majority of an age group pursues general education. In the first case (the Netherlands, the United Kingdom, France) these rates vary from 75 to 85 per cent; in the second case (Japan, the United States) from 40 to 60 per cent. However, in some countries the total as well as the percentage of an age cohort continuing to higher education (see Table 10) is tending to stabilise or decline.

The general education route continues to offer the best assurance of proceeding to higher education. At the same time, in a few countries the proportion of young people being admitted to higher education with a qualification in technical and vocational education is on the increase (Austria, Spain and France for the university sector only). There has also been an increase, notably in Sweden, in the number of entrants without the normal admission requirements (see Table 11). There are, at the same time, signs of some young people deliberately delaying their entry into higher education (see Table 12). The result is that the percentage of new entrants over twenty five is increasing (no fewer than 50 per cent in Sweden and over 65 per cent in Australia for part-time students) (see Tables 13 and 14).

In most countries, the number of new entrants has risen less rapidly since 1975 than during the previous quinquennium and in some countries has even declined (Denmark, Finland, Italy, Japan and the United States for the university sector, and Australia and Yugoslavia for the non-university sector). However, in some countries (e.g. Canada, France and Germany) the situation has improved to a certain extent since 1980 (see Table 15). Admissions to the humanities and the education sectors have tended to fall while for the social sciences they have risen. Admissions to the sciences and to technology remain relatively stable (see Tables 16 and 17).

The same trends in the number of new entrants are also to be found in university enrolments. However, they are less marked in respect of post-graduate enrolments, which generally represent only a small percentage of all enrolments (from 2 to 3 per cent in Japan to 18 per cent in the United States).

The number of part-time students has also increased significantly (85 per cent in the United Kingdom for the universities), above all at the post-graduate level. Enrolments in the non-university sector have also slowed down but not to the same extent as in the university sector. They constitute between 20 per cent and more than 40 per cent of all post-secondary enrolments. Part-time enrolments are also on the increase (see Table 18).

The growth rate in the number completing first degrees and post-graduate degrees has been much weaker for the period since 1975 than in the preceding period. In six of the fourteen countries studied the number has even declined. It is also to be noted that in some countries the growth rate in graduations is lower than the level of enrolments would indicate. In the non-university sector, the slowdown in the rate of graduations is less significant (see Table 19).

Except for a perceptible fall in the number of graduations in the humanities and education, there has been no noteworthy development in the distribution of graduations over disciplines at the first degree level. At the post-graduate level, however, scientific disciplines predominate, although the proportion is showing signs of falling (see Tables 20 and 21). At the non-university level, the distribution remains also generally the same (see Table 22).

Non-Formal Education

As already indicated, data about education and training outside the formal system are incomplete and often hard to interpret because they cover a wide spectrum of programmes from short, ad hoc courses on a precise topic to longer, structured courses which may or may not lead to a qualification; one person may also follow several courses during the same period of time. Programmes may also be provided by a variety of public and private agencies. Nevertheless, such evidence as is available does seem to indicate an increase in adult participation in training programmes (see Table 23).

Certainly, most countries now attach growing importance to offering a 'second chance' to adults who left the education system early or suffer from a disadvantage -- illiterates, immigrants, the unskilled and the physically and mentally handicapped. They also see the necessity for ample provision of updating and retraining programmes for adults in the face of rapidly changing technology, as well as for young people out of work, and more particularly for the least qualified among them. It is, therefore, safe to assume that both the demand and the supply of non-formal educational provision will tend to grow.

III. PARTICIPATION OF WOMEN

During the compulsory cycle of schooling, the distribution of enrolments by gender simply reflects the fact that there are slightly more male than female births. However, wherever there is institutional differentiation at the lower secondary level, girls are almost everywhere more numerous than boys in general education tracks and less so in vocational education tracks.

At the upper secondary level, female participation rates have only marginally risen since 1975, except in those countries where, at about 1965, they were particularly low (in Spain, notably, and in Denmark, Greece, Italy, the Netherlands and the United Kingdom). In Japan, the rate has fallen. In half the 14 countries reviewed (Australia, Canada, Finland, France, Japan, Spain and Sweden) the rate exceeds 50 per cent for the last statistical year recorded. However, this overall rate masks significant differences according to the type of education. In all countries, except for Japan, girls are over-represented in the general education track but under-represented in full-time technical and vocational tracks, except for Denmark (for commercial training), Germany, Japan, Spain and Yugoslavia (for training other than that for qualified workers). They are greatly under-represented in part-time vocational education and in apprenticeship training (see Table 24).

Girls obtain relatively more leaving certificates from the general education track than boys. For example, in Finland they constitute 63 per cent of those who pass and in France 57 per cent. The only exceptions are Germany, Italy for scientific subjects, the Netherlands for the non-university oriented track, the United Kingdom for advanced level passes, and Sweden for three- or four-year technical courses, where they represent only 11 per cent of the graduates. However, in all countries their share of leaving certificates is increasing.

Girls remain in the majority in France for advanced technical courses and in Denmark for full-time vocational courses. In the Netherlands, girls are in the majority for the second cycle of vocational education which permits entry to higher education; but it is to be noted that, whereas half of the certificates awarded to boys are in technical education, nearly three-quarters of the certificates obtained by girls are in the social sciences. In other countries, girls are in the minority, especially in Germany and Italy for long-duration technical courses, and in Denmark for apprenticeships (see Table 25).

As the overall rate of increase of new entrants to higher education has slowed down, the rate of growth for female entrants has increased so that, except in the Netherlands, females now take up more than 40 per cent of the places. Throughout the entire period under review, female entrants have been in the majority in Finland and since 1977 they have been in the majority in the United States and Sweden. In the non-university sector, the gender balance varies according to the education level fixed for the training of paramedical personnel and pre-primary and primary school teachers, two professions in which there is a preponderance of women. Wherever the female participation rate had been traditionally low, it shows a tendency to increase (Germany, Spain, the United States and Yugoslavia). Wherever it was strong it has either stabilised (Australia) or increased (Canada, Denmark) (see Table 26).

However, the net increase in overall female participation in higher education is not reflected in an even distribution across disciplines: two to four times as many women as men embark on literature studies or education. By contrast, the admission rate of women in technological disciplines is very low, being at best no more than 10 per cent (Yugoslavia and Australia for Colleges of Advanced Education) whereas for men it may be as high as 33 per cent. Though slender, the evidence from the non-university sector reveals a similar situation -- a preponderance of women in education and social studies and of men in technological subjects (see Tables 16 and 17).

Whereas the overall rate of entrance to the university and non-university sectors has slackened, or even gone into reverse, the proportion of women entrants continues to increase, but at very different speeds according to the country. Thus, for the last recorded statistical year, the percentage of women in full-time attendance at the under-graduate university level was no more than 22 per cent in Japan and 32 per cent in the Netherlands. On the other hand, it was 47 per cent in Canada and the United States (4-year institutions), and about 50 per cent in France and Finland. At the post-graduate level, when this can be distinguished in the total figures, the female participation rate is much lower -- more than 33 per cent in Canada only. In the non-university sector the situation is quite different. There, leaving aside Germany, Greece and Yugoslavia, women are more strongly represented than in the universities. Thus, in Japan 88 per cent of the enrolments in the non-university sector are women as against 22 per cent in the university sector. It must also be noted that, outside Yugoslavia for non-regular students, the percentage of women is rising more rapidly among part-time than full-time students (see Table 27).

The most striking indication of the changing status of women is to be found in their percentage of total graduates. In 1965, that percentage exceeded 33 per cent in only four of the countries for which statistical evidence is available (Germany, Italy, Sweden and the United States). By 1970, that percentage had also been overtaken in Canada, France (not counted in 1965) and Yugoslavia. By 1979, women comprised more than 40 per cent of graduates in most countries [49 per cent in the United States and 45 per cent of the licences and 49 per cent of the maîtrises in France (5) but less than 25 per cent in Japan and the Netherlands]. At post-graduate level, they are less well represented but have made even more striking progress. Thus, their share doubled between 1965 and 1979 in Australia, Canada, Sweden and the United States. For the last year for which a statistical record is available, they obtained 39 per cent of the masters' degrees in Canada, over 49 per cent in the United States and respectively 24 per cent and nearly 30 per cent of the doctorates in the same two countries, the percentage amounting to 28 in France. On the other hand, in Japan they obtained only a little over 11 per cent of the masters' degrees and 7 per cent of the doctorates (see Table 28).

Finally, the slowdown in growth or the decrease in enrolments and of the number of graduates, at both the secondary and post-secondary levels and particularly in the universities, would have been much more substantial, had not the female participation increased. If this trend continues, it may have important implications for the labour market and for employers, who will have to cope with an increasing demand from women for skilled jobs, some of which were previously held by men; and this, whatever the employment situation.

IV. SOCIO-ECONOMIC INEQUALITIES

Glaring differences in educational enrolments and attainment between the most and least privileged strata of society remain an evident feature of all OECD countries, despite the educational expansion and reforms of recent decades (see Tables 29). The data in these tables are very disparate, covering such areas as access to studies by actual cohorts, the distribution of students at different ages, or by level of education at different times. This is why separate tables are presented for each country and no attempt has been made to regroup them together in one tabulation. It is difficult, therefore, to summarise them except in very general terms. They do, however, illustrate the fact that educational expansion may have achieved the laudable aim of opening access for the less advantaged to higher levels in education systems, but the reality is that their more privileged contemporaries have also taken increasing advantage of the new opportunities. In other words, there is no necessary link between educational expansion and the achievement of greater equality of opportunity; indeed, the declared aim of greater equality appears sometimes to have been a convenient pretext for attracting bigger resources. This suggests that the rhetoric about equality must carefully be distinguished from concrete action.

It is, in any case, particularly difficult to ascertain how far socio-economic group disparities have narrowed over, say, the last twenty years. As any level of education moves from being an elite experience for the few to being that of the many, then the balance of socio-economic groups to be found there inevitably becomes more nearly that of the population as a whole, simply through expansion. To regard this as the successful achievement of greater equality could clearly be highly misleading. Moreover, the meaning of that particular level of education, in educational and labour market terms, may well be significantly altered through such a change, so that any simple comparisons of percentages over time would not be comparisons of like with like. In addition, recent years have witnessed the emergence of new areas of education, including new certificates and qualifications and various non-formal programmes, as well as changing hierarchical orders and strategies whereby some seek to maintain their educational advantage over others. Thus, any simple quantitative comparison between yesterday and today will overlook the most pertinent features of the balance between educational advantage and disadvantage.

This question, however, goes far beyond the technical problem of measuring change. As well illustrated by Jencks in his book on "Inequality" in the early 1970s, the resilience of educational inequalities to change and demonstration of the limited efficacy of educational reforms in reducing social and economic inequalities can be used as an argument both for introducing still more resolute egalitarian reforms or abandoning the egalitarian pursuit. This is not to suggest that no progress has been made in reducing socio-economic disparities in educational enrolment and attainment; but such progress as has been made was, at best, modest and in any case defies simplistic quantitative demonstration.

V. QUALIFICATION LEVELS AND YOUTH UNEMPLOYMENT

Although the statistics presented in Table 30 are somewhat eclectic they show, nevertheless, that fewer young people are leaving school before or at the end of compulsory schooling. Thus, the proportion of early leavers fell from one-third to one-quarter between 1973 and 1978 in France and from 1965 to 1979 in the Netherlands. In Australia, the percentage of leavers from the 8th and 9th year fell also between 1970-1978. But it is in Japan that the most spectacular fall has occurred: in 1965 39 per cent of the age cohort left school at the end of the lower secondary cycle (even if some of them undertook professional training); but by 1979 that percentage had fallen to a mere 4 per cent.

At the same time, the percentage of young people having experienced post-secondary education, whether gaining a qualification or not, has sharply increased. In 1965 or 1970, according to the countries, that percentage was less than 20 per cent in all the countries reviewed. Around 1979 it had exceeded 20 per cent in France, 25 per cent in the Netherlands and Australia, and 35 per cent in Canada. However, it is Japan again which reveals the most striking trend, with the percentage increasing from 12 to 43 between 1965 and 1979.

It is particularly noteworthy that in all the countries appearing in this table the increase in the percentage of women pursuing post-secondary studies has been relatively greater than for men. In Canada this percentage is even higher for women than for men. In Canada, the proportion of women is higher than men.

The general level of educational qualifications is rising, then, in all countries. However, in some of them, and given the tendency -- admittedly unconfirmed in the most recent years -- towards a decelerating increase of new entrants to post-secondary education and of graduates, together with a fall in the size of the age cohort in the last year of the secondary cycle, the rise may not continue. It is possible, of course, that a fall in the number of graduates will raise the value of a degree on the labour market and cause more young people to want to complete the post-secondary cycle.

Despite the overall rise in the level of educational qualifications, there are significant percentages of young people who leave school without any qualification (13 per cent in France, about 17 per cent in the Netherlands and 15 per cent in the United Kingdom). As the next paragraphs will show, it is precisely those young people who are most at risk on the labour market.

Youth Unemployment Trends

The problem of youth unemployment has been fully documented in other OECD studies (6). It is not proposed to do more here than simply highlight general trends (see Graphs 4). In 1970, the national unemployment rate exceeded 2.5 per cent in only three of the countries reviewed (Canada, Italy and the United States). In general, it was higher for women than for men. The rate for young people between 15 and 19 was higher: above 10 per cent in Canada, Italy and the United States but below 6 per cent in the other countries. The rate for 19- to 24-year-olds was lower and, indeed, in several countries near the national norm (Australia, Finland, Germany and the United Kingdom).

By 1975 the situation had deteriorated. Whereas the national norm scarcely reached 4 per cent in six of the ten countries for which data are available, the unemployment rate for the 15-19 age group was between 12 per cent and 19 per cent in Australia, Canada, France, Italy and the United States and it had also risen sharply for the 20-24 age group. Since 1975, the rate has continued to rise, except in Japan and Sweden and to a lesser extent Germany where it was, however, higher for the 15-19 age group, especially girls.

It should be noted that the rise in unemployment has not been linear. Nevertheless, in 1980 the overall unemployment rate was higher than in 1975, except for Germany and the United States. Moreover, the unemployment rate among the young, especially the 20-24 age group, increased more sharply than in the rest of the labour force. Except in Canada (for the young but not the total labour force) and Japan, the unemployment rate has risen more sharply for women than for men; France represents the extreme case : it more than doubled its share of the total labour force and increased by two-and-a-half times in the 15-19 age group. In France, as well as in Italy and Spain, one in three girls in that age group was unemployed in 1980. By contrast, in certain countries the proportion of women among the unemployed young diminished between 1979 and 1981.

Education Level of the Young Unemployed (see Table 31)

In Germany, among the unemployed in the 15-19 age group, the proportion of young people who had not completed a vocational training had increased to 75 per cent by 1980. Those without a school leaving certificate were particularly unlikely to find a job. In Australia, young people who had not completed the secondary cycle constituted in 1981 two-thirds of the young unemployed.

In the other countries for which indicative data exist, a correlation is to be observed between the level of educational qualifications and the unemployment rate. In Denmark, the unemployment rate among the 15-24 age group of those who left school before the end of compulsory schooling attained in 1978 20 per cent for men and 31 per cent for women. In the United States, the rate in 1981 was 24 per cent for men and 32 for women aged 18 to 24 with only eight years of schooling. In France, in 1979 the rate was 21 per cent for men and 51 per cent for women who left school without any certificate.

The unemployment rate is not only ascending for young people without qualifications but also for young people who have completed the secondary cycle (in Canada 16 per cent in 1977 against 9 per cent in 1969; in France 27 per cent for men and 37 per cent for women in 1979 against 9 per cent and 10 per cent respectively in 1973) or even obtained a degree. In Great Britain, in the 'Youth Opportunities Programme' (work experience courses), which is designed for the unemployed aged from 16 to 18, the proportion of young people without qualifications is going down, which seems to indicate that many of those leaving the education system with a qualification experience more and more difficulty in securing a job.

VI. TEACHING AND FINANCIAL RESOURCES

Teachers

Whatever the period, 1965-70, 1970-75 or 1975 to 1980, the number of teachers in primary schools increased more rapidly than the number of pupils, except in Sweden during the first and Japan during the last period. Moreover, even when the number of pupils began to fall in most countries, the number of teachers continued to increase, except in the United Kingdom and Sweden where it declined, though not proportionately with the decline in enrolments. It is noteworthy that the differences in rates of enrolment and teacher increase were more marked during the last than the preceding period, especially in those countries where the fall in enrolments was relatively steep (see Table 32).

In lower secondary education, when the teaching body can be distinguished from that in upper secondary education, a similar pattern applies -- a more rapid increase (except in Italy) or slower decrease in the number of teachers than the number of pupils. However, the imbalance has been less considerable than in the primary cycle, except in Austria, Japan and France.

As for the upper secondary cycle, or that cycle and the lower secondary cycle combined when the teaching body is the same, the imbalance remains but is less than in either the primary or lower secondary sector, except in Australia, Greece and Japan.

In the only two countries, France and Germany, for which data are available, the number of teachers in vocational education increased more rapidly than the number of pupils (7).

Several hypotheses can be put forward to explain the favourable, or

Graph 4

TRENDS IN UNEMPLOYMENT RATES

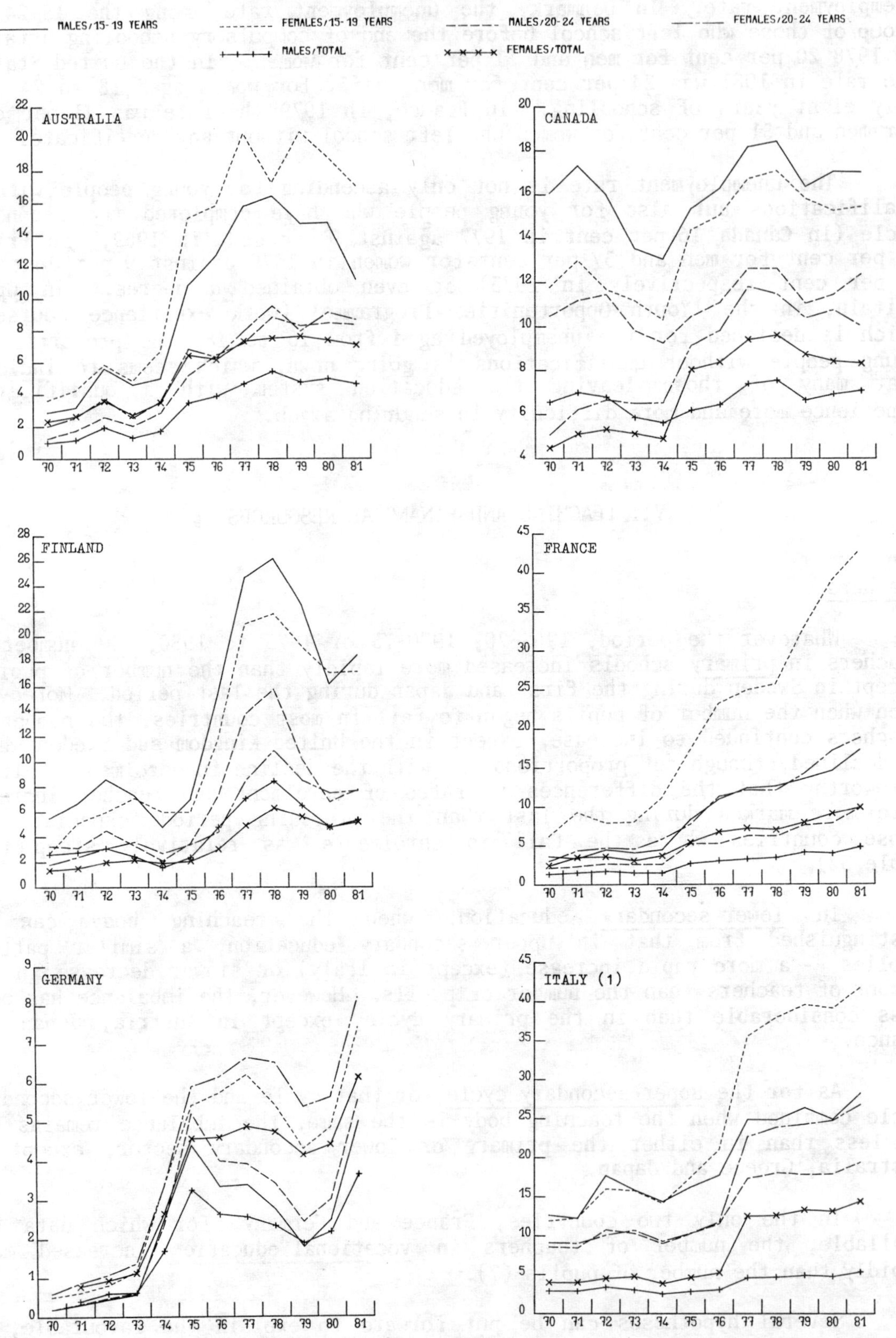

Graph 4 (end)

TRENDS IN UNEMPLOYMENT RATES

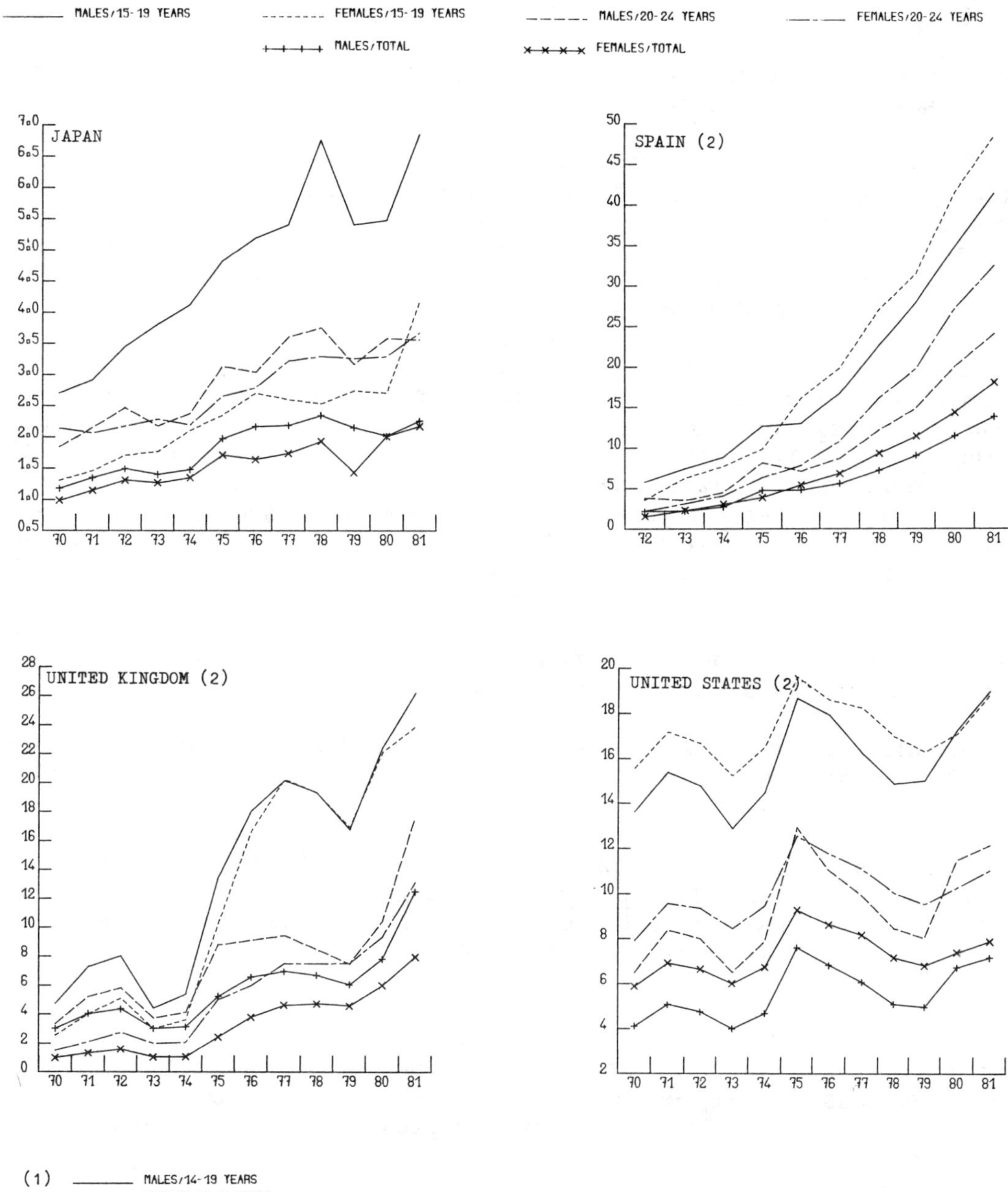

(1) ——— MALES/14-19 YEARS
------- FEMALES/14-19 YEARS

(2) ——— MALES/16-19 YEARS
------- FEMALES/16-19 YEARS

relatively favourable, improvement in the number of teachers, particularly at the primary level. One is that the authorities have been slow to anticipate the effects of a falling birthrate. A second is that it takes time to adjust the intake to teacher training institutions. A third is that teachers' unions have managed to put a brake on reductions. A fourth is that national authorities have deliberately sought to improve the quality of education by lowering teacher/pupil ratios.

The question remains why the situation has differed at the three educational levels. Is it due to a differential cost factor or a change in the preferences of aspiring teachers or the appearance of new salary structures? More positive evidence seems to be required in order that education authorities can make sound projections of the future demand for teachers at the different levels of education.

As an input to the report on Policies for Compulsory Schooling, data were compiled on the distribution of teachers by age. The key finding was that the percentage of teachers under 35 was very high, in some countries attaining 50 per cent. The influx of so many young teachers can be explained by the bulge in the birthrate, the expansion of upper secondary education and measures to improve teacher/pupil ratios. Given that school enrolments are falling and that the external labour market has contracted, it seems inevitable that a large block of young teachers are going to remain in their present posts for a very long time. This situation will have an impact not only on the education provided (older teachers being generally less in touch with pedagogical innovations than young ones just out of college) but also on expenditure, since the salaries of teachers increase with age.

The distribution of teachers by sex varies very considerably according to the educational level. In pre-primary schooling men are seldom found. In primary schooling women comprise up to 90 per cent of the teaching body, except in the Netherlands and Japan, where they comprise just over 50 per cent. Their share, even so, is on the increase. In the lower secondary cycle -- again, when the teaching body can be distinguished from that in the upper secondary cycle -- they are still in the majority but less overwhelmingly so, except in Japan where they are in a minority of one to three.

On the other hand, in upper secondary education (in some countries in secondary education as a whole), women represent an often small minority (except in France where the distribution by sex is almost evenly balanced): in the Netherlands they represent 30 per cent of the teaching staff. Finally, head teachers or principals are men in the great majority of cases, even in primary education.

Teacher supply has become highly problematic for two reasons. The first is that the effects of falling enrolments necessarily takes time to permeate upwards through the system. The second is that the birthrate curve is erratic. This means, for example, that any country may be faced with increased enrolments within a time span of five to ten years. The authorities are increasingly obliged to make critical decisions about the size of the annual intake of recruits to teaching and about the viability of some of the installations concerned with teacher training. Some authorities are seeking simultaneously to avoid staff redundancies and to iron out the differential demand for staff at the various educational levels by redeploying staff from one level to another or to a new function. Their task is often hampered by rigid qualification or tenure regulations or by both.

Public Expenditure

A reliable guide to national commitments to education is the percentage of GDP allocated to public educational expenditure (8) (see Table 33). In this connection three groups of countries can be identified. In the first and largest group (Australia, Austria, Canada, Denmark, Germany, the United Kingdom; Yugoslavia may also belong to this group depending on how very recent trends are interpreted) educational expenditure increased more rapidly than GDP up to 1975 or thereabouts and then increased less rapidly. Before the downturn began, the percentage of GDP was above 5 in all these countries and as high as 7.8 in Denmark and 8.8 in Canada (in 1970, the year when the downturn began in this country). The decrease since about 1975 has varied from 4 per cent in Austria to 20 per cent in Denmark.

In the second group of countries (the Netherlands and the United States), expenditure has more or less kept pace with the rise in GDP. That level is relatively high, being 6.5 per cent for the Netherlands and 8 per cent for the United States.

In the countries in the third group (France, Greece, Japan and Sweden) the percentage of GDP continued to increase up to the last year for which data are available. It is to be noted, however, that whereas in some of these countries the percentage of GDP is relatively high (Japan and, above all, Sweden with 9 per cent) in others the percentage is relatively low (France and Greece).

Falling enrolments, which so far have largely affected the primary school -- the educational level with the lowest unit costs -- do not alone account for decreases in the percentage of GDP devoted to education (9). It seems, therefore, that in some countries and given the economic situation, other factors have also played their part.

Looking at the trend of public expenditure in the main sectors -- i.e. defence, education, health and social security -- we see that it varies a great deal. The share of defence is declining in most of the countries studied, and particularly in the United States, where however it still remains the highest. The share of health remains relatively stable, i.e. between 11 per cent and 15 per cent, except in the United States, where it is smaller but is also increasing steadily. It is the expenditure on social security that represents the largest amount, i.e. up to 40 per cent of total public expenditure (Denmark, France, Germany); in recent years it has tended to fall in some countries (particularly in Australia, Germany and the Netherlands), whereas it has continued to increase in Denmark, the United Kingdom and especially in Japan.

The share of expenditure on education is falling in all countries except Germany, where it is still at the lowest level and in Italy, but it still comes in second position after social security, except in Germany and France where it comes third, after health.

Expenditure per Pupil/Student

The distribution of expenditure over the several levels of education has little significance except in relation to enrolment aggregates. It is proposed, therefore, to concentrate on expenditures per pupil/student, though, regrettably, the data are incomplete, especially for the last few years (see Table 34).

The rate of growth of these expenditures varies a great deal from one educational sector to another. The fastest growth rate has been at the pre-primary level, except in Denmark. The next fastest growth rate has been in special education (data are available for only a few countries). Still, the most striking fact to emerge in all countries is that the increase in expenditure has been much higher for the primary than for the secondary and tertiary sectors throughout the seventies. Expenditure per pupil in the lower secondary cycle, in the few countries where it is a distinct entity, has increased more than in the upper secondary cycle. The weakest growth has been in post-secondary education, especially in the university sector and particularly during the last few years. Indeed, in some countries there has been negative growth in this sector (in the United Kingdom, for example, in 1978 expenditure in constant terms was 85 per cent of the 1968 level for universities and of the 1975 level for polytechnics). But the impact of the demographic factor has to be taken into account here as well. A fall in numbers at a given level leads to diseconomies of scale, and therefore to higher unit costs; conversely, a rise in numbers leads to economies of scale and thus to a fall in costs per pupil.

However, the difference between per-student expenditure in the primary school and per-student expenditure in the other sectors of education remains substantial (see last column of Table 29). Only a pre-primary pupil costs less (except in Germany where it is also true of a middle school pupil). As a rule, the higher the educational level the more the expenditure increases. In France, the gaps are especially wide: a lower secondary pupil costs twice and an upper secondary pupil four times as much as a primary school pupil. At the university level, the cost per student is three times greater in Canada and ten times greater in the Netherlands than for a primary pupil. In the United States, the gap appears narrow but expenditures for primary and secondary pupils cannot be separated. Even allowing for the high cost of equipment in some institutions, the gaps in expenditure between levels of education are quite striking in a number of countries. The explanation no doubt lies in differential salary rates and differential pupil/teacher ratios.

Lastly, when public expenditure on education is considered, it should not be forgotten that other ministries, besides that of Education, as well as other public bodies or subsidised institutions, have responsibilities in this respect, particularly with regard to occupational training. So, if the total amount of public expenditure on education and on training were taken into account, it is possible that, in some countries, and contrary to the expenditure of the Ministry of Education alone, this public expenditure will be seen to have increased in real terms.

NOTES AND REFERENCES

1. Australia, Austria, Canada, Denmark, Finland, France, Germany, Greece, Italy, Japan, the Netherlands, Spain, Sweden, United Kingdom, United States and Yugoslavia. Whenever available, recent data for other countries have also been included in the relevant tables.

2. OECD Data Bank.

3. Compulsory Schooling in a Changing World, OECD, 1983, where the relevant statistical tabulations are presented in detail.

4. The distinction between full-time and part-time education is based on the length of time spent at school. Part-time schooling is often supplemented by in-firm training (apprenticeship, Berufsschulen in Germany, etc.). This twofold training gives the same level of skills that is acquired through full-time education in some countries or through either type in others (for example, the French Certificat d'aptitude professionnelle may be prepared either in full-time vocational schools or through apprenticeship courses.

5. In France, the maîtrise certificate can be obtained after having followed a separate 4-year course, or by one year of further study after the licence (3-year).

6. See, in particular, Youth Unemployment : The Causes and Consequences, OECD, 1980. Youth without Work. Three Countries Approach the Problem, OECD, Paris, 1981, and Improving Youth Employment Opportunities, OECD, Paris, 1984.

7. Data for post-secondary teachers are very difficult to interpret. They are not presented here.

8. In a few countries private expenditure on education is a significant factor. However, it is not discussed here for lack of data.

9. An attempt has been made to see whether there is a relationship between the movement of the GDP percentage on education and the size of the 5 to 24 age group (broadly corresponding to the age for initial education. No linear relationship was discovered.

STATISTICAL ANNEX

Table 1

ANNUAL AVERAGE GROWTH RATE AND, FOR THE LAST YEAR AVAILABLE, DISTRIBUTION OF ENROLMENTS IN 2nd CYCLE SECONDARY EDUCATION

School year beginning in : | Percentage

	1965-70	1970-75	1975-76	1976-77	1977-78	1978-79	1979-80	1980-81	1981-82	1975-LY	Distribution LY
GERMANY											
General (1)	10.1	8.1	-2.5	1.7	5.4	13.9	1.7	14.1		5.7	19.8
Comprehensive (General)	-	28.0	12.7	6.0	2.5	5.6	2.9	2.3		5.3	6.8
Vocational/techni. FT (1)	6.9	15.5	0.5	0.5	8.3	7.8	5.9	7.6		5.1	18.5
Vocational PT	-2.2	-0.2	-1.5	3.5	5.3	5.2	2.3	-2.1		2.1	54.9
AUSTRALIA											
2nd cycle secondary	8.4	3.8	4.8	2.7	1.6	-1.1	-1.0	-0.5		1.1	75.8
Apprenticeship	2.4	4.4	2.1		3.0	2.4	5.2	4.3		3.3	24.2
AUSTRIA		(1970-74)									
General		4.1		0.3	3.6	1.2	-1.0			1.4	16.5
Technical, short		18.6			5.1	28.5				16.2	27.7
Technical, long		12.2			9.5	7.9				8.7	14.8
Vocational PT		5.6		5.5	-0.1	3.5				3.0	41.0
BELGIUM (3)		(1972-75)									
General		-3.2	-3.2	-2.6	-13.1	-11.6	-16.1	-29.1		-12.6	11.3
Technical/vocational		-6.5	-3.1	-4.0	-4.0	-11.4	-17.0	-32.8		-12.1	14.5
Renovated education		24.3	9.5	7.2	17.9	19.6	17.8	14.7		14.5	74.2
CANADA											
General (2)	5.8	0.5	0.1	-0.4	-0.3	-1.5	-2.5	-4.1		-1.4	
DENMARK											
General	12.1	5.7	0.5	1.9	9.2					5.8	37.4
Technical/vocational	6.5	6.7	19.9	17.4	9.7					15.6	28.4
Apprenticeship	-12.0	-2.8	2.6	0.4	5.6					2.8	34.2
SPAIN											
General (4)	11.7	-11.9	3.2	3.9	13.9	5.6	6.6			6.6	55.1
Vocational training	5.0	15.0	17.6	13.6	11.8	13.0	14.0			14.0	26.9
Other secondary	11.5	11.9	6.9	-4.3	44.2	8.8	14.9			4.9	18.0
UNITED STATES											
General (2)	2.5	1.3	0.3	-0.4	-0.04	-3.1	-2.5			-1.1	
FINLAND											
General	5.4	4.0	-0.0	3.0	4.5	4.8	3.7			3.2	50.0
Vocational			4.7	9.0	4.7	6.9	2.7			5.6	47.6
Apprenticeship			-3.8	-5.5	23.4	33.0	22.6			13.9	2.4
FRANCE											
General	-1.1	7.8	3.1	2.2	3.4	2.7				2.8	40.6
Vocational, short	1.5	2.9	0.8	0.5	0.7	0.3				0.6	37.6
Technical	46.5	6.7	6.0	4.4	4.0	3.8				4.5	11.6
Apprenticeship		-4.9	9.0	10.6	7.4					9.0	10.2

./...

Table 1 (cont'd)

ANNUAL AVERAGE GROWTH RATE AND, FOR THE LAST YEAR AVAILABLE, DISTRIBUTION OF ENROLMENTS IN 2nd CYCLE SECONDARY EDUCATION

School year beginning in :

Percentage

	1965-70	1970-75	1975-76	1976-77	1977-78	1978-79	1979-80	1980-81	1981-82	1975-LY	Distribution LY
GREECE											
General		3.7	2.9	3.3	0.9	4.6	5.7	3.5		3.5	85.2
Technical/vocational		6.2	-0.8	-5.2	0.2	-14.7				-5.1	14.8
ITALY											
General	9.7	4.3	1.9	0.3	0.5	2.4	1.3	0.0	-0.6	0.9	24.5
Vocational	8.9	5.9	6.6	7.9	6.7	5.0	2.5	2.6	2.9	4.9	21.2
Technical	3.8	6.6	6.7	3.6	2.9	3.3	0.7	1.1	0.3	2.7	44.4
Teacher education	1.0	-2.2	1.6	2.4	2.1	6.9	5.1	2.2	2.1	3.2	9.9
JAPAN											
General	-3.9	2.0	3.2	1.7	2.3	3.1	4.4	2.6		2.9	68.7
Vocational training	-3.0	-1.8	-2.2	-3.3	-2.0	-1.3	-0.3	-1.0		-1.7	31.3
NETHERLANDS											
General FT		9.5	6.2	4.1	3.2	2.2	1.7			3.5	38.9
Technical/vocational FT		6.3	8.5	10.2	7.5	5.9	8.4			8.1	29.0
General PT						18.0	-5.2				3.4
Technical/vocational PT		-7.2	6.1	-0.3	5.1	7.1	11.2			5.8	6.3
Young worker education (5)		-5.5	-1.9	7.2	5.8	6.8	-3.8			2.8	22.3
UNITED KINGDOM (6)											
Secondary		6.5	5.1	1.0						3.0	37.2
Further educ. non adv. FT		12.9	5.9	2.0						3.9	17.0
" " PT (7)		0.1 (8)		-1.2							45.9
SWEDEN		1971-1975									
3/4 yr. courses		-3.8	-0.9	2.8	4.7	6.3	7.7	7.9		4.7	40.4
2 yr. courses		8.3	2.7	5.3	7.7	7.6	9.7	8.6		6.9	46.6
Special courses (9)		-10.0	-0.5	-5.1	-3.3	3.9	2.4	-8.2		-1.8	13.0
YUGOSLAVIA	1965-1969	1969-1975									
General + common core (10)	1.0	8.7	29.5	37.0	17.5					28.0	64.3
Teacher education	-6.5	-13.0	4.4	-14.7	-10.3					-6.9	0.6
Skilled worker training	8.4	-1.8	-7.9	-23.7	-16.2					-15.9	15.9
Other technical/vocational	-2.2	6.2	-6.4	-12.5	-24.7					-14.5	19.2

LY = Last year available. FT = Full-time - PT = Part-time

(1) Including evening classes and colleges of secondary education.
(2) As from the 9th year of study.
(3) French and German linguistic systems only.
(4) Old system for 1965-70, new system as from 1975; the two series of data are not comparable.
(5) With or without a contract of apprenticeship.
(6) Pupils aged 16 and over although in 1971 compulsory schooling stopped at 15.
(7) Including evening classes and not including pupils over 20.
(8) Including advanced level courses.
(9) Courses of variable duration - a few weeks to 1 year or more - preparing for specific trades.
(10) Introduced in 1975 and explaining the large increase in general education and the decline in other types.

Table 2

ENROLMENT RATE AT 16 YEARS, BY TYPES OF EDUCATION

School year beginning in : Percentage

	1965		1970		1975		1976		1977		1978		1979		1980		1981		1982	
	M	F	M	F	M	F	M	F	M	F	M	F	M	F	M	F	M	F	M	F
GERMANY																				
Secondary, 1st cycle (1)	9.7		10.5	8.4	16.2	14.3			22.4		23.0	22.2	23.1	22.1	23.8	23.1	21.0			
Secondary, 2nd cycle																				
General (2)	12.6		18.0	14.7	19.9	19.2			22.5		21.3	22.9	22.7	23.8	22.9	24.6	24.4			
Technical/vocat.FT	5.2		6.8	9.5	8.4	15.3			10.8		11.6	18.6	12.7	19.4	13.2	19.4	12.1			
Technical/vocat.PT	65.4		62.9	58.2	51.8	44.4			40.1		40.9	32.2	39.0	30.5	37.3	29.0	34.6			
Total FT	27.5		35.3	32.6	44.5	48.8			55.7		55.9	63.7	58.5	65.3	59.9	67.1	57.5			
Total FT + PT	(92.9)		98.2	90.8	96.3	93.2			95.8		96.8	95.9	97.5	95.8	97.2	96.1	92.1			
AUSTRALIA FT			(1971)																	
Secondary (3)			56.6	48.3	56.2	54.3	57.7	56.9	56.7	58.0	58.4	59.7	57.6	59.2	56.4	58.5	54.6	57.9		
TAFE (4)					1.1	3.8									3.1	5.6	3.8e	5.7e		
CAE					0.2	0.2									0.1	0.2	0.1	0.1		
Universities					0.1	0.1									0.1	0.1	0.1	0.1		
PT																				
TAFE					14.3	6.1									16.0	9.5	20.2e	11.9e		
Total FT					57.6	58.4									59.7	64.4	58.6	63.8		
Total FT + PT					71.9	64.5									75.7	73.9	78.8	75.7		
AUSTRIA																				
Compulsory schooling													15.0		14.0		13.8			
Secondary 2nd cycle/teacher training											15.3		15.8		15.7					
Vocational, short													15.4		15.6		15.3			
Vocational, long													11.0		12.0		13.1			
Non University															1.0		0.9			
University																				
Vocational PT													27.9		28.5		28.3			
Total FT													56.7		58.4		58.8			
Total FT + PT													84.6		86.9		87.1			
CANADA			(1971)																	
Secondary			85.1		88.2		85.5		84.6		87.8		87.7		88.6		87.4			
Post-secondary			0.5		0.9		(1.0)		(1.0)		(1.0)		(1.0)		1.1		1.2			
Total			85.6		89.1		86.5		85.6		88.8		88.7		89.7		88.6			
DENMARK																				
Basic school									69.3											
Secondary, 2nd cycle																				
General									10.8											
Technical/vocational									5.0											
Total									85.1		85		85		86					
SPAIN													Tot.	F						
Secondary, general and teacher training	11.5		22.3		32.0		29.4		31.2		32.8	37.1	41.5	40.5						
Vocational training	2.5		4.5		9.7		11.5		11.8		16.9	10.7	15.0	11.6						
Other secondary			2.6		2.1		2.1		2.2		1.1	1.7	1.5	1.8						
Higher					0.2		0.2		-			-								
Total	14.0		29.4		44.0		43.2		45.2		50.8	49.5	58.0	54.0						

./...

Table 2 (cont'd)

ENROLMENT RATE AT 16 YEARS, BY TYPES OF EDUCATION

School year beginning in : Percentage

	1965	1970	1975	1976	1977	1978	1979	1980	1981	1982
	M F	M F	M F	M F	M F	M F	M F	M F	M F	M F
UNITED STATES *										
Secondary								92.9 92.9	94.2 93.2	
Higher								0.5 0.5	0.4 0.6	
Total								93.4 93.4	94.6 93.8	
FRANCE			(1974)							
Secondary, 1st cycle	10.3	11.4	9.3	7.5	7.1	5.9	6.1	5.6 6.2	6.3 7.4	
Vocational, short	19.2	23.6	26.7	28.3	28.8	29.1	29.5	30.4 28.9	31.0 30.1	
Secondary, 2nd cycle general	22.7	25.3	28.2	29.1	30.4	35.6	36.4	29.4 44.0	29.5 42.6	
Secondary, technical		2.2	4.1	4.7	4.6					
N. University							0.2			
Apprenticeship							10.7	16.0 4.8	16.8 4.9	
Total FT	52.3	62.6	68.4	69.6	70.8	70.6	72.0	65.4 79.1	66.8 80.1	
Total FT + PT							82.9	81.4 83.9	83.6 85.0	
GREECE		(1972)								
Secondary, general		45.6	49.0							
Secondary, techn/vocat.		8.8	9.7							
Non University		0.1								
University										
Total		54.4	58.7							
ITALY	(1966)	(1973)								
Secondary, 1st cycle	2.5	2.2	2.5			1.6 0.8			17.9 [bracket: 1st cycle to Gen. and teacher train.]	
Secondary, 2nd cycle										
Gen. and teacher train.	14.1	19.1	[bracket: Gen./Technical/Vocational]			[bracket: Gen./Technical/Vocational]				
Technical	11.6	16.8	50.9			49.8 50.3			19.5	
Vocational	5.0	8.8							10.9	
Total	33.2	46.9	53.4			51.4 51.1			48.3	
NEW ZEALAND										
Secondary								67.8	69.0	67.4
Techn. Instit. FT and PT								4.1	3.0	4.1
Teacher Colleges								0.0		
University										
Total FT								71.9	72.0	71.5
Full year continuing second educ. PT								2.2	2.3	2.0
Total FT + PT								74.1	74.3	73.5
* UNITED STATES (16 and 17 years)	88.0 86.9	91.3 88.6	90.7 87.2	90.5 87.7	90.0 87.7	89.5 88.8	90.8 87.6	89.1 88.8	90.7 90.5	

./...

Table 2 (cont'd)

ENROLMENT RATE AT 16 YEARS, BY TYPES OF EDUCATION

School year beginning in : Percentage

	1965		1970		1975		1976		1977		1978		1979		1980		1981	
	M	F	M	F	M	F	M	F	M	F	M	F	M	F	M	F	M	F
NETHERLANDS FT			(1971)		(1974)													
Secondary, 1st cycle																		
General (3)			21.7	18.8			24.6	24.0	24.5	24.5	24.2	24.8	24.1	24.7	23.9	24.7		
Vocational			24.8	5.9			34.9	22.6	34.9	22.2	34.7	22.3	34.2	22.5	34.7	22.3		
Secondary, 2nd cycle																		
General			18.8	18.0			23.7	25.7	24.2	26.7	24.2	27.5	23.7	27.9	23.6	28.7	47.5(5)	54.3(5)
Vocational/technical			5.8	11.7			6.2	11.0	6.3	11.5	6.6	11.8	7.1	11.6	7.7	12.0	44.0(6)	35.2(6)
Higher			0.6	0.3			0.3	0.1	0.2	0.2	0.2	0.1	0.2	0.1	0.1	0.1	0.0	0.1
PT education			16.7	10.6			7.8	10.9	7.6	9.8	8.1	9.7	7.9	9.0	7.0	7.8	6.2	7.1
Total FT			71.7	54.7	88.0	78.0	89.7	83.4	90.0	85.1	89.9	86.5	89.1	86.7	90.1	87.8		
Total FT + PT			88.4	65.3	95.3	89.6	97.5	94.3	97.6	94.9	98.0	96.2	97.0	95.7	97.1	95.6	97.7	96.7
UNITED KINGDOM FT													(8)					
Secondary			36.3	34.9	50.5	50.8	51.3	52.4	50.3	51.6			27.1	30.0				
Further education,non-ad.			5.7	6.1	8.0	10.7	7.5	10.9	7.7	11.3			10.7	16.4				
Further educ.n-adv. PT(7)			33.0	20.1	24.7	18.5	24.0	18.9	21.9	16.8			29.0	20.0				
Total FT			42.0	41.0	58.5	61.5	58.8	63.3	57.9	62.9			37.9	46.5				
Total FT + PT			75.0	61.1	83.2	80.0	82.8	82.2	79.8	79.7			66.9	66.5				
SWEDEN			(1969)															
Basic school (3)			11.7		5.0													
Secondary 2nd cycle			58.6		69.3						77.9							
Higher					0.1						0.0							
Total			70.3		74.4						77.9							
Other (9)			0.2		0.9						1.1							
SWITZERLAND																		
Primary															1.9		1.9	
Secondary, 1st cycle															25.9		26.0	
Secondary, 2nd cycle															55.9		56.8	
Higher															0.0		0.1	
Total															83.7		84.8	
YUGOSLAVIA																		
Basic school	20.2				16.7													
Secondary, 2nd cycle																		
general and teacher trai.	13.2				13.3													
Skilled worker training	10.3				14.4													
Other technical/ vocational	12.6				15.4													
Common core					15.3													
Total	56.3				75.1													

Table 2 (cont'd)

FT = Full-time - PT = Part-time

P = Provisional

(e)= Estimates.

(1) Including pupils still in upper primary and special education.
(2) Including some pupils still in the 1st cycle in gymnasium or comprehensive school.
(3) Including special and primary education.
(4) Technical and further education including apprentisceship.
(5) General secondary, 1st and 2nd cycles.
(6) Vocational secondary, 1st and 2nd cycles.
(7) Including evening classes.
(8) Age at 31st August, i.e. at beginning of academic year and not at 31st december as for the previous years.
(9) Adult education, popular education, training for the labour market.

Table 3

ENROLMENT RATE AT 17 YEARS, BY TYPES OF EDUCATION

School year beginning in :

Percentage

	1965		1970		1975		1976		1977		1978		1979		1980		1981		1982	
	M	F	M	F	M	F	M	F	M	F	M	F	M	F	M	F	M	F	M	F
GERMANY																				
Secondary, 1st cycle	3.0		2.8	1.5	4.0	2.9			5.4		6.5	5.1	6.5	5.1	4.2	3.4	3.9			
Secondary, 2nd cycle (1)																				
General	10.9		15.8	11.9	18.8	17.2			18.9		20.2	20.2	20.8	21.5	21.4	22.8	22.7			
Technical/vocat. FT	2.9		5.6	9.4	6.9	13.4			10.7		9.3	16.2	10.1	17.0	10.8	17.5	12.7			
Technical/vocat. PT	54.6		61.7	46.5	60.3	46.9			52.4		57.9	45.6	56.7	44.4	55.5	42.8	50.0			
Total FT	16.8		24.2	22.8	29.7	33.5			35.0		36.0	41.6	37.4	43.6	36.4	43.7	39.3			
Total FT + PT	71.4		85.9	69.3	90.0	80.4			87.3		93.9	87.1	94.1	88.0	91.9	86.5	89.3			
AUSTRALIA FT			(1971)																	
Secondary (2)			32.5	24.4	31.4	28.9	31.4	30.7	31.0	32.0	30.4	32.6	30.3	32.6	28.2	30.7	28.1	31.1		
TAFE					2.7	3.4									4.0	4.8	5.2	5.2		
CAE			0.9	1.6	1.7	2.9									1.4	2.4	1.3	2.2		
Universities			2.5	2.0	2.7	2.1									2.2	1.9	2.1	1.9		
PT																				
TAFE					25.7	8.1									25.5	11.2	28.6	11.9		
CAE					0.3	0.1									0.4	0.2	0.3	0.2		
Universities					0.1	0.1									0.1	0.1	0.1	0.1		
Total FT					38.5	37.3									35.8	39.8	36.7	40.4		
Total FT + PT					64.6	45.6									61.8	51.3	65.7	52.6		
AUSTRIA																				
Compulsory schooling													0.4		0.5		0.4			
Sec. 2nd cycle/Teach trai													14.5		14.4		14.8			
Vocational short													11.1		11.4		12.0			
Vocational long													9.5		10.4		10.8			
Non University															1.0		1.0			
University															0.1		0.1			
Vocational PT													44.3		44.0		44.6			
Total FT													35.5		37.8		39.1			
Total FT + PT													79.8		81.8		83.7			
CANADA			(1971)																	
Secondary			63.6		60.7		59.0		58.3		57.1		58.7		58.7		60.1			
Post-secondary			6.3		7.8		8.4		9.6		10.3		10.9		11.1		11.5			
Total			69.9		68.5		67.4		67.9		67.4		69.6		69.8		71.6			
DENMARK																				
Basic school									10.4											
Secondary, 2nd cycle																				
General									22.3											
Technical/vocational									28.4											
Higher									0.0											
Total									61.4		64		65		68					

./...

Table 3 (cont'd)

ENROLMENT RATE AT 17 YEARS, BY TYPES OF EDUCATION

School year beginning in :

Percentage

	1965		1970		1975		1976		1977		1978		1979		1980		1981		1982	
	M	F	M	F	M	F	M	F	M	F	M	F	M	F	M	F	M	F	M	F
SPAIN													Tot.	F						
Secondary, general	7.3		13.1		20.2		24.4		18.0(3)		25.5	28.1	31.3	33.5						
Vocational training	2.7		3.2		6.4		7.9		8.4		12.4	7.4	10.9	8.3						
Other secondary			3.2		2.9		2.7		2.1		1.0	1.6	1.4	1.7						
Higher																				
University	2.0		2.9		6.1		7.6		7.9		1.5	0.1	1.6	1.5						
Other NU			0.4		1.5		1.9		3.5		0.7	0.7	0.7	0.7						
Total	12.0		22.8		37.1		44.5		39.8		41.1	37.9	45.9	45.7						
UNITED STATES																				
Secondary															80.9	77.4	82.4	80.9		
Higher															4.1	7.0	4.2	6.3		
Total															85.0	84.5	86.6	87.1		
FRANCE																				
Secondary, 1st cycle	2.0		1.0		0.5		0.3		0.3				0.3		0.3	0.4	0.3	0.4		
Vocational, short	10.4		15.1		18.4		19.9		20.1		20.6		21.2		21.1	22.8	22.1	23.8		
Secondary, 2nd cycle	24.2		27.1		29.1		30.7		31.4		32.7		33.1		27.4	40.2	27.8	40.7		
Non University													1.2		1.1	1.1	1.1	1.1		
Universities (4)													1.3		1.4	1.2	1.4	1.2		
Apprenticeship													10.7		16.8	5.1	16.7	5.1		
Total FT (4)	36.6		43.2		48.0		50.9		51.8		53.3		57.1		51.3	65.7	52.7	67.2		
Total FT + PT (4)													67.8		68.1	70.8	69.4	72.3		
GREECE			(1972)																	
Secondary, general			40.0		43.5															
Secondary, technical/vocat			8.8		9.6															
Non university																				
University			0.1																	
Total			48.9		53.2															
ITALY	(1966)		(1973)																	
Sec.general and teach edu	9.4		17.9														16.9			
Technical	14.2		14.8														17.9			
Vocational	3.2		5.8														7.5			
Total	26.8		38.5		43.3						44.4	42.1					42.3			
NEW ZEALAND																				
Secondary															32.9		34.0		32.0	
Tech. Inst. FT and PT															11.3		8.9		9.7	
Teacher Colleges															0.5		0.6		0.2	
University															1.6		1.7		1.6	
Total FT															46.3		45.2		43.5	
Full year cont. sec. ed.PT															3.1		3.3		2.9	
Total FT + PT															49.4		48.5		46.4	

./...

Table 3 (cont'd)

ENROLMENT RATE AT 17 YEARS, BY TYPES OF EDUCATION

School year beginning in :

Percentage

	1965		1970		1975		1976		1977		1978		1979		1980		1981		1982	
	M	F	M	F	M	F	M	F	M	F	M	F	M	F	M	F	M	F	M	F
NETHERLANDS FT			(1971)		(1974)															
Secondary, 1st cycle																				
General			8.7	5.9	9.3	6.9	10.0	8.1	10.3	8.6	9.7	8.6	9.8	8.8	9.5	8.9				
Vocational			10.2	1.4	12.9	2.3	18.4	6.7	18.7	7.2	18.1	7.5	17.7	7.7	17.3	7.9				
Secondary, 2nd cycle																				
General			20.3	15.2	25.1	21.9	26.9	24.8	27.5	26.1	27.7	27.0	26.6	27.6	26.1	28.1	35.4(5)	37.9(5)		
Vocational/technical			10.4	9.8	11.9	13.4	13.2	15.2	13.4	17.6	13.9	18.2	14.6	18.5	15.9	19.7	36.1(6)	30.0(6)		
Higher																				
University			1.2	0.3									0.1		0.1		1.1	1.4		
Non university			1.9	2.0	1.8	1.5	1.8	1.8	1.7	1.8	1.6	1.7	1.4	1.5	1.3	1.4				
PT education			23.9	7.2	18.4	10.4	13.0	8.3	13.6	8.8	14.0	8.9	14.4	9.2	13.4	9.0	12.4	9.0		
Total FT			52.7	34.6	61.0	46.0	70.3	56.6	71.6	61.3	70.9	62.9	70.2	64.1	70.1	66.1	72.6	69.3		
Total FT + PT			76.6	41.8	79.4	56.4	83.3	64.9	85.2	70.1	84.9	71.8	84.6	73.3	83.5	75.1	85.0	78.3		
UNITED KINGDOM FT														(8)						
Secondary			21.3	19.3	21.0	20.5	21.2		21.4	21.2			17.6	17.4						
Further edu., non-advanc.			5.4	5.7	7.7	10.9	9.7		8.1	12.4			6.1	10.8						
Further edu., advanced					0.2	0.2			0.2	0.2			0.3	0.3						
Universities			0.3	0.2	0.3	0.2	0.5		0.3	0.3			0.6	0.5						
Furt. edu. non-adv . PT(7)			[39.6	21.2	[34.7	21.5	26.5		30.6	20.1			31.8	19.8						
Furth. edu. advanced PT(7)							0.1													
Total FT			27.0	25.2	29.1	31.8	31.3		29.9	34.0			24.6	29.0						
Total FT + PT			66.6	46.4	63.8	53.3	57.9		60.5	54.1			56.4	48.8						
SWEDEN			(1969)																	
Basic school/special			1.6		0.9															
Secondary			52.9		61.3						69.1									
Higher			-		0.0						0.0									
Total			54.5		62.2						69.1									
Other (9)			0.7		1.8						1.1									
SWITZERLAND																				
Primary															0.6		0.6			
Secondary, 1st cycle															3.6		3.7			
Secondary, 2nd cycle															74.7		75.8			
Higher															0.1		0.1			
Total															79.1		80.2			
YUGOSLAVIA																				
Skilled worker training	16.0				20.4															
Other technical/vocation.	13.5				19.8															
Second.general/teach.trai	12.1				18.8															
Total	41.6				59.0															

Table 3 (cont'd)

FT = Full-time - PT = Part-time.

P = Provisional

(1) Including some pupils still in the 1st cycle.
(2) Technical and Further education including apprenticeship.
(3) The general introduction of the "baccalauréat" reform explains rate disparities compared with previous years.
(4) Data on higher education U and NU do not include certains schools such as health, commerce and so on.
(5) General secondary, 1st and 2nd cycles.
(6) Vocational secondary, 1st and 2nd cycles.
(7) Including evening classes.
(8) Age at 31st August, i.e. at beginning of academic year and not at 31st December as for the previous year.
(9) Adult education, popular education, training for the labour market.

Table 4

ENROLMENT RATE AT 18 YEARS, BY TYPES OF EDUCATION

School year beginning in : Percentage

	1965		1970		1975		1976		1977		1978		1979		1980		1981		1982	
	M	F	M	F	M	F	M	F	M	F	M	F	M	F	M	F	M	F	M	F
GERMANY																				
Secondary, 1st cycle	0.4		0.6	0.2	0.9	0.5			0.5		0.7	0.4	0.6	0.4	0.6	0.4				
Secondary, 2nd cycle																				
general	9.0		12.7	8.9	16.4	14.3			15.3		16.4	15.1	17.8	17.5	18.3	18.8				
technical/vocat. FT(1)	4.4		14.8	7.9	6.1	11.8			9.1		6.8	12.1	7.2	12.5	7.6	12.7				
technical/vocat. PT	25.0		39.5	18.5	44.4	23.6			37.3		46.6	31.4	49.5	34.1	48.2	33.5				
Higher																				
university	0.0		0.8	1.0	0.7	0.7			0.7		0.6	1.0	0.2	0.2	0.1	0.1				
non university	0.1		0.3	0.2	0.4	0.3			0.3		0.3	0.2	0.1	0.1	0.1	0.1				
Total FT	13.8		19.2	18.2	24.5	27.6			25.9		24.8	28.8	25.9	30.7	26.7	32.1				
Total PT	38.8		58.7	36.7	68.9	51.2			63.2		71.4	60.2	75.4	64.8	74.9	65.6				
AUSTRALIA FT			(1971)																	
Secondary			10.0	5.0	8.0	5.4	8.0	5.7	7.4	6.1	7.2	6.1	7.1	6.3	6.1	5.5	5.5	4.8		
TAFE (2)					2.7	2.0									3.9	4.1	4.5	4.0		
CAE			2.4	3.9	4.2	6.9									3.6	6.0	3.5	5.4		
Universities			6.5	4.6	7.0	5.2									5.6	4.6	5.4	4.6		
PT																				
TAFE					29.8	8.6									31.0	13.2	32.4	12.8		
CAE					0.8	0.4									0.9	0.6	0.9	0.5		
Universitiés					0.5	0.3									0.4	0.3	0.4	0.3		
Total FT					21.9	19.5									19.2	20.2	18.9	18.8		
Total FT + PT					53.0	28.8									51.5	34.3	52.6	32.4		
AUSTRIA																				
Compulsory schooling															0.0		0.0			
Secondary, 2nd cycle													14.3		14.0		13.7			
Vocational short													5.7		5.6		4.1			
Vocational long													8.1		9.0		9.7			
Non University															0.5		0.3			
University															4.4		4.8			
Vocational PT													45.7		44.3		43.9			
Vocational FT													28.1		33.5		32.6			
Total FT + PT													73.8		77.8		76.5			
CANADA			(1971)																	
Secondary			27.3		22.2						20.6		20.5		21.6		22.9			
Post-secondary			16.5		18.5						18.4		18.5		18.7		19.2			
Total			43.8		40.7						39.0		39.0		40.3		42.1			
DENMARK																				
Basic school									1.0											
Secondary, 2nd cycle																				
general									22.8											
technical/vocational									30.1											
Higher									0.8											
Total									55.3		55		58		61					

./...

Table 4 (cont'd)

ENROLMENT RATE AT 18 YEARS, BY TYPES OF EDUCATION

School year beginning in : Percentage

	1965		1970		1975		1976		1977		1978		1979		1980		1981		1982	
	M	F	M	F	M	F	M	F	M	F	M	F	M	F	M	F	M	F	M	F
SPAIN																				
Secondary, general and													Tot.	F						
teacher training	5.1		7.8		9.9		11.5		10.5		10.9	13.6	13.8	15.2						
Technical/vocational	2.2		4.9		5.8		6.4		7.3		8.9	4.7	7.8	5.8						
Other secondary	0.6		1.5		1.8		1.9		1.4		1.2	1.8	1.3	1.5						
Higher U	3.0		5.2		11.2		13.2		14.3		9.1	6.8	7.7	7.1						
NU											4.3	4.1	3.4	3.8						
Total	10.9		19.4		28.7		33.1		33.5		34.4	31.0	34.0	33.4						
UNITED STATES *																				
Secondary															22.0	14.2	22.2	14.2		
Higher															31.0	37.2	35.1	39.8		
Total															53.0	51.3	57.4	53.9		
FRANCE																				
Secondary, 1st cycle	0.5		0.1		0.1		0.1		0.0		0.0		0.0							
Vocational, short	3.5		5.1		5.8		5.8		5.9		6.2		6.7		7.0		7.9			
Secondary, 2nd cycle	16.9		17.8		17.7		18.0		18.1		18.6		19.3		19.7		20.6			
N. University (3)	0.6				4.3		4.5						5.6		5.9		5.9			
Universities(3)	4.9				5.6		5.9						7.3		7.5		7.8			
Apprenticeship													3.6		2.9		3.0			
Total FT	26.4				33.5		34.3						38.9		40.1		42.2			
Total FT + PT													42.5		43.0		45.2			
GREECE			(1972)																	
Secondary, general			13.0		14.2															
Secondary, technical/ vocational			8.5		11.3															
Non university			2.4		2.1															
University			5.2		7.3															
Total			29.1		34.9															
ITALY (4)	(1966)																			
Secondary, general and teacher training	7.7																11.8			
Technical	[12.4																16.2			
Professional	[																4.4			
Total	20.1				32.9						35.4	28.4					32.4			
* UNITED STATES (18 and 19 years)	55.6	37.7	54.4	41.6	49.9	44.2	48.2	44.4	48.4	44.0	47.8	43.0	46.6	43.4	47.1	45.8	50.5	47.5		

./...

Table 4 (cont'd)

ENROLMENT RATE AT 18 YEARS, BY TYPES OF EDUCATION

School year beginning in : Percentage

	1965		1970		1975		1976		1977		1978		1979		1980		1981		1982	
	M	F	M	F	M	F	M	F	M	F	M	F	M	F	M	F	M	F	M	F
NEW-ZEALAND																				
Secondary															6.4		6.5		5.6	
Techn. Institutes FT/PT															14.4		13.1		12.4	
Teacher Colleges															1.6		1.6		1.1	
University															9.7		10.2		10.1	
Total FT															32.1		31.4		29.2	
Full year conti. sec.ed. PT															3.6		3.6		3.3	
Total FT + PT															35.7		35.0		32.5	
NETHERLANDS FT			(1971)		(1974)															
Secondary, 1st cycle																				
general			2.4	1.4	2.6	1.7	3.1	2.1	3.2	2.1	3.1	2.2	3.2	2.5	3.2	2.5				
vocational			3.0	0.3	3.9	0.5	5.9	1.2	5.9	1.4	5.6	1.5	5.3	1.6	5.2	1.7				
Secondary, 2nd cycle																				
general			13.5	6.6	16.2	10.2	17.4	11.7	17.6	12.2	17.5	12.9	17.2	13.3	16.8	14.2	19.6	17.0 (5)		
vocational/technical			10.9	6.2	13.2	7.3	15.1	9.0	15.7	11.3	15.9	12.9	16.7	13.7	17.8	15.0	25.0	19.1 (6)		
Higher																				
university			4.3	1.4	3.5	1.7	3.5	1.8			3.9	2.0	3.6	2.1	3.5	2.0	3.5	2.2		
non university			4.9	4.9	5.7	5.4	5.9	6.1	5.8	6.4	5.8	6.2	5.5	5.7	5.1	5.5	4.8	5.6		
PT education			23.1	5.8	16.6	10.4	13.9	5.0	14.7	5.5	13.9	5.8	14.3	6.3	14.4	7.1	13.3	7.4		
Total FT			39.0	20.9	45.1	26.7	50.9	31.9			51.7	37.7	51.4	39.0	51.6	41.0				
Total FT + PT			62.1	26.7	61.7	37.1	64.8	36.9			65.6	43.5	65.7	45.3	66.0	48.1	66.2	51.3		
UNITED KINGDOM FT													(9)							
Secondary			7.4	5.4	6.9	5.5	6.6		6.9	5.9			2.2	1.5						
FE. educ. Non-advanced			4.4	3.1	5.1	5.1			5.5	6.0			4.0	4.3						
FE. "Advanced"			2.3	4.7	2.4	3.8	5.6		2.3	2.8			3.0	3.4						
Universities			4.8	3.0	4.6	3.2	6.8		4.8	3.3			6.3	4.7						
FE.Advanced courses PT(7)							0.5													
FE. Non-advanced PT(7)			35.5	15.0	33.8	17.9	24.6		30.2	17.1			28.5	16.4						
Total FT			18.9	16.2	19.0	17.7	19.0		19.5	18.1			15.5	14.0						
Total FT + PT			54.4	31.2	52.8	35.6	44.1		49.7	35.2			44.0	30.4						
SWEDEN			(1969)																	
Secondary			39.9		34.4						35.0									
Higher			0.2		0.2						0.8									
Total			40.1		34.6						35.8									
Other (8)			2.3		6.5						4.8									

./...

Table 4 (cont'd)

ENROLMENT RATE AT 18 YEARS, BY TYPES OF EDUCATION

School year beginning in :

Percentage

	1965		1970		1975		1976		1977		1978		1979		1980		1981		1982	
	M	F	M	F	M	F	M	F	M	F	M	F	M	F	M	F	M	F	M	F
SWITZERLAND																				
Primary															0.2		0.2			
Secondary, 1st cycle															0.3		0.3			
Secondary, 2nd cycle															67.5		70.1			
Higher															0.9		0.9			
Total															69.0		71.6			
YUGOSLAVIA																				
Skilled worker training	15.0				18.4															
Other technical/ vocational	12.6				17.0															
Secondary general/ and teach. training	13.0				14.1															
Higher																				

FT = Full-time - PT = Part-time
P = Provisional

(1) Including some pupils in part-time education.
(2) Technical and Further education including apprenticeship.
(3) Data or higher education U and NU do not include certain schools such as health, commerce and soon.
(4) Higher education not included.
(5) General secondary, 1st and 2nd cycles.
(6) Vocational secondary " " " ".
(7) Including evening classes.
(8) Adult education, popular education, training for the labour market.
(9) Age at 31st August, i.e. at beginning of academic year and not at 31st December as for the previous years.

Table 5

ENROLMENT RATE AT 19 YEARS, BY TYPES OF EDUCATION

School year beginning in : Percentage

	1965		1970		1975		1976		1977		1978		1979		1980		1981		1982	
	M	F	M	F	M	F	M	F	M	F	M	F	M	F	M	F	M	F	M	F
GERMANY																				
Secondary, 1st cycle	0.0		0.2	0.1	0.2	0.1			0.2		0.3	0.2	0.3	0.2						
Secondary, 2nd cycle																				
general	6.2		6.7	3.3	8.7	5.9			7.0		7.8	5.5	9.2	6.9	10.0	8.4	9.1			
technical/vocat. FT (1)	3.4		4.4	6.4	5.6	9.5			8.2		5.8	10.5	6.0	10.0	6.3	10.5	8.7			
technical/vocat. PT	9.4		15.0	5.1	19.0	8.0			16.9		22.9	13.7	26.4	15.4	28.5	18.5	24.0			
Higher																				
university	0.7		2.9	4.3	3.1	5.1			3.7		2.9	5.3	2.7	4.8	2.3	4.3				
non university FT	0.5		0.9	1.1	0.8	1.0			0.9		0.7	0.9	0.6	1.0	0.5	0.9				
Total FT	10.8		15.1	15.2	18.4	21.6			20.0		17.5	22.4	18.8	22.9	19.1	24.1				
Total FT + PT	20.2		30.1	20.3	37.4	29.6			36.9		40.4	36.1	45.2	38.3	47.6	42.6				
AUSTRALIA FT			(1971)																	
Secondary (2)			1.8	0.7	1.8	1.3	1.7	1.4	1.5	1.3	1.8	1.8	1.7	1.9	1.6	1.9	1.6	1.8		
TAFE (3)					1.8	1.4									2.3	2.1	2.8	2.3		
CAE			3.0	4.5	5.2	8.2									4.5	7.4	4.5	7.0		
Universities			8.3	5.0	8.5	6.1									7.1	5.6	7.0	5.6		
TP																				
TAFE					24.3	7.1									26.1	10.9	27.8	11.0		
CAE					1.3	0.6									1.3	0.9	1.3	0.8		
Universities					0.7	0.5									0.6	0.5	0.7	0.5		
Total FT					17.3	17.0									15.5	17.0	15.9	16.7		
Total FT + PT					43.6	25.2									43.5	29.3	45.7	29.0		
AUSTRIA																				
Compulsory schooling													0.0		0.0		-			
Sec. 2nd cycle/teach. train													7.1		6.4		2.8			
Vocational short													2.0		2.0		1.1			
Vocational long													7.9		8.3		9.3			
Non University															1.7		0.2			
Universities															8.1		8.7			
Vocational PT													23.5		24.1		23.5			
Total FT													17.0		26.5		22.1			
Total FT + PT													40.5		50.6		45.6			
CANADA			(1971)																	
Secondary			7.5		5.2						4.5		4.6		4.9		5.6			
Post-secondary			22.4		22.9						22.8		22.8		22.6		24.4			
Total			29.9		28.1						27.3		27.4		27.5		30.0			
DENMARK																				
Basic school									0.2											
Secondary, 2nd cycle																				
general									12.9											
technical/vocational									28.7											
Higher									5.2											
Total									47.7		47		47		50					

./...

Table 5 (cont'd)

ENROLMENT RATE AT 19 YEARS, BY TYPES OF EDUCATION

School year beginning in : Percentage

	1965		1970		1975		1976		1977		1978		1979		1980		1981		1982	
	M	F	M	F	M	F	M	F	M	F	M	F	M	F	M	F	M	F	M	F
SPAIN													T							
Secondary, general	3.6		4.9		4.8		5.8		6.0		4.7	5.8	5.7	6.5						
Technical and vocational	2.6		4.3		3.9		4.2		4.4		4.9	2.7	4.4	3.5						
Other secondary	0.4		1.1		1.7		1.6		1.4		1.1	2.2	1.2	1.4						
Higher U	3.2		6.7		12.2		14.4		14.4		10.7	8.1	9.1	8.4						
NU											5.9	5.4	5.6	5.5						
Total	9.8		17.0		22.6		26.1		26.2		27.3	24.2	26.0	25.3						
UNITED STATES																				
Secondary															3.4	2.6	5.1	3.3		
Higher															37.6	37.9	37.6	37.5		
Total															41.0	40.5	42.7	40.8		
FRANCE																				
Vocational, short	1.5		1.7		1.5		1.5		1.6		1.6		1.8		2.0		2.1			
Secondary, 2nd cycle	8.3		7.9		6.8		6.1		6.3		6.4		6.9		7.2		7.6			
NU (4)	1.4				5.4		5.7						7.9		8.9		9.4			
Universities (4)	7.1				8.2		8.9						9.9		10.5		10.3			
Apprenticeship													0.6		0.5		0.6			
Total FT	18.3				21.9		22.2						26.5		28.3		29.4			
Total FT + PT													27.1		28.8		30.0			
GREECE			(1972)																	
Secondary, general			4.8		5.3															
Secondary, technical/vocat.			8.1		13.2															
Non University			2.6		4.0															
University			6.9		10.9															
Total			22.4		33.4															
ITALY (5)			(1973)																	
Sec. general and teach.trai	3.7		4.0														5.3			
Technical	7.8		7.2														8.5			
Professional			1.6														1.8			
Total	11.5		12.6														15.6			
NEW ZEALAND																				
Secondary															1.0		1.3		1.3	
Tech. Inst. FT and PT															13.6		13.6		13.4	
Teacher Colleges															1.8		1.9		1.7	
University															11.2		11.7		11.5	
Total FT															27.6		28.5		27.9	
Full year conti. sec. ed PT															3.4		3.4		3.0	
Total FT + PT															31.0		31.9		30.9	
NETHERLANDS																				
Secondary, 1st cycle			(1971)		(1974)															
general			0.3	0.1	0.3	0.1	0.4	0.2	0.4	0.3	0.4	0.3	0.3	0.2	0.3	0.2				
vocational			0.9	0.1	0.8	0.1	1.3	0.2	1.3	0.3	1.2	0.3	1.1	0.4	1.1	0.4				

./...

Table 5 (cont'd)

ENROLMENT RATE AT 19 YEARS, BY TYPES OF EDUCATION

School year beginning in : Percentage

	1965		1970		1975		1976		1977		1978		1979		1980		1981		1982	
	M	F	M	F	M	F	M	F	M	F	M	F	M	F	M	F	M	F	M	F
NETHERLANDS (cont'd)																				
Secondary, 2nd cycle																				
general			5.9	1.6	7.2	2.6	7.1	3.2	7.3	3.2	7.2	3.2	7.2	3.6	6.9	3.7	7.1(6)	4.4(6)		
vocational/technical			8.5	3.5	10.4	3.8	12.4	4.6	12.8	5.2	13.6	6.4	13.8	6.8	14.6	7.6	16.8(7)	9.4(7)		
Higher																				
university			6.8	2.3	6.0	2.7					7.0	3.5	6.7	3.6	6.3	3.6	6.2	3.5		
non university			7.9	5.8	9.5	7.4	10.0	8.6	10.0	8.7	9.5	9.0	9.3	8.7	9.0	8.4	8.8	8.4		
PT education			15.8	4.8	12.6	5.0	11.5	4.9	11.7	5.0	13.2	5.3	11.0	5.7	11.2	6.2	11.4	7.0		
Total FT			30.3	13.4	34.2	16.8					38.8	22.6	38.4	23.3	38.2	24.0				
Total FT + PT			46.1	18.2	46.8	21.8					52.0	27.9	49.4	29.0	49.4	30.2	50.3	32.7		
UNITED KINGDOM FT													(9)							
Secondary			0.9	0.3	0.7	0.4		0.5	0.7	0.4			0.1	0.1						
Further education N. adv.			2.6	1.3	3.2	2.3			3.3	2.5			1.4	1.3						
Further " advanc.			4.4	7.4	4.4	6.4		2.9	4.2	5.0			4.3	4.6						
Universities			7.8	4.0	7.8	5.0		11.7	7.9	5.2			8.1	5.5						
F. Educ. Advanced PT (8)																				
F. Educ. non advanc. PT(8)			28.7	10.9	26.7	15.6		19.0	26.4	15.3			18.8	13.6						
Total FT			15.7	13.0	16.1	14.0		15.1	16.1	13.2			14.0	11.4						
Total FT + PT			44.4	23.9	42.8	29.6		35.2	42.5	28.5			32.8	25.0						
SWEDEN			(1969)																	
Secondary			18.2			12.9						10.9								
Higher			1.2(11)			5.0						4.4								
Total						17.9						15.3								
Other (10)			1.8			7.0						6.8								
SWITZERLAND																				
Primary																0.1		0.1		
Secondary, 1st cycle																0.1		0.1		
Secondary, 2nd cycle																45.4		45.8		
Higher																3.9		3.9		
Total																49.5		49.9		
YUGOSLAVIA																				
Skilled worker training	9.0					6.8														
Other technical/vocational	11.4					11.8														
Secondary, general and training	10.8					9.1														
Higher																				

Table 5 (cont'd)

P = Provisional

FT = Full-time - PT = Part-time.

(1) Including some pupils in part-time education.
(2) Including some pupils older than 19.
(3) Technical and Further education including apprenticeship.
(4) Including Preparatory classes to the "Grandes Ecoles". Data on higher education U and NU do not include certain schools such as health, commerce and so on.
(5) Higher Education not included.
(6) General secondary, 1st and 2nd cycles.
(7) Vocational secondary, 1st and 2nd cycles.
(8) Including evening classes.
(9) 19 and 20 years old. Age at 31st August, i.e. at beginning of academic year and not at 31st December as for the previous years.
(10) Adult education, popular education, training for the labour market.
(11) Excluding universities.

Table 6

RATES OF TRANSFER INSIDE AND OUTSIDE SECONDARY EDUCATION (1)

(Year of origin)

Percentage

Destination (t1) / Origin (t0)	1965		1970		1975		1976		1977		1978		1979		1980	
	M	F	M	F	M (1974)	F	M	F	M	F	M	F	M	F	M	F
DENMARK																
7th Basic school to																
Basic school	43.0		51.1	43.8	41.2	41.2	97.0	99.7								
Middle school	40.0		40.6	51.3	55.3	55.3	-	-								
Exit	17.7		8.3	4.9	3.6	3.6	3.0	0.3								
9th Basic school to																
Basic school	11.3		44.0	54.0	54.2	67.6	50.7	65.3								
Middle school	2.2		2.1	2.6	2.0	2.9	1.9	2.6								
Gymnasium			0.1	0.1	0.3	0.4	0.6	1.0								
Exit	86.3		53.6	43.1	42.7	28.7	46.2	30.6								
2nd Middle school (9th yr) to																
Basic school	0.2		0.4	0.4	2.7	2.3	1.4	1.3								
Middle school	76.6		75.0	77.3	75.1	76.8	76.6	77.7								
Gymnasium	20.2		22.3	20.2	17.5	17.6	17.2	17.7								
Exit	2.6		1.5	1.5	3.3	2.3	3.6	2.5								
10th Basic school to																
Middle school	0.9		3.0	2.0	3.5	4.4	1.8	2.5								
Gymnasium	0.3		1.1	0.2	2.4	1.0	1.7	1.0								
Exit	97.1		94.7	97.3	93.1	94.0	95.3	96.0								
3rd Middle school (10th yr) to																
Gymnasium	14.1		24.1	16.8	32.0	27.2	32.1	28.8								
Exit	85.4		75.0	82.8	67.1	72.0	66.7	70.5								
1st Gymnasium (10th-11th yr) to																
Middle school	0.6		0.9	1.5	0.3											
Gymnasium	92.4		86.8	87.8	90.5											
Exit	4.7		6.0	8.0	7.6											
FRANCE 6e-4e (6th to 8th yr) to																
Pre-vocational education							38.3						37.5			
Vocational "							44.8						46.4			
Exit							16.9						16.1			
Transfers as % of total enrolments							11.7						10.8			
Exits as % of total enrolments							2.0						1.7			
3e (10th yr.) to																
Pre-vocational education							0.2						0.2			
vocational							23.8						25.5			
2nd cycle general							55.8						55.3			
Exit							12.6						9.4			
Transfers as % of total enrolments							93.4						90.4			
Exits as % of total enrolments							11.8						8.5			

./...

Table 6 (cont'd)

RATES F TRANSFER INSIDE AND OUTSIDE SECONDARY EDUCATION (1)

(Year of origin)

Percentage

Destination (t1) / Origin (t0)	1965		1970		1975		1976		1977		1978		1979		1980	
	M	F	M	F	M	F	M	F	M	F	M	F	M	F	M	F
FRANCE (cont'd)																
Pre-vocational to																
Other pre-vocational							22.1						21.6			
Vocational							14.9						19.8			
Exit							63.0						58.6			
Transfers as % of total enrolments							87.2						78.2			
Exits as % of total enrolments							55.0						45.8			
1st and 2nd yrs vocational to																
General							0.8						-			
Pre-vocational							-						4.3			
Exit							99.2						95.7			
Transfers as % of total enrolments							17.7						13.7			
Exits as % of total enrolments							17.5						13.1			
3rd vocational to																
General							5.3						6.1			
Exit							94.7						93.9			
Transfers as % total enrolments							93.9						91.8			
Exists as % of total enrolments							89.0						86.2			
2e and lère (11-12th yr.) to																
Vocational							28.5						34.8			
Exit							71.5						65.2			
Transfers as % of total enrolments							8.1						8.3			
Exits as % of total enrolments							5.8						5.4			
ITALY			(1971)		(1973)											
Middle school to																
Higher secondary			68.8		66.9				74.2		74.5		74.5			
Vocational			6.8		0.8											
Exit			24.4		32.3											
Transfers as % of total enrolments			30.8		31.5											
Exits as % of total enrolments			7.5		10.2											
Higher secondary to																
Vocational			9.1		1.1											
Universities			39.5		37.2				74.6		74.6		72.7			
Exit			51.4		61.7											
Transfers as % of total enrolments			24.8		25.8											
Exits as % of total enrolments			12.8		15.9											
JAPAN																
Graduates 1st cycle sec. to																
2nd cycle sec.	71.6	69.6	81.6	82.7	91.0	93.0	91.7	93.5	92.2	94.0	92.7	94.4	93.0	95.0	93.1	95.4
Vocational							3.6	2.5	3.5	2.5	3.2	2.4	3.1	2.1	3.0	2.0
Exit	28.3	30.4	18.4	17.3	9.0	7.0	4.7	4.0	4.3	3.5	4.1	3.2	3.9	2.9	3.9	2.6

./...

Table 6 (cont'd)

RATES OF TRANSFER INSIDE AND OUTSIDE SECONDARY EDUCATION (1)

(Year of origin)

Percentage

Destination (t1) / Origine (t0)	1965		1970		1975		1976		1977		1978		1979		1980	
	M	F	M	F	M	F	M	F	M	F	M	F	M	F	M	F
JAPAN (cont'd)																
2nd cycle sec. to Higher	25.4		25.0	23.5	33.8	34.6	32.8	35.1	32.2	34.3	31.9	33.7	30.5	33.4	30.3	33.5
vocational							15.0	14.2	16.4	16.2	18.6	17.0	21.1	17.9	22.2	18.2
Exit	74.6		75.0	76.5	66.2	65.4	52.2	50.7	51.4	49.5	49.5	49.3	48.4	48.7	47.5	48.3
NETHERLANDS																
1st cycle general without diploma to					(1974)											
2nd cycle general			65.8	59.1	66.0	67.5	67.1	69.1	63.8	66.2	64.4	67.9	62.9	67.0		
1st cycle vocational			14.4	10.3	19.0	15.2	21.5	17.5	23.1	18.3	24.3	18.4	23.8	17.3		
2nd cycle vocational			3.5	3.7	1.5	1.4	1.4	1.2	1.4	0.9	1.6	1.1	1.7	1.3		
Apprenticeship and PT			6.7	3.9	3.3	3.2	3.8	4.1	3.5	3.6	2.7	2.6	3.6	4.1		
Exit			9.6	23.0	9.7	12.7	5.5	7.7	7.5	10.7	6.3	9.7	7.2	10.1		
Transfers as % of total enrolments			14.2	14.3	15.2	13.7	14.8	13.5	15.4	13.9	15.7	14.0	16.4	14.9		
Exists as % of total enrolments			1.4	3.3	1.5	1.7	0.8	1.0	1.2	1.5	1.0	1.4	1.2	1.5		
1st cycle general with diploma to																
2nd cycle general			34.3	18.3	38.9	27.0	38.7	29.7	40.2	31.4	37.6	31.7	33.1	30.9		
1st cycle vocational			0.6	0.1	0.8	0.2	1.0	0.2	1.2	0.4	1.8	0.4	2.1	0.4		
2nd cycle vocational (2)			36.4	28.3	42.6	35.1	45.2	39.8	44.6	37.9	46.4	39.6	46.6	41.2		
Apprenticeship and PT			8.3	5.5	4.4	8.0	6.8	9.8	6.9	9.8	6.0	8.7	7.6	10.6		
Exit			20.3	47.8	13.3	29.7	8.3	21.8	7.1	20.6	8.1	19.5	5.0	16.6		
1st cycle vocat. without diploma to																
1st cycle general			6.2	4.6	10.6	14.4	9.7	12.0	8.0	11.7	6.8	11.8	5.8	9.3		
2nd cycle vocational			0.3	-	0.6	0.1	0.3	-	0.2	-	0.3	0.2	1.3	1.0		
Apprenticeship and PT			32.8	10.4	36.4	22.2	53.4	63.5	48.9	51.6	45.3	51.2	50.3	59.8		
Exit			60.6	85.0	50.9	62.7	34.1	23.4	39.6	34.6	44.7	34.6	39.4	26.8		
Transfers as % of total enrolments			8.0	14.9	6.6	8.7	5.4	5.9	5.6	6.6	6.8	6.4	6.5	5.7		
Exits as % of total enrolments			4.8	12.7	3.4	5.3	1.8	1.4	2.2	2.3	3.0	2.2	2.6	1.5		
1st cycle vocat. with diploma to																
1st cycle general					0.2	0.1	1.0	1.2	1.1	1.2	0.9	1.1	1.3	1.7		
2nd cycle vocational (2)			22.0	42.0	22.9	48.1	26.9	40.3	24.3	40.1	22.7	39.1	23.5	39.7		
Apprenticeship PT			66.8	5.9	46.8	16.4	49.9	27.7	49.7	28.5	48.1	27.0	47.0	27.5		
Exit			11.3	51.9	30.1	35.5	22.2	30.9	24.9	30.2	28.3	32.7	28.2	31.1		
2nd cycle vocat. without diploma to																
non-university higher			24.7	0.1	10.0	0.5	10.3	0.7	8.3	0.5	8.6	0.6	10.2	0.0		
Apprenticeship PT			15.1	1.9	4.0	1.3	4.2	2.1	5.0	1.0	3.4	0.3	4.6	0.2		
Exit			60.2	97.9	85.7	97.8	85.0	97.0	86.3	98.3	87.6	99.0	84.3	98.1		
Transfers as % of total enrolments			12.1	10.9	14.2	11.8	12.6	12.6	13.4	16.3	13.6	16.2	13.1	16.2		
Exits			7.3	10.7	12.2	11.5	10.7	12.2	11.6	16.0	11.9	16.0	11.0	15.9		

./..

Table 6 (cont'd)

RATES OF TRANSFER INSIDE AND OUTSIDE SECONDARY EDUCATION (1)

(Year of origin)

Percentage

Origin (t0) / Destination (t1)	1965		1970		1975		1976		1977		1978		1979		1980	
	M	F	M	F	M	F	M	F	M	F	M	F	M	F	M	F
NETHERLANDS (cont'd)																
2nd cycle vocational with diploma to																
Non-university higher			8.9	5.3	9.3	0.9	10.4	1.5	12.9	3.1	10.4	1.9	13.4	3.0		
Apprenticeship PT			6.1	17.0	6.3	14.7	5.3	14.7	3.8	20.5	4.1	17.5	4.7	15.9		
Exit			85.0	77.7	84.4	84.4	84.3	83.9	83.3	76.4	85.5	80.6	82.6	81.1		
2nd cycle general without diploma to																
2nd cycle vocational			4.3	7.3	9.0	7.0	11.3	8.4	13.0	9.9	12.0	8.0	13.9	8.1		
Non-university higher			6.3	3.6	4.3	1.7	4.9	2.8	3.5	2.7	2.1	2.4	2.2	2.1		
Apprenticeship PT			5.4	3.5	4.5	5.2	7.8	7.1	8.3	6.6	0.5	1.3	8.0	8.1		
Exit			83.9	85.6	82.0	86.1	74.6	80.1	74.0	79.3	84.3	86.4	74.5	81.1		
Transfers as % of total enrolments			5.8	6.3	6.5	6.3	5.4	5.3	5.5	5.4	6.4	6.0	7.0	7.2		
Exits as % of total enrolments			4.9	5.4	5.3	5.4	4.0	4.2	4.1	4.3	6.0	5.2	5.2	5.8		
2nd cycle general with diploma to																
2nd cycle vocational			0.2	3.4	0.9	4.0	1.4	4.2	1.7	4.0	2.8	4.4	4.1	5.1		
Non-university higher			27.8	30.2	36.9	34.2	39.9	37.9	41.9	39.8	39.8	37.5	37.8	36.5		
University higher			43.8	15.3	33.1	16.6	-	-	-	-	-	-	27.4	15.4		
Apprenticeship PT			1.4	1.7	1.3	2.2	1.6	2.1	1.6	2.3	1.7	2.0	1.6	2.6		
Exit (3)			26.8	49.3	27.7	43.1	57.0	55.7	54.8	53.8	55.7	55.7	20.5	40.4		

PT - Part-time.

(1) Not including repeaters in the same type of education, consequently the total cannot be equal to 100 per cent.
(2) Including a number of pupils entering non-university-type higher education.
(3) Including pupils entering higher education, for 1976, 1977 and 1978.

Table 7

RATES OF RETENTION IN 2nd CYCLE SECONDARY EDUCATION 1965-1979 (1)

Percentage

	1965		1970		1975		1976		1977		1978		1979		1980		1981	
	M	F	M	F	M	F	M	F	M	F	M	F	M	F	M	F	M	F
AUSTRALIA - As percentage of number of pupils who started secondary school																		
10th year of study			78.7	76.2	82.0	82.2	86.5	86.7	87.1	88.3	88.3	89.5	88.5	90.4	89.5	91.5	90.3	92.6
11th " "			46.0	38.7	48.2	47.1	51.4	52.6	50.3	54.4	51.1	55.8	50.4	55.8	50.8	57.3	51.6	59.0
12th " "			31.1	23.7	34.1	31.6	34.6	35.3	34.0	36.6	33.1	37.3	32.4	37.2	31.9	37.3	32.0	37.8
CANADA - As percentage of pupils enrolled in 9th year of study 3 years earlier																		
12th year of study	51.1		77.5		74.2		78.2		77.0		77.9		77.5		77.9		78.2	
UNITED STATES - As percentage of pupils who started 5th year of study and are still enrolled in :	(1966)				(1974)													
10th year of study	90.8		92.8		95.9		95.8		95.9		96.3		97.6		98.4			
11th " "	84.2		86.0		87.1		86.9		87.6		88.3		87.4		88.6			
12th " "	76.1		79.0		78.3		78.6		78.9		80.0		79.4		79.8			
Graduates	73.2		75.0		74.4		74.9		74.4		74.6		74.3		74.4			
FRANCE - Proportion of a given generation still enrolled at (2) :																		
Age 15			81.2		91.7		92.6		91.2									
16			62.9		69.6		70.6		70.8		71.6							
17			44.1		49.9		51.7		52.7		54.3		55.4					
18			24.9		25.2		26.2		27.0		27.8		29.0					
JAPAN - Graduates of 2nd cycle secondary education in relation to 1st cycle graduates 3 years earlier	59.6		72.0		85.0		85.9		86.4		88.4		88.5		88.6		88.6	
UNITED KINGDOM (England and Wales) - As percentage of number of pupils aged 13 (1965 and 1970) or 14 (as from 1975) 2 to 4 years earlier - secondary schools only																		
Grant-aided schools																		
Age 15	40.5	39.6	55.1	54.6														
16	23.9	21.8	32.4	31.7	23.1	24.2	24.5	25.9	24.7	26.8	23.4	25.6	25 (3)					
17	12.5	10.2	17.7	16.9	17.6	18.0	18.4	18.8	18.9	19.5	18.5	19.1	18 (3)					
18	5.1	3.2	6.6	4.8	6.4	5.2	6.5	5.4	6.8	5.9	6.5	5.7	6 (3)					
Non-grant-aided schools																		
Age 15	89.0	87.6	93.7	88.9														
16	76.2	62.7	80.0	67.2	77.2	61.6	68.6		68.2		67.3							
17	51.0	34.4	57.7	44.6	61.8	52.6	57.2		57.7		57.3							
18	17.3	8.4	18.7	11.2	19.1	14.0	16.9		17.8		17.3							

(1) Or nearest year.
(2) Excluding higher education but including the preparatory classes for the "Grandes Ecoles" and the higher technician sections.
(3) England only.

Table 8

ANNUAL GROWTH RATE AND, FOR THE LAST YEAR AVAILABLE, DISTRIBUTION OF THE NUMBER OF GRADUATES IN THE DIFFERENT TYPES OF 2nd CYCLE SECONDARY EDUCATION

Percentage

	1965-70		1970-75		1975-76		1976-77		1977-78		1978-79		1979-80		1980-81		1975-LY		Distribution LY	
	M	F	M	F	M	F	M	F	M	F	M	F	M	F	M	F	M	F	M	F
													(1978-80)							
GERMANY																				
General	10.6		7.2		15.0		9.7		6.8				0.0		17.1		9.7		17.6	
Technical/vocational leading to higher			47.0		16.0		-1.6		-4.9				1.3		15.6		5.3		6.7	
PT education			-0.6		6.6		-0.3		-0.8				6.3		4.8		3.3		60.1	
FT education			3.9		-3.7		-2.8		21.7				16.9		2.4		6.9		15.6	
AUSTRIA			1970-1973																	
General			3.7						7.5											
CANADA																				
High school	11.1		3.2		8.2(1)		2.1		-0.8		0.9		1.6				2.3			
DENMARK																				
Gymnasium					-3.6		1.9		11.9								3.4			
HF courses (2)					4.7		-4.9		-2.0								-0.7			
SPAIN (3)																				
General			23.0		31.5		-67.5		117.3		7.9		0.8				18.0		59.6	
Vocational training	-7.1		9.2		134.8		39.6		2.1		-0.1		33.8				42.0		40.4	
UNITED STATES	1966-70		1970-74																	
High school	2.4	2.6	1.4	1.7	-0.4	0.3	-0.4	0.3	-0.8	-0.4	-0.3	0.2	-1.9	-2.6			-0.8	-0.4		
FINLAND																				
General	5.6	7.1	5.7	6.7	4.0	4.3	-0.8	4.3	6.9	5.3	-5.7	-0.7	0.0	6.3			0.9	3.9	32.3	
Vocational	3.5	5.2	1.9	0.9	-1.0		5.0		4.8		5.4		2.7				3.4		67.7	
FRANCE																				
General (Bac) (4)	7.0		2.2		10.3	9.0	-0.5	2.1	1.4	2.1	0.4	1.6					2.9	3.7	25.8	35.2
Vocational short	0.4	1.2	4.3	4.3	6.6	11.2	7.5	3.6	2.8	6.0	2.2	3.5					4.8	6.1	64.3	52.0
Technical long (4)	85.0	55.0	6.1	11.2	-0.4	2.7	7.8	11.4	8.4	6.2	1.4	1.7					4.3	5.5	10.0	12.8
GREECE																				
General	3.7		7.6	8.3	-2.0	2.4													57.9	80.6
Technical/vocation.	7.0	11.2	8.7	6.0	2.4	9.3													42.1	19.4
JAPAN																				
High School	4.9		-1.1		-0.2		5.9		-0.8		-0.7		1.1		1.8		1.3			
ITALY																				
Classical/scientific "Maturity"	8.9	13.3	4.5	9.9	2.5	-2.2	5.3	9.8	-3.2	-5.7							1.5	0.6	23.9	22.4
Teacher "Maturity"	11.9	9.5	-8.0	-3.5	23.1	-2.2	6.2	2.0	5.3	-2.5							11.5	-0.9	2.8	16.5
Technical "Maturity"	27.5	17.4	2.7	11.7	1.2	4.0	1.8	15.5	2.4	4.0							1.8	7.8	46.8	24.8
Vocational/artistic "Maturity"					22.4	20.6	5.0	20.1	-2.3	-3.6							8.4	12.4	8.1	8.4
Teacher "Licence"	17.9		1.3			2.8		4.3		28.6								11.9		8.9
Vocational/artistic qualification	4.4	5.3	1.7	5.2	-3.1	3.6	2.4	4.2	-0.8	-0.8							-0.5	2.3	18.4	19.0

./...

Table 8 (cont'd)

ANNUAL GROWTH RATE AND, FOR THE LAST YEAR AVAILABLE, DISTRIBUTION OF THE NUMBER OF GRADUATES IN THE DIFFERENT TYPES OF 2nd CYCLE SECONDARY EDUCATION

Percentage

	1965-70		1970-75		1975-76		1976-77		1977-78		1978-79		1979-80		1980-81		1975-LY		Distribution LY	
	M	F	M	F	M	F	M	F	M	F	M	F	M	F	M	F	M	F	M	F
NETHERLANDS	(1967-70)																			
General short			15.9	9.3	3.6	8.8	2.3	5.9	17.7	6.1	-0.5	-0.5	-1.0	4.3			4.4	4.9	35.5	35.7
General long	-0.2	6.8	-2.0	7.7	9.3	17.5	5.2	2.6	-0.6	1.7	0.0	0.0	0.6	2.5			2.9	4.9	28.1	20.2
Vocat., 2nd cycle FT			8.5	3.1	5.9	-10.3	7.9	-30.0	7.4	15.8	8.9	19.3	6.3	2.9			7.3	-0.5	29.5	35.7
" " PT			-10.0	5.3	12.5	8.3	-5.6	3.8	2.9	-1.9	17.1	0.0	-4.9	-3.8			4.4	1.3	6.8	8.4
UNITED KINGDOM - School leavers by highest qualification																				
GCE A level/SCE H Grade	3.3	5.1	1.6	2.0	3.3	4.3	2.6	3.2											17.4	16.0
GCE O level/CSE/SCE O Grade	1.7	3.6	8.6	9.0	10.3	10.1	1.6	3.0											32.4	38.0
No higher grade	0.4	0.8	2.8	2.8	5.0	5.9	2.7	1.9											50.3	45.8
SWEDEN			(1972-75)																	
3/4 yr. courses			-4.5		-2.5		3.7		1.1		3.6		7.8				2.7		33.4	18.5
2 yr. courses (5)			1.9		3.7		4.5		8.6		3.6		5.8				5.2		45.9	40.1
Special courses (5)			-4.5		0.7		0.7		-0.9		-2.0		-6.5				-1.6		20.7	41.4
YUGOSLAVIA																				
General	6.9		3.3		13.3														25.1	
Teacher education	2.3		-20.0		16.7														0.7	
Technical	2.2		5.6		8.1														29.5	
Vocational	6.2		2.0		4.6														44.7	

FT = Full-time - PT = Part-time.

LY = Last year available.

(1) This high rate is due to the reorganisation of the educational system of one of the Provinces.
(2) HF courses = leading to the higher preparatory examination.
(3) The reorganisation of secondary education and vocational training explain the variations between 1976/77 and 78.
(4) Including "certificats de fin d'études secondaires générales et professionnelles" as from 1976.
(5) Courses of variable duration - a few weeks to 1 year or more - attached to different gymnasium sections and preparing for specific trades.

Table 9

2nd CYCLE SECONDARY DIPLOMAS GIVING ACCESS TO HIGHER EDUCATION AND RELATION WITH POPULATION OF CORRESPONDING AGE

Thousand

Diplomas giving access to	1965	1970	1975	1976	1977	1978	1979	1980	1981
GERMANY University									
°/oo population 18 yrs		108	142	161	167	175		168	
"Fachhochschulen"(NU)									
°/oo population 18 yrs		5	52	60	56	51		52	
Total °/oo		113	194	220	223	226		220	
AUSTRIA Higher			(1973)						
Number		14.5	16.2		14.1	15.1			
°/oo population		153	159		122	128			
CANADA Higher Number	134.2	227.3	266.4	288.2	294.2	292.0	294.6	299.3	
°/oo population 18 yrs	367	557	580	618	618	608	626	624	
DENMARK Higher									
Number			17.9	17.7	17.6	18.3			
°/oo population 18 yrs			240	238	237	247			
SPAIN University									
orientation course		(1969)							
Number	21.7	33.8	132.8	174.7	56.8(1)	123.5	133.2	153.2	
°/oo population	38	62	226	293	92	198	214	241	
UNITED STATES Higher									
°/oo population 17 yrs		757		749		745		736 P	
FINLAND Higher Number		13.4	18.3	24.8	25.4	26.9	26.2	27.2	28.7
°/oo population 19 yrs	167	206	299	309	336	343	358	378	
FRANCE Bac. general/to U									
Number	105.7	138.6	154.1	151.2	152.6	155.4	158.9		
°/oo population	135	162	183	179	180	182			
Bac technician/to NU	-	28.6	50.8	50.9	56.2	60.1			
°/oo population		33	60	60	66	71			
Total °/oo	135	195	243	239	246	253			
GREECE Higher Number	34.1	40.8	64.6	63.8					
°/oo population	230	319	480	466					
ITALY University									
Diplom general number	42.3	69.9	96.0	97.7	104.9	100.3	100.3	100.3	
°/oo population	54	93	179	121	130	120	110	114	
Teacher (primary) Number	31.3	50.2	40.4	40.6	40.9	40.3	39.0	42.0	
°/oo population	40	59	50	50	51	48	43	48	
Technical/voc./artistic									
Number	99.1	112.5	171.4	176.7	189.6	192.6	190.1	196.5	
°/oo population	198	183	213	219	234	230	209	223	
Total °/oo	232	335	382	390	415	398	362	385	

./...

Table 9 (cont'd)

2nd CYCLE SECONDARY DIPLOMAS GIVING ACCESS TO HIGHER EDUCATION AND RELATION WITH POPULATION OF CORRESPONDING AGE

Thousand

Diplomas giving access to	1965	1970	1975	1976	1977	1978	1979	1980	1981
JAPAN Higher Number	1.160.1	1.403.0	1.327.4	1.325.1	1.403.3	1.392.3	1.383.5	1.399.3	1.424.3
°/oo population	505	742	844	838	863	876	881	880	870
NETHERLANDS University	(1967)								
Number	21.4	22.2	23.7	26.7	27.8	27.9	27.9	28.3	
°/oo population	101	100	105	115	118	116			
Non university									
Diplom general (havo)									
Number	6.9	18.8	33.5	35.6	37.1	41.4	41.2		
°/oo population	32	84	148	153	158	172			
Technical Number		37.8	44.1	43.1	37.6	41.0	46.3	47.5	
°/oo population		170	195	186	160	171			
Total °/oo		354	448	454	436	459			
UNITED KINGDOM Univers.(2)	(1967)								
Number	87.0	99.0	109.2	113.3	116.5				
°/oo population	106	129	134	135	137				
NU (3) Number	77.8	84.2	99.3	111.3	113.0				
°/oo population	95	109	122	133	133				
Total °/oo	201	238	256	268	270				
SWEDEN		(1972)							
3/4 yr. courses Higher Number		31.8	27.7	27.0	28.0	28.3			
°/oo population		236	253	245	255	259			
2 yr. courses Number		38.7	40.9	42.4	44.3	48.1			
°/oo population		287	375	384	404	441			
Total °/oo		523	628	629	659	700			
YUGOSLAVIA University									
Number	28.4	37.1	45.1	51.1	54.7				
°/oo population	90	98	115	134	145				
Technical and teachers training colleges Number	41.0	44.8	56.7	61.4	68.9				
°/oo population	129	118	144	161	183				
Total °/oo	219	216	259	295	328				

(1) This figure relates to repeaters only due to the extension of one year of the duration of education leading to the new BUP (comprehensive unified baccalaureate).
(2) Pupils obtaining GCE Advanced level with 2 or more A Grades or SCE with 3 or more H grades.
(3) Pupils obtaining GCE Advanced level with 1 A grade or SCE with 1 or 2 H grades or GCE/CSE/SCE ordinary with 5 or more passes.

Table 10

PROPORTION OF A GENERATION (1) ENTERING HIGHER EDUCATION, UNIVERSITY-TYPE (U) AND NON-UNIVERSITY-TYPE (NU)

Per mil

	1965	1970	1975	1976	1977	1978	1979	1980	1981
GERMANY									
U	91	116	144	140	135	139	133	139	
NU	31	37	51	54	50	47	51	56	
Total	122	153	195	194	185	186	184	195	
AUSTRALIA Universities		(1973) 121	168	165	159	161	160	162	162
CAE U Level			68		94	106	111	117	127
CAE NU Level			128.		96	97	85	81	79
Total			364		349	364	356	360	368
AUSTRIA									
U		(1972) 88	86			114	122	126P	132P
NU							49	49	50
Total							171	175P	182P
BELGIUM									
U			118	128	130	127	135	129	129
DENMARK									
U	74	118	175	163	147	145	143	145	
NU			178	182	156(2)	155(2)	147(2)	182	
Total			353	345	303(2)	300(2)	290(2)	327	
SPAIN									
U	67	145	198	194	206	// 125	166	177	
NU			107	114	129	// 109	107	106	
Total			305	308	335	234	273	283	
UNITED STATES									
U	284	309	279	270	274	275	279	278	279
NU	147	242	321	289	299	298	312	330	338
Total	431	551	600	559	573	573	591	608	617
FINLAND									
U	135	116	160	152	151	151	157	187	
NU	71	77	95						
Total	206	193	255						
FRANCE									
U			218	213	213	216	217	213	225
NU (3)		38	57	68	74	73	102	105	115
Total			275	281	290	289	319	318	340
ITALY (4)									
Total	135	256	311	304	292	286	271	276	251

./...

Table 10 (cont'd)

PROPORTION OF A GENERATION (1) ENTERING HIGHER EDUCATION, UNIVERSITY-TYPE (U) AND NON-UNIVERSITY-TYPE (NU)

Per mil

	1965	1970	1975	1976	1977	1978	1979	1980	1981
JAPAN									
U	109	176	276	266	263	268	258	255	250
NU	35	67	114	110	113	114	112	110	108
Total	144	243	390	376	376	382	370	365	358
NETHERLANDS (4)									
U	61	83	// 85	87	93	90	92	93	93
NU						165	166	165	164
Total						255	258	258	257
UNITED KINGDOM	(1968)								
Universities FT	82	83	91	91	94	95	93		
Universities FT and "Advanced Further education" (5)		199		274	280	286	285		
SWEDEN									
Total	134	229	248	266	// 228	243	251		
YUGOSLAVIA (6)									
U	129	159	195	201	216	240			
NU	70	66	75	89	89	92			
Total	199	225	270	290	305	332			

P = Provisional. FT: Full Time

// indicates a change of classification.

(1) Average of age groups normally corresponding to entry into higher education.
(2) Without preprimary teacher training.
(3) As the number of institutions taken into account vary from year to year, data are not really comparable.
(4) 1st year students.
(5) Full time and part time for England and Wales only. Include courses of university and non university level.
(6) Regular 1st year students.

Table 11

RATES OF TRANSFER FROM SECONDARY EDUCATION (BY TYPE) TO HIGHER EDUCATION

Academic year beginning in : Percentage

	1965	1970	1975	1976	1977	1978	1979	1980	1981
AUSTRALIA									
Total			53.9	51.3	48.7	45.8	47.3	42.5	
University			28.4	26.9	25.0	23.1	22.6	22.0	
CAE			25.5	24.4	23.6	22.7	24.7	20.4	
CANADA									
High school			P	P	P	P	P	P	
Total		51.7	54.5	52.4	52.6	51.3	51.4	51.5	
University		25.0	24.1	23.2	21.9	22.6	23.2	23.4	
Non university		26.7	30.4	29.2	30.7	28.7	28.2	28.1	
DENMARK	(1966)								
Universities and Centres	59.3	54.6	53.8						
SPAIN - Relation between pupils enrolled in pre-university year or COU and pupils who spent the previous year taking a 6th year of general baccalaureate or a 7th year of technical baccalaureate.	51.7	50.2	82.5	(1)	88.7	81.7	88.3		
UNITED STATES									
High school									
U + NU		48.9	50.3	48.5	50.0	49.6	49.0	48.6	
FRANCE		(1973)							
Preparatory classes for "Grandes Ecoles"									
General Baccalaureat		12.1	12.1			12.9			
Technical Baccalaureat		0.3	0.2			0.8			
Universities									
General Baccalaureat		53.3	54.7			55.5			
Technical Baccalaureat		13.5	15.0			16.5			
University Institutes of Technology									
General Baccalaureat		6.4	6.9			7.3			
Technical Baccalaureat		14.0	13.3			14.7			
Higher Technician									
General Baccalaureat		6.4	7.7			8.9			
Technical Baccalaureat		18.1	18.6			19.0			
Total									
General Baccalaureat		78.2	81.4			84.6			
Technical Baccalaureat		45.9	47.1			51.0			

./...

Table 11 (cont'd)

RATES OF TRANSFER FROM SECONDARY EDUCATION (BY TYPE) TO HIGHER EDUCATION

Academic year beginning in : Percentage

	1965		1970		1975		1976		1977		1978		1979		1980		1981	
	M	F	M	F	M	F	M	F	M	F	M	F	M	F	M	F	M	F
JAPAN (2)																		
Universities	20.7	4.6	27.3	6.5	40.4	12.5	40.9	13.0	39.6	12.6	40.8	12.5	39.3	12.2	39.3	12.3	38.6	12.2
Junior colleges	1.7	6.7	2.0	11.2	2.6	19.9	2.4	20.6	2.3	20.7	2.3	21.0	2.1	20.9	2.0	21.0	1.9	20.8
Technical colleges	0.3	0.0	0.8	0.0	1.1	0.0	1.1	0.0	1.1	0.0	1.1	0.0	1.1	0.0	1.1	0.0	1.1	0.0
NETHERLANDS - 1st year university students in relation to graduates in pre-university education			(1971)															
	79.4	52.7	94.6	69.7	94.0	60.7	93.0	61.9	91.5	58.6	86.0	58.8	91.9	64.7	91.9	66.4		
UNITED KINGDOM - Destination of qualified secondary school leavers																		
Universities																		
3 or more A levels			68.2	57.6	66.9	55.2			66.0	54.9								
2 A levels			20.9	11.3	21.7	14.8			18.7	13.7								
1 A level			1.7	0.7	0.7	1.2			1.4	0.7								
5 or more 0 levels			0.2	0.1	0.1	0.1			0.2	0.0								
1 to 4 0 levels			0.0	0.0	0.0	0.0			0.0	0.0								
Further Education																		
3 or more A levels			15.4	28.1	13.6	24.4			15.4	22.7								
2 A levels			41.4	61.3	38.0	45.9			40.4	44.4								
1 A level			41.7	61.0	35.6	46.3			36.8	42.8								
5 or more 0 levels			26.5	42.2	27.7	40.2			24..0	38.1								
1 to 4 0 levels			16.6	25.8	14.7	27.3			13.3	28.4								
Total universities and Further Education																		
3 or more A levels			83.6	85.7	80.5	79.6			81.4	77.6								
2 A levels			62.3	72.6	59.7	60.7			59.1	58.1								
1 A level			42.8	61.7	36.3	47.5			38.2	43.5								
5 or more 0 levels			26.7	42.3	27.8	40.3			24.2	38.1								
1 to 4 0 levels			16.6	25.8	14.7	27.3			13.3	28.4								

(1) Due to the extension of one year of education leading to the new BUP (comprehensive unified baccalaureat), only repeaters were enrolled in COU that year.

(2) The proportion of secondary education graduates wishing to enter higher education is as follows :

Universities	39.7	11.1	51.9	17.1	52.0	17.5	51.3	16.8	49.7	15.9	49.3	16.1
Junior colleges	1.8	16.4	2.1	23.5	2.0	24.0	2.0	24.2	2.0	24.3	1.8	24.3

P. Provisional

Table 12

TIME LAG BETWEEN OBTAINING 2nd CYCLE SECONDARY DIPLOMA AND ENTERING HIGHER EDUCATION

Percentage

	1965		1970		1975		1976		1977		1978		1979		1980		1981	
	M	F	M	F	M	F	M	F	M	F	M	F	M	F	M	F	M	F
GERMANY																		
Same year									46.4	81.0	46.1	78.1	40.0	71.5				
1 year after									34.9	11.0	34.1	12.0	34.7	15.3				
2 yrs or more									18.7	8.0	19.8	9.9	25.3	13.2				
AUSTRALIA - University FT																		
Following calendar year					[92.2	92.6	85.9	85.5	83.6	82.8	82.2	81.0	81.5	79.8	80.4	77.4		
1 year after							7.4	7.2	8.1	8.0	8.1	7.7	7.9	9.4	8.4	9.9		
More than 1 year after					4.5	4.4	3.8	3.7	4.8	4.7	4.3	3.9	5.0	4.2	5.1	4.2		
Other (1)					3.3	3.0	2.9	3.6	3.5	4.5	5.3	7.3	5.3	6.2	5.9	8.2		
CAE FT																		
Following calendar year						82.7			79.4	86.2	78.8	85.4	78.8	85.8	77.3	83.8	79.4	83.7
1 year after						7.8			10.8	7.1	10.0	7.0	9.3	6.7	10.1	7.5	9.5	7.9
More than 1 year after						9.5			9.8	6.7	11.2	7.6	11.9	7.5	12.5	8.7	11.1	8.4
Universities PT																		
Following calendar year					[46.3	33.0	31.7	27.1	33.8	27.0	30.7	17.2	30.1	18.4	26.8	14.2		
1 year after							8.4	7.3	7.2	7.8	7.6	8.3	7.0	8.1	7.3	7.0		
More than 1 year after					28.5	37.6	29.6	33.8	30.7	30.8	20.4	22.2	16.6	18.1	19.8	20.6		
Other (1)					25.3	29.4	30.3	31.8	28.3	34.4	41.3	52.3	45.5	54.9	45.1	57.9		
CAE PT																		
Following calendar year						48.0			45.3	45.5	40.4	38.3	41.1	42.4	39.8	41.2	40.6	35.5
1 year after						13.0			14.3	11.0	13.0	14.6	14.5	11.9	14.5	12.3	13.1	13.3
More than 1 year after						39.0			40.4	43.5	46.6	47.1	44.3	45.7	45.7	46.5	46.3	51.2
UNITED STATES																		
Same year					54.5	56.9	53.1	56.4	55.4	52.9	56.9	57.1	55.4	52.9				
1 to 3 yrs after					21.2	23.2	22.8	21.3	20.7	21.1	23.8	19.5	25.1	20.1				
4 yrs and over after					24.3	19.9	24.1	22.4	24.0	25.9	19.3	23.4	19.5	27.1				
FRANCE																		
Total University + IUT																		
Same year						74.3						79.0			72.9			
1 year after						11.8						5.8			5.2			
2 yrs or more after						12.7						12.3			11.7			
Indeterminate						1.2						2.9			10.2			
UIT																		
Same year						86.6						92.3			91.1			
1 year after						10.3						4.9			5.8			
2 yrs or more after						3.0						2.2			2.4			
Indeterminate						0.1						0.6			0.7			

./...

Table 12 (cont'd)

TIME LAG BETWEEN OBTAINING 2nd CYCLE SECONDARY DIPLOMA AND ENTERING HIGHER EDUCATION

Percentage

	1965		1970		1975		1976		1977		1978		1979		1980		1981	
	M	F	M	F	M	F	M	F	M	F	M	F	M	F	M	F	M	F
NETHERLANDS																		
University - Transfer rate and lag by secondary diploma																		
Gymnasium			(1971)		(1974)													
Same year	75.5	63.4	85.8	68.3	79.6	56.9												
1 to 3 years after	13.9	12.7																
4 yrs or more after	2.4	2.0																
Total	91.8	78.1																
HBS (Atheneum in 1974)																		
Same year	44.2	21.1	53.4	29.3	69.4	39.3												
1 to 3 yrs after	11.7	6.2																
4 yrs or more after	4.0	3.6																
Other	59.9	30.9																
SWEDEN																		
No more than one semest. after									16.3			17.0	16.6		17.2			
No more than 7 semesters after									49.3			47.8	47.3		51.6			

FT = Full-time - PT = Part-time

(1) Including qualifications obtained through adult education or "concessional" which are classified in the "other" category by all universities only for 1978.

Table 13

DISTRIBUTION BY AGE OF NEW ENTRANTS INTO UNIVERSITY-TYPE HIGHER EDUCATION

Academic year beginning in :

Percentage

	1965		1970		1975		1976		1977		1978		1979		1980		1981	
	M	F	M	F	M	F	M	F	M	F	M	F	M	F	M	F	M	F
GERMANY			Tot.		Tot.													
17 yrs and under					0.1	0.1			0.2	0.3	0.1	0.2	0.1	0.1				
18 yrs			9.6	12.6	5.1	7.3			4.2	8.0	4.2	8.4	1.0	1.7				
19 yrs			30.3	43.5	25.0	40.2			16.5	37.9	16.7	38.3	17.0	41.9				
20 - 24 yrs			51.3	38.5	54.8	41.0			71.0	46.2	71.5	46.1	75.3	49.3				
25 yrs and over			8.7	5.5	14.9	11.3			8.1	7.6	7.4	7.5	6.6	7.0				
AUSTRALIA (1) FT			(1971)															
17 yrs and under			41.9	52.8	44.9	48.8	43.7	49.2	42.5	45.4	34.2	38.2	34.1	37.2	33.2	35.9		
18 yrs			38.4	36.8	36.5	33.8	37.0	32.1	35.8	33.6	30.7	30.4	30.5	30.4	30.7	30.9		
19 yrs			8.9	4.5	8.2	6.3	8.6	5.9	9.4	7.4	11.4	8.8	11.1	10.2	11.7	10.5		
20 - 24 yrs			8.5	3.7	6.9	4.3	6.7	5.1	8.1	6.2	15.9	12.0	16.6	12.4	16.9	12.9		
25 yrs and over			2.4	2.1	3.5	6.8	4.0	7.6	4.2	7.3	7.7	10.6	7.7	9.7	7.5	9.7		
AUSTRALIA (1) PT			(1971)															
17 yrs and under			13.7	9.0	13.0	8.0	8.9	5.0	11.8	4.6	4.3	1.5	4.8	2.3	4.9	2.2		
18 yrs			20.3	11.2	17.3	8.5	15.7	5.5	15.6	5.4	6.2	2.5	6.7	2.8	7.3	3.6		
19 yrs			6.3	7.3	6.0	3.7	6.3	3.8	4.6	3.5	3.6	2.1	3.4	2.6	3.2	2.6		
20 - 24 yrs			27.5	31.2	19.1	19.6	17.6	18.2	17.5	17.4	25.3	24.6	24.2	23.2	23.2	23.5		
25 yrs and over			32.1	41.2	44.5	60.3	51.5	67.5	50.6	69.1	60.6	69.2	60.9	69.0	61.2	68.1		
AUSTRIA	(1970)		(1972)															
17 yrs and under																		
18 yrs	19.9	41.6	29.3	46.4	32.8	48.9					29.5	44.1	28.9	43.7				
19 yrs	22.4	32.2	25.9	28.9	25.2	29.2					31.4	29.7	30.7	29.5				
20 - 24 yrs	52.0	21.0	38.7	20.2	35.4	17.2					32.9	20.7	34.4	20.0				
25 yrs and over	5.7	5.1	6.1	4.5	6.6	4.8					6.1	5.5	6.0	6.8				
BELGIUM																		
17 yrs and under													3.4	5.0	3.7	4.8	3.5	4.3
18 yrs													53.9	69.9	58.1	70.3	59.4	71.0
19 yrs													19.3	14.6	19.9	15.1	19.6	14.6
20-24 yrs													20.8	9.4	16.0	8.3	15.1	8.5
25 yrs et over													2.6	1.1	2.3	1.5	2.4	1.6
CANADA (2) FT																		
17 yrs and under											2.2	3.1	2.2	3.0	2.0	2.8	2.1	2.8
18 yrs											18.7	24.2	18.8	23.5	18.7	22.4	18.3	22.1
19 yrs											30.9	32.6	32.6	34.4	32.9	35.0	32.8	35.0
20 yrs											15.9	12.3	15.2	12.2	15.2	11.8	15.7	12.1
21-24 yrs											21.9	18.4	21.0	17.5	21.5	18.0	21.1	17.7
25 and over											9.6	8.8	9.4	8.8	9.5	9.7	9.8	10.0
Unknown											0.8	0.6	0.8	0.6	0.2	0.3	0.2	0.3
DENMARK																		
under 21 yrs			48.8		44.5													
21 - 26 yrs			43.9		42.0													
27 yrs and over			7.2		13.5													

./...

Table 13 (cont'd)

DISTRIBUTION BY AGE OF NEW ENTRANTS INTO UNIVERSITY-TYPE HIGHER EDUCATION

Academic year beginning in :

Percentage

	1965		1970		1975		1976		1977		1978		1979		1980		1981	
	M	F	M	F	M	F	M	F	M	F	M	F	M	F	M	F	M	F
SPAIN																		
17 yrs and under			13.9	15.3	28.2	21.7	34.2	39.5	34.6	37.5	3.9	3.0	8.4	8.9				
18 yrs			20.7	19.8	21.4	24.1	22.8	23.6	22.3	22.3	21.8	18.6	33.1	38.9				
19 yrs			16.5	17.2	14.8	15.0	14.2	12.4	12.2	10.7	17.3	16.0	12.0	14.0				
20 - 24 yrs			34.1	33.3	23.6	27.4	18.6	16.8	14.0	13.0	35.5	45.1	24.6	25.8				
25 yrs and over			14.8	14.5	12.1	11.8	10.2	7.8	16.9	16.5	21.9	17.3	21.9	12.4				
UNITED STATES (3)			(1971)															
17 yrs and under			2.7	4.4	2.8	5.0	3.0	5.0	2.6	4.2	2.6	4.1	2.3	3.6	2.1	3.3		
18 yrs			70.5	78.4	70.6	77.1	71.5	77.0	71.7	77.0	72.5	77.9	71.0	77.2	69.1	75.9		
19 yrs			18.6	12.8	19.4	13.7	19.2	13.7	19.9	14.2	20.2	14.4	20.9	14.9	22.1	15.8		
20 - 21 yrs			3.5	1.9	3.8	1.9	3.5	2.0	3.6	2.2	3.1	1.8	3.7	2.0	3.8	2.3		
22 - 25 yrs			3.6	.9	2.1	.9	1.9	.9	1.5	1.1	1.1	.8	1.5	1.0	1.9	1.1		
26 yrs and over			1.2	1.6	1.3	1.5	1.1	1.3	.8	1.5	.6	1.0	.7	1.2	1.0	1.5		
FINLAND																		
17 yrs and under					0.0	0.0	0.0	0.0	0.1	0.1	0.1	0.1	0.1	0.1				
18 yrs					1.8	2.0	1.8	2.0	1.6	2.6	1.8	2.2	1.8	2.3				
19 yrs					30.1	32.3	29.0	34.1	30.1	33.2	29.0	35.1	30.0	36.1				
20 - 24 yrs					53.5	51.2	53.0	50.5	53.1	49.3	52.6	48.3	54.4	47.9				
25 yrs and over					14.6	14.5	16.1	13.3	15.1	14.8	16.5	14.3	13.7	13.7				
FRANCE	(2)												(1980)					
17 yrs and under	6.2	8.3			7.7		8.2		7.9		5.4	8.9	5.6	8.0				
18 yrs	18.2	23.1			26.8		31.2		32.6		26.2	37.5	26.9	37.3				
19 yrs	22.9	24.5			22.9		25.0		25.1		26.6	24.6	25.4	24.3				
20 - 24 yrs	40.5	37.3			27.2 (4)		24.3 (4)		23.9 (4)		28.6(4)	19.0	28.0(4)	20.3				
25 yrs and over	12.3	6.7			15.4 (5)		11.3 (5)		10.5 (5)		13.1(5)	9.9	14.1(5)	10.1				
GREECE (2)																		
18 yrs and under	28.3	43.6	24.4	37.2	31.5	46.5	42.8	60.5										
19 yrs	20.9	27.8	23.0	30.8	18.4	21.5	18.5	20.2										
20 - 24 yrs	31.6 (4)	25.1 (4)	32.7	25.9	25.9	20.1	22.0	12.9										
25 yrs and over	19.2 (5)	3.5 (5)	20.0	6.1	24.1	11.9	16.7	6.4										
ITALY	(1964)		(1967)		(1973)													
18 yrs and under	0.3	4.4	10.6	26.9	9.5	22.6												
19 yrs	14.2	27.3	31.3	36.5	36.8	43.5												
20 - 24 yrs	72.4	44.4	48.1	31.5	38.7	26.5												
25 yrs and over	13.0	9.5	10.0	5.1	15.0	7.4												

./...

Table 13 (cont'd)

DISTRIBUTION BY AGE OF NEW ENTRANTS INTO UNIVERSITY-TYPE HIGHER EDUCATION

Academic year beginning in :

Percentage

	1965		1970		1975		1976		1977		1978		1979		1980		1981	
	M	F	M	F	M	F	M	F	M	F	M	F	M	F	M	F	M	F
NETHERLANDS			(1971)															
under 18 yrs			8.9	8.1	0.4	0.5							0.5	0.5				
18 yrs			25.2	28.8	30.0	33.8							30.0	32.1				
19 yrs			21.1	25.0	27.9	28.3							25.8	26.8				
20 - 24 yrs			31.8	26.2	30.1	24.5							30.9	24.9				
25 and over			13.0	11.9	11.6	12.9							12.8	15.8				
UNITED KINGDOM (universities)																		
18 yrs and under	44.6	55.9	42.2	54.0	39.9	47.6			40.3	45.9	40.6	45.9	57.1	62.5				
19 yrs	34.3	30.1	32.1	28.0	30.9	29.5			30.9	30.3	30.6	29.7	21.7	18.3				
20 yrs	8.4	5.7	9.7	7.1	10.5	8.7			10.7	9.3	10.6	9.1	6.3	5.9				
21 - 24 yrs	8.4	4.4	10.8	6.6	12.3	8.0			11.8	8.2	11.9	8.4	9.4	6.8				
25 yrs and over	4.2	3.9	5.2	4.3	6.3	6.2			6.3	6.2	6.2	6.9	5.4	6.5				
UNITED KINGDOM (Further education - advanced)																		
18 yrs and under			17.6	27.1														
19 yrs			24.2	25.8														
20 yrs			14.7	11.2														
21 - 24 yrs			25.2	16.1														
25 yrs and over			18.2	19.7														
SWEDEN																		
Technical occup.																		
21 yrs and under									63		61		58					
22 - 24 yrs									19		21		20					
25 and over									18		18		22					
Adm. eco., soc.occup.																		
21 yrs and under									49		50		46					
22 - 24 yrs									22		22		23					
25 and over									29		28		31					
Med., paramed. occup.																		
21 yrs and under									30		27		27					
22 - 24 yrs									19		18		18					
25 and over									51		55		55					
Teaching																		
21 yrs and under									34		29		27					
22 - 24 yrs									21		19		20					
25 and over									45		52		53					
Communic., cult. occup.																		
21 yrs and under									31		31		29					
22 - 24 yrs									25		24		24					
25 and over									44		45		47					

./...

Table 13 (cont'd)

FT = Full-time - PT = Part-time

(1) Students beginning a Bachelor's degree at university.

(2) 1st year students.

(3) Includes all full-time students enrolled for the first time in Junior Colleges, 4-year institutions and universities.

(4) 20-23 years.

(5) 24 and over.

Table 14

DISTRIBUTION BY AGE OF NEW ENTRANTS INTO NON-UNIVERSITY-TYPE HIGHER EDUCATION

Academic year beginning in :

Percentage

	1965		1970		1975		1976		1977		1978		1979		1980		1981	
	M	F	M	F	M	F	M	F	M	F	M	F	M	F	M	F	M	F
GERMANY																		
17 yrs and under									0.5	0.6	0.0	0.1	0.0	0.0				
18 yrs									4.4	8.2	3.8	8.1	2.8	4.7				
19 yrs									7.3	22.5	7.5	23.6	7.1	25.5				
20 - 24 yrs									74.6	59.1	76.2	59.6	76.8	60.3				
25 yrs and over									13.2	9.6	12.5	8.6	13.3	9.5				
AUSTRALIA (1) FT																		
17 yrs and under					33.1	45.6			33.1	41.1	33.9	42.3	33.8	42.9	34.6	42.2	32.2	37.7
18 yrs					31.3	31.2			32.6	32.1	31.7	32.9	30.9	32.4	29.3	31.5	32.4	33.1
19 yrs					11.8	6.5			11.7	7.2	11.1	7.3	11.1	6.9	11.0	7.6	11.5	9.6
20 - 24 yrs					12.6	5.9			12.7	7.7	13.7	7.5	14.5	8.2	15.1	8.4	13.8	9.0
25 yrs and over					11.1	10.8			9.9	10.0	11.1	10.0	9.7	9.5	9.9	10.1	9.8	10.3
AUSTRALIA (1) PT																		
17 yrs and under					10.1	11.0			10.4	11.2	10.8	10.0	10.4	10.5	11.1	10.2	10.2	7.4
18 yrs					13.8	14.6			11.8	12.4	10.7	11.2	11.6	10.1	10.1	10.1	9.2	7.7
19 yrs					7.9	6.5			8.3	6.2	6.8	4.9	6.8	5.6	5.3	5.2	5.3	5.7
20 - 24 yrs					26.5	18.9			26.0	19.2	24.7	20.5	23.3	20.5	23.6	20.0	20.2	17.5
25 yrs and over					41.7	49.0			43.6	51.1	47.1	53.3	47.4	53.3	49.2	54.0	54.1	60.9
FRANCE (IUT)													(1980)					
17 yrs and under							4.0		3.7				2.7	5.5				
18 yrs							31.7		33.1				29.9	44.5				
19 yrs							35.3		35.3				36.7	33.3				
20 - 24 yrs							26.8		25.8				28.9	15.6				
25 yrs and over							2.2		2.1				1.8	1.1				
GREECE (2)																		
18 yrs and under					19.9	33.5	27.9	43.7										
19 yrs					33.3	38.3	29.5	32.7										
20 - 24 yrs					40.0	26.2	37.2	27.3										
25 yrs and over					11.7	2.0	5.4	1.3										

FT = Full-time - PT = Part-time

(1) New entrants into CAE regardless of diploma prepared (U or NU).
(2) Enrolled in 1st year.

Table 15

ANNUAL GROWTH RATE AND, FOR THE LAST YEAR AVAILABLE, DISTRIBUTION OF NUMBER OF NEW ENTRANTS INTO HIGHER EDUCATION, UNIVERSITY TYPE (U) AND NON-UNIVERSITY TYPE (NU)

Percentage

	1965-70	1970-75	1975-76	1976-77	1977-78	1978-79	1979-80	1980-81	1975-LY	Distribution LY
GERMANY (1)										
U	8.3	5.3	-1.0	-0.5	6.3	-0.3	8.2	11.4	4.0	71.3
NU	6.9	7.5	6.2	-4.3	-1.6	12.1	14.7	10.3	6.2	28.7
AUSTRALIA		(1973-75)		(1975-77)						
University		20.5		5.5	8.7	3.8	3.1	2.8	4.8	8.5
CAE (diploma/ associate dip.)		(2)		-11.6	2.5	-10.4	-4.8	-2.0	-5.3	1.5
AUSTRIA (Regular Austrian students)			(1972-74)		(1974-78)					
University			1.0		10.5	11.8	6.6		9.6	72.6
NU							5.4	4.1		27.4
BELGIUM		(1972-75)								
Total		0.0	8.5	2.5	-2.0	5.8	-4.1	0.7	1.9	
CANADA (3)										
U						1.0	2.7	5.7	3.1	48.0e
NU							5.4	5.5		52.0e
DENMARK										
U (4)	7.5	5.3	-7.2	-10.6	-1.6	-0.7	3.9		-3.5	44.4
NU			1.0		-0.7(5)	-5.0(5)				55.6
SPAIN										
U	16.6(6)	8.8(6)	1.1	6.5	-42.7	32.8	6.3		0.8	59.8
NU			8.8	14.5	-13.3	-1.6	-0.6		1.6	40.2
UNITED STATES						(1977-79)				
University			-4.0	0.9		2.0	-3.7	-0.8	-0.9	13.9
Other 4-year institutions			-1.3	1.6		1.5	0.1	-0.8	0.2	29.8
NU			-9.6	3.1	-0.8	6.5	4.8	1.3	0.9	56.3
FINLAND										
U	-0.6	5.2	0.0	-4.8	-5.0	5.3			-1.2	61.3
NU	3.6	3.1								38.7
FRANCE										
Universities and engineering schools		6.9(7)	-2.2	0.3	1.7		-0.8	6.3	1.1	66.3
NU (IUT and higher technicians)		10.2(8)	1.9	10.4	4.1		3.4	10.3	6.0	33.7
ITALY (3)										
University	13.0	4.5	-0.1	-2.9	6.4	-3.1	0.7	-7.3	-1.0	
JAPAN										
U	6.1	4.9	-0.8	1.9	-0.6	-4.2	1.2	0.2	-0.4	69.8
NU	10.2	6.7	-0.1	4.9	-1.1	-2.3	0.7	0.5	0.4	30.2
NETHERLANDS (3)										
University		0.5	6.8	8.5	-0.5	2.9	2.1	1.3	3.2	36.2
NU						2.0	1.0	0.7		63.8

./...

Table 15 (cont'd)

ANNUAL GROWTH RATE AND, FOR THE LAST YEAR AVAILABLE, DISTRIBUTION OF NUMBER OF NEW ENTRANTS INTO HIGHER EDUCATION, UNIVERSITY TYPE (U) AND NON-UNIVERSITY TYPE (NU)

Percentage

	1965-70	1970-75	1975-76	1976-77	1977-78	1978-79	1979-80	1975-LY	Distribution LY
UNITED KINGDOM FT + PT	(1968-70)								
University	3.3	3.0	3.1	4.7	2.4	1.1		3.3	
"Further edu." advanced									
SWEDEN Before the reform									
Universities	9.5	-1.5	8.5						
After the reform									
Total Higher education					-2.6	-8.5			
"Cours normaux"					7.0	-1.3			
"Cours séparés"					-12.2	-17.9			
YUGOSLAVIA (3)	(1965-69)	(1969-75)							
(Regular and non regular									
U	8.6	7.8	0.3	5.1	8.1			4.4	59.3
NU	2.0	8.9	-3.6	-1.4	-3.0			-2.7	40.7

LY : Last year available.
P = Provisional
FT = Full-time / PT = Part-time.

(1) Not including foreign students in 1965.
(2) Universities only.
(3) First year students.
(4) Classification by type of institution.
(5) Not including pre-primary teacher training.
(6) Not including university colleges.
(7) 1965-1975, universities only.
(8) 1971-1975.

(e) estimates.

Table 16

DISTRIBUTION BY DISCIPLINES OF NEW ENTRANTS INTO UNIVERSITY EDUCATION

Academic year beginning in : Percentage

	1965		1970		1975		1976		1977		1978		1979		1980		1981	
	M	F	M	F	M	F	M	F	M	F	M	F	M	F	M	F	M	F
GERMANY			(1973)															
Enrolments (000)	43.1	20.7	70.9	52.5	72.3	50.5	74.8	46.8	69.2	51.8	73.4	55.2	74.9	53.3	78.5	60.2		
Humanities				36.1	22.3	46.6	19.0	46.2	20.1	42.3	20.3	44.6	20.2	43.8	19.3	43.0		
Social sciences				19.8	23.8	15.2	25.7	17.1	24.3	18.7	25.1	16.8	25.8	18.0	27.3	19.8		
Education							included in other disciplines											
Science				22.4	22.8	18.8	20.7	17.9	19.8	18.7	19.8	18.3	19.9	16.9	20.1	17.2		
Technology				9.8	19.4	2.4	23.1	2.6	22.5	2.9	20.2	2.4	19.1	2.5	18.2	2.5		
Medical science				4.2	4.7	3.6	4.9	5.1	6.6	5.6	7.1	6.0	7.3	7.0	7.8	6.7		
Law							included in social Sciences											
Others				7.7	6.9	13.4	6.5	11.1	6.7	11.7	7.5	11.8	7.7	11.8	7.3	10.9		
Teacher education as % of Total					23.0	47.1	17.4	40.8	14.9	36.1	14.6	35.5	15.1	34.9	12.9	31.2		
AUSTRALIA Universities			(1973)															
Enrolments (000)			17.1	10.8	24.0	16.6	24.1	17.0	23.3	17.0	23.5	18.0	23.3	18.9	23.1	19.7	22.7	19.9
Humanities			20.4	51.5	23.0	47.6	23.6	47.9	23.2	47.9	23.5	46.9	23.0	45.0	21.7	44.7	21.6	43.1
Social sciences			21.5	13.8	22.1	16.6	21.1	15.4	20.9	16.0	21.5	15.3	21.9	17.7	24.5	20.2	23.3	20.0
Education			2.1	4.9	4.7	8.3	4.4	8.1	4.1	7.7	4.6	9.1	4.2	9.0	2.8	6.3	3.0	6.4
Science			20.5	15.8	19.6	13.6	19.8	14.6	20.4	14.1	20.3	15.2	20.5	14.6	20.0	14.4	21.0	14.5
Technology			14.5	0.5	12.2	0.5	11.8	0.4	11.7	0.4	12.1	0.7	12.1	0.9	12.2	0.9	13.4	1.3
Medical science			7.9	6.9	5.9	6.1	6.3	5.7	6.6	5.7	6.6	5.3	6.5	5.1	6.4	5.1	5.9	5.3
Law			6.4	3.5	6.6	4.2	6.6	4.3	7.1	4.7	6.1	4.1	6.4	4.4	6.6	5.0	6.3	5.4
Others			6.8	3.2	5.9	3.1	6.3	3.6	5.9	3.4	5.3	3.5	5.4	3.3	5.8	3.2	5.5	5.7
AUSTRALIA CAE																		
Enrolments (000)					12.0	4.4			15.1	8.7	16.8	10.6	16.7	12.6	17.5	13.4	18.5	14.8
Humanities					7.7	27.4			10.4	24.7	11.5	28.5	11.1	24.6	10.1	24.6	11.5	25.9
Social sciences					40.3	21.3			39.4	18.1	40.1	20.	38.9	19.0	37.7	20.0	34.4	19.3
Education					4.8	18.6			10.3	29.5	7.2	19.3	10.0	25.1	9.3	25.4	10.4	24.2
Science																		
Technology					37.4	12.1			30.0	8.5	27.9	9.1	26.2	9.5	29.9	10.3	29.8	9.9
Medical science					2.7	15.0			2.9	13.1	2.7	12.3	2.6	11.2	2.6	9.2	2.6	9.2
Others					7.0	5.5			6.9	6.2	10.6	10.8	11.1	10.6	10.3	10.5	11.3	11.5
AUSTRIA Regular Austrian students			(1972)		(1974)								P		P			
Enrolments (000)			5.6	3.4	5.4	4.0					7.2	6.3	8.1	7.0	8.6	7.5	9.1	8.1
Humanities			26.7	58.8	27.5	52.5					12.5	36.5	15.6	35.2				
Social sciences			19.6	14.7	13.7	15.0					16.7	15.9	18.6	18.3				
Education											1.4	1.6	1.0	1.3				
Science					included in Humanities				8.3	9.7	7.1	8.7						
Technology			25.0	5.9	27.5	5.0					22.2	3.2	20.5	3.5				
Medical science			14.3	17.6	15.7	20.0					15.3	19.4	14.4	18.2				
Law			8.9	2.9	11.8	5.0					16.7	11.1	16.7	11.6				
Others			5.4		3.9	2.5					6.9	2.5	6.1	3.1				

./...

Table 16 (cont'd)

DISTRIBUTION BY DISCIPLINES OF NEW ENTRANTS INTO UNIVERSITY EDUCATION

Academic year beginning in :

Percentage

	1965		1970		1975		1976		1977		1978		1979		1980		1981	
	M	F	M	F	M	F	M	F	M	F	M	F	M	F	M	F	M	F
BELGIUM Total			(1972)															
Enrolments (000)			18.5		18.5		20.1		20.6		20.2		21.4		20.5		20.6	
Humanities			14.4		16.4		17.8		17.8		18.5		17.4		18.8		17.2	
Social sciences			16.4		14.4		12.2		14.0		14.1		15.0		15.4		17.4	
Education			6.0		6.6		6.1		6.2		6.4		6.5		6.4		6.2	
Science			12.0		12.8		12.1		11.7		12.2		12.8		12.2		12.7	
Technology			6.3		6.7		6.4		6.4		6.1		6.4		6.3		6.4	
Medical Science			23.7		20.8		22.2		21.0		20.0		19.5		16.9		15.7	
Law			12.4		12.2		11.8		12.0		11.8		11.5		12.9		13.2	
Others			8.8		10.1		11.4		10.9		10.8		11.0		11.2		11.1	
CANADA (5) FT																		
Humanities											3.6	6.2	3.4	5.7	3.3	5.6	3.1	5.0
Social sciences											17.9	13.9	17.8	15.1	17.1	15.5	17.4	16.0
Education											5.4	14.0	4.6	12.6	4.7	12.9	4.6	12.7
Science											7.4	7.1	7.9	7.1	8.6	6.9	9.3	6.9
Technology											16.2	1.9	17.1	2.2	16.9	2.3	16.4	2.4
Medical Science											5.4	8.6	4.7	8.1	4.7	8.1	4.5	7.9
Law											4.0	2.4	3.8	2.6	3.5	2.6	3.3	2.5
Others											40.1	45.9	40.7	46.6	41.2	46.1	41.4	46.6
DENMARK	(1966)																	
Enrolments (000)	5.4	2.2	6.9	3.2	8.3	4.8	7.4	4.8	6.6	4.2	6.5	4.2	6.3	4.3	6.5	4.5		
Universities					77.2		74.0	85.1	69.6	78.2	68.8	80.0	68.5	78.2	67.4	77.5		
Others institutions					22.8		26.0	14.9	30.4	21.8	31.2	20.0	31.5	21.8	32.6	22.5		
of which Education					5.4		2.5	2.9	5.6	6.5	4.1	4.4	5.3	5.9	4.7	6.1		
Technology					8.3		13.8	1.8	13.7	2.6	15.7	2.5	15.3	3.0	16.7	3.6		
Medical science					2.9		2.4	4.3	2.3	5.3	2.2	5.7	2.0	6.1	2.1	5.6		
Others					6.3		7.2	5.9	8.8	7.4	9.2	7.3	8.9	6.8	9.1	7.3		
SPAIN Universities and assimilated (1)																		
Enrolments (000)	26.8	8.6	55.0	21.5	78.5	47.5	77.7	49.7	81.6	54.1	48.4(2)	29.4(2)	59.3	44.0	60.6	49.2		
Humanities	9.2	38.4	14.9	46.8	12.2	30.4	13.6	30.5	14.3	31.2	15.6	30.4	16.7	34.3	17.4	35.3		
Social sciences	12.7	8.7	11.1	4.5	17.2	10.4	17.0	10.1	17.4	9.9	16.9	10.1	14.7	9.2	14.6	9.2		
Education							included in Humanities											
Science	28.5	24.7	19.8	20.8	14.8	15.1	14.0	13.1	13.9	13.3	13.2	11.4	15.3	16.1	17.0	17.1		
Technology	12.3	0.6	25.1	3.0	20.3	2.6	17.2	2.5	17.6	3.0	15.1	3.1	16.4	3.5	18.0	3.3		
Medical science	24.0	19.9	18.3	17.4	21.1	28.9	21.0	29.1	17.5	25.7	17.6	25.3	14.5	19.4	11.6	16.0		
Law	12.9	7.4	9.9	6.8	12.9	11.9	15.6	14.2	17.5	16.1	20.7	18.3	21.4	16.0	20.4	17.6		
Others	0.4	0.3	1.0	0.8	1.6	0.6	1.4	0.5	1.8	0.8	0.9	1.4	1.0	1.5	1.0	1.5		
UNITED STATES Universities (3)																		
Enrolments (000)					218.5	190.5	208.7	183.9	207.9	188.3			214.6	199.8	207.7	191.3	204.3	191.7
Humanities					13.9	15.8	12.8	14.3	8.1	13.7			8.5	14.0	7.8	13.1		
Social sciences					22.1	18.5	22.9	18.8	28.4	23.9			30.7	28.2	28.0	28.2		
Education					2.5	12.2	2.7	11.0	2.4	9.9			1.6	8.1	1.6	6.7		
Science					17.5	12.1	16.7	11.4	12.1	8.9			10.0	7.6	10.2	7.3		
Technology					24.7	8.4	25.8	8.7	21.5	3.9			24.1	5.1	26.3	6.2		
Law et Medical Sc.					1.6	12.9	2.0	14.7	14.1	26.8			11.9	23.5	12.0	23.7		
Others					17.5	20.1	17.0	21.1	13.2	12.7			13.0	13.7	14.1	14.9		

./...

Table 16 (cont'd)

DISTRIBUTION BY DISCIPLINES OF NEW ENTRANTS INTO UNIVERSITY EDUCATION

Academic year beginning in : Percentage

	1965		1970		1975		1976		1977		1978		1979		1980		1981	
	M	F	M	F	M	F	M	F	M	F	M	F	M	F	M	F	M	F
UNITED STATES (cont'd)																		
Others inst. 4 yrs																		
Enrolments (000)					389.1	384.9	369.2	385.1	367.3	399.4			369.5	413.6	370.3	413.8	366.5	410.7
Humanities					15.0	15.8	14.8	16.3	9.5	13.7			8.8	12.4	9.3	12.1		
Social sciences					25.0	21.6	27.1	22.5	31.3	27.2			32.1	29.5	31.1	29.4		
Education					6.5	21.0	6.8	19.2	5.5	19.0			5.8	17.2	5.1	15.9		
Science					15.0	8.7	15.1	9.2	10.9	7.4			9.8	6.7	8.4	5.9		
Technology					19.7	6.0	17.5	5.9	18.8	2.4			20.1	3.8	23.0	4.6		
Law et Medical Sc.					1.6	12.4	1.3	11.7	8.4	18.4			8.6	17.6	8.6	18.7		
Others					17.3	14.4	17.3	15.2	15.4	11.6			14.8	12.7	14.6	13.3		
FINLAND																		
Enrolments (000)	4.9	5.1	5.2	4.5	6.0	6.5	6.1	6.4	5.8	6.1	5.5	5.8	5.9	6.0	5.7	6.2		
Humanities													10.7	21.9	9.0	24.4		
Social sciences													21.3	18.1	22.0	19.2		
Education													9.9	22.5	9.3	20.1		
Science													17.1	13.5	15.6	12.9		
Technology													23.2	3.3	26.6	3.1		
Medical science													4.5	8.4	4.6	8.3		
Law													5.9	3.3	5.9	3.6		
Others													7.4	9.1	7.0	8.4		
FRANCE Universities																		
and engineering schools																		
Enrolments (000)	90.3 (4)				184.1		180.0		180.5		183.6		183.8		182.3		193.7	
Humanities and human sciences					35.0		35.3		34.3		35.0				32.5			
Economic science and Law					25.6		24.7		25.0		24.3				28.8			
Education																		
Science					13.8		14.7		15.5		15.9				19.0			
Technology					4.7		4.2		4.5		4.5				7.5			
Medical science					17.1		17.3		16.0		15.0				10.3			
Law															1.9			
Others					3.8		3.9		4.6		5.3							
GREECE																		
Enrolments (000)															10.7			12.6
																		(1982) 15.7
ITALY (5)																		
Enrolments (000)	105.5		123.4	70.9	144.0	98.5	141.8	100.4	134.6	100.5	139.2	110.9	134.3	108.0	134.7	109.4	123.7	102.7
Humanities	30.0		11.6	57.5	9.2	38.8	9.1	36.2	9.2	36.5	9.9	36.1	9.7	35.1				
Social sciences	24.6		21.1	10.4	19.6	13.0	20.8	13.8	21.8	14.3	22.4	15.3	24.1	16.7				
Education																		
Science	14.1		15.0	13.5	12.1	17.2	11.6	17.2	11.8	16.5	11.4	15.3	11.7	14.0				
Technology	13.3		21.1	2.8	21.5	4.0	21.1	4.4	80.0	3.9	20.0	3.9	19.9	4.2				
Medical science	7.0		14.3	6.8	15.6	11.1	14.7	11.3	13.0	10.2	11.7	9.5	9.9	8.2				
Law	7.0		12.8	6.6	15.4	12.4	15.2	12.8	15.4	12.9	15.8	14.2	16.3	15.7				
Others	3.9		4.1	2.4	6.6	3.6	7.5	4.4	8.8	5.7	8.8	5.7	8.4	6.1				

./...

Table 16 (cont'd)

DISTRIBUTION BY DISCIPLINES OF NEW ENTRANTS INTO UNIVERSITY EDUCATION

Academic year beginning in : Percentage

	1965		1970		1975		1976		1977		1978		1979		1980		1981		1982	
	M	F	M	F	M	F	M	F	M	F	M	F	M	F	M	F	M	F	M	F
JAPAN																				
Enrolments (000)	249.9		333.0		423.9		420.6		428.4		425.7		407.6		412.4		413.2		414.5	
Humanities			14.1		15.1		15.4		15.6		15.6		16.1		16.2		16.2			
Social sciences			42.1		42.6		41.8		41.6		41.4		40.8		40.4		40.2			
Education			7.0		7.5		7.8		7.7		7.6		7.9		7.8		7.9			
Science			3.2		2.8		2.9		3.0		3.1		3.1		3.1		3.1			
Technology			20.9		19.5		19.4		19.6		19.4		19.0		19.2		19.3			
Medical science			2.1		4.6		4.8		4.9		5.0		5.2		5.2		5.2			
Others			10.7		7.9		7.9		7.7		7.8		8.0		8.1		8.1			
NEW ZEALAND																				
Enrolments (000)															11.4		11.3		11.2	
of which FT															8.7		8.5		8.7	
PT															2.7		2.8		2.5	
NETHERLANDS																				
Enrolments (000)	10.2	2.4	14.4	4.0	13.3	5.8	13.8	6.3	14.8	7.0	14.5	7.2	14.7	7.7	15.0 P	8.2P	14.8	8.6		
Humanities	6.7	22.4	5.4	14.6	13.4	30.8	14.6	31.9	13.4	30.8	12.8	30.4	12.2	28.8	11.7	26.2				
Social sciences	28.2	33.9	31.6	43.1	25.2	32.5	25.4	32.9	25.4	33.9	26.1	33.0	29.1	34.6	29.9	35.5				
Education																				
Science	14.0	10.6	13.1	9.8	14.9	7.7	14.5	7.6	14.8	7.4	13.7	6.9	12.9	6.6	12.4	6.0				
Technology	22.0	2.1	21.9	2.9	18.5	1.8	18.7	1.6	19.7	1.9	20.0	2.3	18.8	2.2	20.1	2.3				
Medical science	14.2	15.3	10.5	13.4	10.4	9.1	9.4	9.1	8.1	8.5	8.5	7.6	8.0	8.0	7.8	8.9				
Law	11.2	12.9	14.0	12.4	12.1	13.7	11.9	12.6	13.4	13.6	13.5	15.9	13.6	15.2	13.4	16.6				
Others	3.4	2.9	3.5	3.8	5.5	4.4	5.4	4.4	5.1	3.8	5.4	3.9	5.3	4.6	4.7	4.4				
UNITED KINGDOM (6)	(1968)																			
Enrolments (000)	42.1	17.9	43.6	20.4	26.1		49.3	27.2	51.1	29.0	51.5	30.4								
Humanities	8.2	25.9	7.4	22.2	7.1	22.1	6.9	21.6	6.7	21.5	6.6	21.2								
Social sciences	20.0	24.2	20.0	22.6	24.2	25.4	23.9	25.6	23.1	25.2	22.9	25.7								
Education	1.0	2.2	1.1	3.1	0.6	2.2	0.4	2.3	1.2	3.1	1.2	3.6								
Science	30.0	24.6	28.7	22.4	26.0	19.9	19.7		26.1	20.0	26.8	19.8								
Technology	23.1	0.9	23.1	1.3	21.5	1.7	22.4	2.0	22.9	2.3	22.5	2.4								
Medical science	8.5	8.1	8.8	9.2	9.2	9.9	8.9	9.9	8.6	10.1	8.5	9.7								
Law																				
Others	9.2	14.0	10.8	19.2	11.6	18.8	11.4	18.8	11.5	17.7	11.2	17.5								

./...

Table 16 (cont'd)

DISTRIBUTION BY DISCIPLINES OF NEW ENTRANTS INTO UNIVERSITY EDUCATION

Academic year beginning in :

Percentage

	1965		1970		1975		1976		1977		1978		1979		1980		1981	
	M	F	M	F	M	F	M	F	M	F	M	F	M	F	M	F	M	F
SWEDEN Before the reform																		
Enrolments (000)	10.3	7.2	16.1	11.4	14.4	12.7	15.3	14.1										
Humanities	17.9	48.7	15.6	38.1	16.0	32.4	15.6	32.4										
Social sciences	35.0	31.4	46.5	43.2	44.0	48.0	45.6	48.2										
Education			0.7	1.2	0.5	0.8	0.6	0.7										
Science	21.1	10.3	17.4	7.1	13.8	6.4	12.8	6.4										
Technology	13.5	0.9	11.5	1.3	15.4	1.9	15.3	2.3										
Medical science	3.9	5.2	2.6	5.2	4.0	5.5	3.9	5.0										
Law	6.7	2.6	4.8	3.1	5.1	4.0	5.2	4.1										
Others	1.8	0.8	1.0	0.9	1.2	1.0	1.1	1.0										
After the reform																		
Enrolments (000) (7)									24.9		25.6		26.2					
Technical occupations									16.7		15.9		17.2					
Adm, eco., soc. occup									26.0		27.0		24.7					
Med., paramed.occup.									22.2		22.5		24.0					
Teaching									31.4		31.0		30.8					
Communic.,cult.occup.									3.7		3.6		3.4					
YUGOSLAVIA (8)			(1969)															
Enrolments (000)	35.1	19.1	46.4	29.0	71.1	47.2	72.5	46.1	77.1	47.6	83.0	51.8						
Humanities	9.1	21.8	8.0	22.2	6.6	13.1	6.9	13.4	6.6	13.2								
Social sciences	17.9	19.2	20.7	23.9	28.3	34.5	25.1	32.3	23.7	31.3								
Education	2.6	2.6	5.3	0.8	1.8	1.3	2.2	1.6	2.9	3.1								
Pure Science	7.4	9.9	5.4	8.6	5.5	6.6	5.5	6.3	5.2	6.1								
Technology	35.2	15.1	34.0	12.5	30.0	9.5	31.7	9.5	33.2	9.5								
Medical science	6.0	11.5	3.9	8.3	3.5	7.8	3.2	7.8	3.4	7.6								
Law	12.5	14.6	20.7	23.9	28.3	34.5	25.1	32.3	23.7	31.3								
Others	9.4	5.3	11.2	6.4	7.5	4.7	7.3	4.5	8.2	4.6								

(1) Higher technical schools and university colleges, excluding the latter in 1965 and 1970.
(2) Generalisation of the new BUP (Comprehensive unified Baccalaureate) explains the fall in the number of new entrants.
(3) Full-time and part-time students enrolled for the first time. About 92 % of students enrolled for the first time in universities and 88 % of those in other 4-year institutions are full-time students. The distribution by disciplines refers to full-time students only.
(4) Universities only.
(5) 1st year students.
(6) Full-time new entrants in universities only.
(7) Total of higher education excluding students enrolled in separate courses : 23,4 in 1977 ; 20.4 in 1978 and 16.8 in 1979.
(8) 1st year students, regular or not.

Table 17

DISTRIBUTION BY DISCIPLINES OF NEW ENTRANTS INTO NON-UNIVERSITY-TYPE HIGHER EDUCATION

Academic year beginning in :

Percentage

	1965		1970		1975		1976		1977		1978		1979		1980		1981	
	M	F	M	F	M	F	M	F	M	F	M	F	M	F	M	F	M	F
GERMANY			(1973)															
Enrolments (000)		21.9	41.3		33.3	10.5	35.1	11.4	32.0	12.5	30.3	13.5	33.3	15.8	38.4	17.9		
Humanities			2.4		0.9	5.7	0.5	3.0	0.5	3.0	0.8	4.9	0.6	3.2	0.5	3.1		
Social sciences			38.0		27.0	59.0	28.8	61.6	29.0	63.8	29.6	64.4	34.6	66.7	37.8	67.5		
Science			1.9		2.4	1.9	2.6	2.1	2.1	1.8	2.6	2.1	2.9	2.1	3.2	2.6		
Technology			51.1		63.7	18.1	62.3	17.7	61.5	16.8	60.3	14.3	55.7	14.7	53.1	15.4		
Others			6.5		6.0	15.3	5.9	15.5	7.0	14.6	6.7	14.2	6.2	13.3	5.4	11.4		
AUSTRALIA (1)																		
Enrolments (000)					12.9	18.1			9.4	14.9	9.2	15.7	8.1	14.2	8.2	13.1	8.9	11.9
Humanities					6.8	6.9			5.3	6.0	8.9	10.3	9.8	11.9	10.7	12.7	9.5	14.0
Social Sciences					18.3	5.1			17.7	4.4	17.1	7.0	16.0	5.5	13.8	6.0	13.8	6.9
Education					43.1	71.2			41.9	70.1	31.2	61.0	29.8	56.7	29.4	51.7	35.0	51.1
Science																		
Technology					9.6	0.7			11.3	1.4	16.4	3.0	18.7	4.7	19.7	4.1	19.8	4.5
Medical science					3.9	6.3			4.7	8.4	4.6	7.9	4.3	9.6	5.0	11.3	4.9	11.8
Other					18.4	9.8			19.1	9.7	21.7	10.7	21.3	11.7	21.5	14.1	17.0	11.8
AUSTRIA																		
Enrolments (000)													1.7	4.3	1.7	4.6	1.9	4.6
CANADA (2) FT																		
Humanities													6.2	8.4	6.3	8.2	6.0	7.7
Social Sciences													24.8	39.4	24.4	39.5	24.7	39.2
Education													0.1	0.2	0.1	0.1	0.0	0.1
Technology and assimil.													32.1	4.6	32.5	4.5	32.2	4.5
Medical science													2.5	17.7	2.4	17.3	2.5	17.1
Other													34.0	29.4	34.2	30.2	34.4	31.2
Unknown													0.2	0.2	0.2	0.2	0.2	0.2
DENMARK																		
Enrolments (3) (000)						13.4	5.6	7.9	5.8	5.8	5.9	5.6	5.9	5.1	6.2	7.6		
Humanities						2.7	1.8	3.3	2.1	4.4	2.1	4.6	1.8	5.2	1.5	3.6		
Social sciences						43.0	55.5	40.4	54.5	58.3	52.1	53.6	53.4	51.0	52.0	39.5		
Education (3)						43.4	27.0	51.2	23.1	30.0	24.1	34.0	23.8	35.0	25.0	50.2		
Science																		
Technology						6.1	12.3	0.1	17.6	0.6	18.3	0.6	17.5	0.7	18.2	0.6		
Medical science						2.5	0.5	3.9	0.5	5.1	0.8	5.3	1.1	6.4	0.8	5.0		
Law																		
SPAIN Univ. schools																		
Enrolments (000)					40.5	22.2	41.9	26.3	46.8	31.3	41.4	26.3	39.9	26.7	38.9	27.3		
Social sciences					13.3	6.4	13.5	6.8	15.6	7.9	16.0	10.1	16.3	11.5	17.9	14.1		
Education					25.9	87.3	27.1	87.2	29.3	85.5	26.1	81.0	25.4	80.0	21.5	75.5		
Technology					60.7	6.3	59.4	6.0	57.2	6.6	57.9	8.9	58.3	8.5	60.6	10.4		

./...

Table 17 (cont'd)

DISTRIBUTION BY DISCIPLINES OF NEW ENTRANTS INTO NON-UNIVERSITY-TYPE HIGHER EDUCATION

Academic year beginning in :

Percentage

	1965		1970		1975		1976		1977		1978		1979		1980		1981	
	M	F	M	F	M	F	M	F	M	F	M	F	M	F	M	F	M	F
UNITED STATES (4)																		
2-year institutions																		
Enrolments (000)					733.1	627.5	605.9	624.6	596.9	671.7	583.4	675.3	610.4	730.2	640.7	763.6	646.8	775.4
Humanities					10.0	7.7	9.4	8.4	5.3	7.3			5.7	7.2	5.3	6.7		
Social sciences					24.1	36.4	26.0	36.3	28.2	38.0			27.8	39.7	24.2	39.5		
Education					4.3	12.0	3.7	11.6	3.5	10.4			3.1	10.4	2.7	10.0		
Science					6.7	4.2	6.6	4.8	5.4	4.3			5.6	3.5	4.4	3.9		
Technology					27.9	9.9	27.4	9.7	30.0	4.5			32.8	5.4	38.0	7.3		
Law and Medical Sc.					2.0	14.2	1.4	11.8	7.6	23.3			7.0	20.8	7.4	18.9		
Other					24.9	15.7	25.4	17.3	19.9	12.2			18.2	13.3	17.7	13.6		
FINLAND																		
Enrolments (000)	2.5	3.2	2.6	4.2	2.7	5.2												
Humanities	4.4		4.7		3.0													
Social sciences	9.3		10.5		10.6													
Education	14.8		14.0		13.2													
Science																		
Technology	27.1		27.7		30.3													
Medical science	41.7		39.0		39.4													
Law	2.7		4.0		3.5													
Other																		
FRANCE (5)																		
Enrolments (000)			32.6		48.0		57.8		62.5		62.4		86.5		89.4		98.6	
Primary and secondary sectors			53.9		47.7		40.3		41.1		41.8							
Tertiary sector			46.1		52.3		44.3		45.2		48.2							
Education			-		-		15.4		13.6		9.9							
GREECE																		
Enrolments (000)															14.6		14.7	
JAPAN																		
Enrolments (000)	80.6		126.7		174.9		174.7		183.2		181.2		177.0		178.2		179.1	
Humanities			27.5		28.6		28.3		29.0		29.2		29.7		29.6		29.8	
Social sciences			11.2		10.4		9.8		9.2		9.1		8.7		8.7		8.7	
Education			17.6		22.7		24.8		24.7		24.0		24.6		24.7		24.2	
Science			0.1		0.0		0.0											
Technology			7.4		5.6		5.0		4.9		5.1		4.8		4.7		4.6	
Medical science			2.1		2.8		2.8		3.1		3.4		3.4		3.6		3.8	
Law																		
Other			34.0		29.8		29.2		29.1		29.2		28.8		28.7		28.8	

./...

Table 17 (cont'd)

DISTRIBUTION BY DISCIPLINES OF NEW ENTRANTS INTO NON-UNIVERSITY-TYPE HIGHER EDUCATION

Academic year beginning in :

Percentage

	1965		1970		1975		1976		1977		1978		1979		1980		1981	
	M	F	M	F	M	F	M	F	M	F	M	F	M	F	M	F	M	F
NETHERLANDS																		
Enrolments (000)											39.8		40.6		41.0		41.3	
YUGOSLAVIA (6)																		
Enrolments (000)	31.7	18.1	30.8	23.1	55.6	34.5	54.0	32.9	53.4	32.3	50.9	32.2						
Social sciences	41.6	40.9	39.0	42.9	51.1	62.0	51.3	59.0	53.7	58.2								
Education	28.7	48.6	24.7	42.9	11.9	21.4	13.9	24.0	13.5	24.5								
Science																		
Technology	25.9	5.0	31.8	7.8	34.5	9.3	31.9	8.5	29.8	8.0								
Medical science	1.3	5.0	1.0	5.6	1.1	6.7	0.9	7.6	0.9	8.4								
Law																		
Other	2.5	0.5	3.6	0.9	1.4	0.6	2.0	0.9	2.1	0.9								

(1) Diplomas and Associate diploma dans les CAE.
(2) First-year students.
(3) Excluding pre-primary teacher training for years 1977 to 1979 inclusive.
(4) Full-time and part-time students enrolled for the first time of which about 50 % are full-time students. The distribution by disciplines relates to full-time students only.
(5) Without teacher training colleges.
(6) 1st year students, regular or not.

Table 18

ANNUAL GROWTH RATE OF ENROLMENTS IN HIGHER EDUCATION
AND, FOR THE LAST YEAR AVAILABLE, DISTRIBUTION OF UNIVERSITY STUDENTS BY LEVEL
OF QUALIFICATION PREPARED AND PROPORTION OF NON UNIVERSITY STUDENTS AMONG TOTAL STUDENTS

Percentage

	1965-70	1970-75	1975-76	1976-77	1977-78	1978-79	1979-80	1980-81	1981-82	1975-LY	Distribution LY
GERMANY											
U	6.4	10.6	3.6	3.8	3.4	3.6	5.1	4.4		4.0	78.3
NU	3.3	10.2	8.2	5.3	4.5	5.6	10.7	11.2		7.6	11.7
AUSTRALIA											
University FT + PT	6.0										
1st degree		4.2	3.7	2.2	1.3	0.2	1.1	1.3		1.6	79.4
Master		9.9	5.1	5.7	3.1	4.5	3.2	7.1		4.8	9.3
Doctorate		2.7	6.0	3.8	5.5	1.7	3.8	3.7		4.1	3.8
Non-degree course	4.5	4.6	2.6	6.8	-4.8	-2.5	2.0	4.2		1.4	7.5
Total FT		5.7	3.6	2.3	-1.5	-2.7	-0.1	0.9		0.4	
Total PT		3.5	4.3	3.9	5.8	5.1	3.9	3.9		4.5	
CAE FT + PT											
1st degree			22.5	23.3	17.7	12.2	9.4	6.6		5.3	80.3
Master			41.3	21.1	25.8	30.1	9.4	19.5		4.5	1.0
Post-graduate diploma			4.7	18.5	18.9	16.2	13.9	11.3		13.9	18.7
Diploma and associate dipl. (NU)			2.6	-9.1	-3.9	-7.2	-9.0	-7.5		-5.7	16.0(1)
Total FT			10.4	2.8	-0.7	-2.6	-4.8	-2.0		0.5	
Total PT			8.8	6.5	18.4	12.2	10.5	8.8		10.9	
AUSTRIA											
Total (2)	1.9	9.4	8.7	7.8	8.4	8.5 //	7.5	7.7		8.1	89.6
NU							0.8	3.1			10.4
BELGIUM											
Total		(1972-75) 1.3	4.1	2.9	0.3	3.2	2.9	0.7		2.4	10.4
CANADA											
1st degree FT	8.1	3.7	1.5	-0.7	-2.0	0.9	2.5	4.9		1.2	52.5
Post-graduate FT	14.0	3.8	2.7	0.1	1.1	0.8	7.0	5.5		2.9	7.0
NU FT	19.0	5.9	2.1	6.9	3.4	0.9	3.5	4.8		3.6	40.5
1st degree PT	16.8	2.2	3.1	12.1	2.0	6.7	6.9	3.0		5.6	87.1
Post-graduate PT	13.2	13.4	2.6	3.4	3.6	3.3	5.0	0.8		3.1	12.9
DENMARK											
Universities	9.0	7.8	// 4.9	-1.5	-2.1	-5.6	-0.8			-1.0	77.9
Other U institutions	5.4	6.4	// 7.1	5.8	1.6	0	5.4			3.9	22.1
NU	7.0	6.3	//-16.5	-3.4	-5.3	0.3	18.8			-1.9	38.3
SPAIN											
U	11.1	13.1	5.5	14.9	-5.8	2.4	2.1			3.8	26.3
NU	11.5	4.5	13.9	11.9	-1.7	1.4	0.1			5.1	73.7

./...

Table 18 (cont'd)

ANNUAL GROWTH RATE OF ENROLMENTS IN HIGHER EDUCATION
AND, FOR THE LAST YEAR AVAILABLE, DISTRIBUTION OF UNIVERSITY STUDENTS BY LEVEL
OF QUALIFICATION PREPARED AND PROPORTION OF NON UNIVERSITY STUDENTS AMONG TOTAL STUDENTS

Percentage

	1965-70	1970-75	1975-76	1976-77	1977-78	1978-79	1979-80	1980-81	1981-82	1975-LY	Distribu-tion LY
UNITED STATES											
1st degree and prof. (3)											
FT + PT		7.0	2.4	0	2.4	2.3	5.7			2.6	2.3
Post-graduate FT + PT		4.2	5.5	-1.1	0.1	-0.8	2.6			1.3	11.1
4-year institu. FT		1.4	-1.0	1.7	-0.8	1.9	2.7	1.7	-0.6	0.9	38.1
" " PT		4.7	-9.3	4.5	1.5	3.4	3.6	3.7	-2.2	0.7	11.1
2-year institu. FT (NU)		8.7	-5.5	-0.6	-5.8	2.2	10.2	-0.3	3.3	1.0	14.5
" " PT (NU)		15.9	0.5	7.6	3.4	6.3	5.6	4.0	0.5	4.7	22.9
FINLAND											
U	7.0	5.4	3.2	2.8	0.6	1.1	1.3			1.8	
FRANCE											
Univers. 1st and 2nd cy.	9.4	1.5	1.5	2.2	2.0		0.7	3.0		1.8	69.9
" 3rd cycle	10.3	18.3	0.6	-0.3	1.4	2.0					15.1
Grandes Ecoles (4)	4.1	16.4	-6.3	2.7							15.0
NU	7.4	7.0	0.4	9.6	0.4	-1.8	3.1	9.6		3.6	17.4
GREECE											
U	5.9	5.7	-0.4	1.7	-0.8	-11.9	6.2	1.1		-0.7	75.7
NU	7.0	9.5	7.2	-3.7	13.3	-12.6	3.1	6.7		5.7	24.3
ITALY U											
Regular students	13.5	5.6	3.5	0.1	2.0	-1.3	-0.5			-0.8	72.9
Non-course students	2.5	10.5	9.9	6.4	9.2	5.2	5.8			7.3	27.1
JAPAN											
Univers. 1st degree	8.5	4.2	3.0	2.6	1.3	-0.8	-0.7	-0.9		0.8	96.9
" Master	10.8	4.0	7.7	2.0	-1.9	-2.2	1.2	4.0		1.8	2.1
Doctorate	2.6	2.4	5.3	4.4	4.4	4.6	1.8	1.0		3.5	1.0
Junior Colleges NU	12.9	6.1	3.2	2.6	1.7	-1.7	-0.9	0.3		0.9	17.0
Technical colleges NU	43.7	4.6	-3.4	2.7	-1.5	-3.2	0.1	0.4		-0.8	0.8
NETHERLANDS											
U	9.8	3.0	6.4	6.4	4.3	4.3	0.4	1.7		3.9	41.5
NU FT		9.1	6.5	4.6	2.5	2.2	1.7	1.7		3.2	36.6
NU TP		1.8	1.8	3.0	9.1	11.0	9.6			6.9	21.9
UNITED KINGDOM											
Universities FT											
1st degree	2.5	2.5	4.6	4.5	3.1	2.5				3.7	83.9
Post-graduate	5.7	3.4	0.6	-2.7	0.8	-3.0				-1.1	16.1
Further education FT	5.0	2.5	-4.5	-5.0	-4.2					-4.5	
Universities PT											
1st degree	-5.3	0.5	-0.1	9.4	-2.4	7.2				3.0	14.3
Post-graduate	15.7	3.2	4.5	4.2	3.7	5.9				6.4	85.7
Further education PT	-1.2	3.7	2.3	8.2	8.7					4.7	
Open University		26.0	3.2	8.0	6.7	3.1				5.3	

./...

Table 18 (cont'd)

ANNUAL GROWTH RATE OF ENROLMENTS IN HIGHER EDUCATION
AND, FOR THE LAST YEAR AVAILABLE, DISTRIBUTION OF UNIVERSITY STUDENTS BY LEVEL
OF QUALIFICATION PREPARED AND PROPORTION OF NON UNIVERSITY STUDENTS AMONG TOTAL STUDENTS

Percentage

	1965-70	1970-75	1975-76	1976-77	1977-78	1978-79	1979-80	1980-81	1981-82	1975-LY	Distribution LY
SWEDEN											
Before the reform. Total	12.6	-1.7	3.5								
of which Post-graduate	11.6	3.3	4.8								
After the reform. Total					5.7	-1.4	2.4				
1st degree											30.1
Post-graduate											6.3
NU											63.6
YUGOSLAVIA											
U. Regular students	10.0	6.9	4.4	6.9	6.0					5.8	
U. Non-regular students	3.3	16.8	6.3	5.3	8.2					6.6	
NU Regular students	5.2	1.8	15.8	2.4	0.2					5.9	17.9
NU Non-regular students	1.4	12.1	-10.9	-1.2	-7.3					-6.5	41.1

// changement of classification or reform.

P = Provisional.

FT = Full-time - PT = Part-time .

LY = Last year.

(1) In relation to total enrolments in universities and CAEs.
(2) University only as from 1979.
(3) First professional degrees include diplomas in odontology, medicine, law, theology and some other fields related to medical sciences.
(4) As the number of schools taken into account may vary from year to year the data are not really comparable.

Table 19

ANNUAL GROWTH RATE OF GRADUATES IN HIGHER EDUCATION
AND, FOR THE LAST YEAR AVAILABLE, DISTRIBUTION OF UNIVERSITY-LEVEL GRADUATES
ACCORDING TO LEVEL OF QUALIFICATION AND PROPORTION OF NON UNIVERSITY GRADUATES AMONG TOTAL GRADUATES

Percentage

	1965-70	1970-75	1975-76	1976-77	1977-78	1978-79	1979-80	1980-81	1975-LY	Distribution LY
GERMANY										
Graduates and equivalents	5.6	5.1	8.8	-1.5	0.7	-3.0			1.1	86.3
Doctorates	8.0	0.9	0.9	-0.9	3.5	0.8			1.1	13.7
Non-university	3.6	10.0	-8.2	13.7	-7.5	10.7			1.7	28.2
AUSTRALIA										
"Bachelor" Universities + CAEs	10.7(1)	10.1(1)	14.0	9.5	9.5	10.5	2.9		9.3	74.0
"Master" Universities + CAEs	11.7(1)	11.8(1)	14.0	9.7	7.1	4.9	-2.3		6.7	4.4
Doctorates	13.4	2.7	6.9	-6.0	5.4	10.0	-4.3		2.4	1.8
Post-graduate diploma Universities	14.4	12.3	2.9	-2.5	0.0	-12.4	-7.8		4.0	7.2
Graduate diploma CAE			20.0(2)	20.3	4.2	11.3	1.5		11.5	12.5
Diploma/associate diploma CAE (NU)			14.7(2)	-0.6	-3.1	-9.5	-6.3		-1.0	25.7
AUSTRIA										
Diploma	3.5	1.2	-2.8	20.2	-0.2				3.1	64.1
Doctorate	7.1	-2.1	0.3	-4.8	11.1				2.4	35.9
CANADA										
Bachelor	12.1	4.5	4.9	2.2	-2.4	-0.8	-1.7		0.4	73.8
Master	16.5	3.8	7.1	2.1	-2.3	0.7	4.1		2.3	11.3
Doctorates	8.4	0.8	0.5	6.9	-0.9	-3.6	4.7		1.5	1.6
Diploma/certificate 1st cycle	..	12.6	10.3	31.5	-1.1	-5.8	22.4		6.1	12.1
Diploma/certificate 2nd and 3rd cycl	22.5	7.9	-9.0	39.5	-13.5	5.9	-12.3		0.4	1.2
NU	14.1	5.4	7.1	6.9	4.6	-2.1	1.5		3.5	37.0
DENMARK										
University diploma	21.5	5.5	9.0	4.1	3.9	-0.1			4.2	
Dipl. other institutions (3)	3.4	7.3	-1.3	3.8	-7.3	6.4			0.3	
NU (3)	6.7	4.5	4.5	3.2	-7.6	26.2			4.7	
SPAIN										
University schools diploma (1st cy.)	1.9	3.1	7.1	17.9	11.4	12.0			12.0	50.7
Licences	10.9	14.1	18.1	18.6	8.3	17.5			15.6	46.6
Doctorates			-16.2	1.3	2.0	-3.9			-4.2	2.7
UNITED STATES										
Bachelor	10.1	2.0	-0.7	0.2	0	0.9			0.1	69.9
First professional (4)	4.0	10.6	2.7	3.5	3.4	1.9			2.9	5.3
Master	10.4	6.3	1.7	-1.7	-3.4	-1.0			-1.1	22.4
Doctorates	12.0	1.2	-2.4	-3.3	1.9	-0.4			-1.1	2.4
FRANCE										
Licences	6.7	-1.5	13.8		-6.8				0.8	43.6
Engineer's Diploma	2.5	2.4	-0.9	3.5	5.4				2.0	11.6
Master		4.0	51.2(5)							29.7
Doctorat	11.8	6.3	5.0		5.5				5.6	15.1(7)
NU. (DUT, BTS, capacité droit)	22.0(6)	8.1	5.9							27.9(7)

./...

Table 19 (cont'd)

ANNUAL GROWTH RATE OF GRADUATES IN HIGHER EDUCATION
AND, FOR THE LAST YEAR AVAILABLE, DISTRIBUTION OF UNIVERSITY-LEVEL GRADUATES
ACCORDING TO LEVEL OF QUALIFICATION AND PROPORTION OF NON UNIVERSITY GRADUATES AMONG TOTAL GRADUATES

Percentage

	1965-70	1970-75	1975-76	1976-77	1977-78	1978-79	1979-80	1980-81	1975-LY	Distribution LY
GREECE										
1st degree	13.0	10.1	-7.0	-10.1					-8.5	96.3
Post-graduate diploma			0.9	-25.0					-13.0	0.7
Doctorate	-2.6	3.7	14.0	3.1					8.4	3.0
NU	7.0	9.5	126.7							31.4
ITALY										
"Laureati"	16.2	3.3	4.7	-1.5	..	-29.0	-0.1		0.0	93.6
"Diplomati" (NU)	3.0	12.7	32.6	78.3	21.8	-0.8	-4.0		25.6	6.4
JAPAN										
1st degrees	8.2	5.5	4.2	4.2	5.1	5.0	1.0	2.0	3.6	95.3
Master	15.0	7.7	-1.2	11.6	5.5	0.8	-3.7	0.4	2.2	3.8
Doctorate	8.9	-1.6	6.9	5.7	-2.3	8.3	4.9	7.6	5.2	1.0
"Junior colleges" (NU)	16.5	4.2	7.0	6.1	1.6	5.0	-0.5	-1.9	2.9	28.8
Technical colleges (NU)	126.7	6.0	2.8	-5.3	0.1	4.3	-6.3	-0.2	-0.8	1.4
NETHERLANDS										
University degrees	13.0	6.6	1.4	1.9	3.9	2.0			3.2	24.7
NU FT		5.6	3.3	0.8	11.7	-1.8	4.3		3.7	57.2
NU PT		17.5	0.8	5.2	3.3	2.1	75.1		17.3	18.1
UNITED KINGDOM	(1968-71)	(1971-75)								
1st degrees (8)	8.1	4.4	0.4	1.0	4.9				2.1	74.6
Higher degrees (8)	11.1	5.9	4.3	-1.4	4.2				2.3	18.6
Higher certificates/diplomas	5.0	-0.7	1.1	-3.0	-1.5				-1.2	6.9
NU (9)	3.6	5.8	9.2	5.6	8.0				7.6	16.8
SWEDEN Before the reform										
1st degrees (10)	17.6(11)	-7.0	1.1							97.3
Higher degrees	15.4	-4.0	-25.4							2.7
NU (only teacher training schools)	9.5	-2.5	-12.7							32.5
After the reform										
Total Higher education					3.4	0.3				
1st degree										37.9
Post-graduate										2.2
NU										59.9
YUGOSLAVIA										
1st cycle graduates (12)	-19.5	6.3	9.0	3.0					6.0	9.1
2nd cycle graduates (12)	1.8	9.1	9.7	8.5					9.1	82.6
3rd cycle graduates (12)	15.1	15.7	3.6	21.3					12.1	6.0
Doctorates	23.0	14.1	17.6	-17.9					-1.7	2.2
Higher school diplomas (NU)	11.2	4.2	-3.8	3.3					-0.3	41.1

LY : Last year available.

./...

Table 19 (cont'd)

Notes

(1) Universities only.
(2) 1974-76.
(3) Types of education taken into account as from 1975 do not correspond exactly to those for previous years.
(4) First professional diplomas include diplomas in odontology, medicine, law, theology and a few other disciplines related to medicine.
(5) Increase mainly due to creation of Masters in law and economics.
(6) Creation of IUTs during this period.
(7) Not including "doctorats d'Etat" in humanities and science and engineering doctorates.
(8) Including teacher diplomas and degrees awarded by the CNAA, the Open University and London University.
(9) Certificates and diplomas lower than first degree, HND and HNC.
(10) Including diplomas lower than first degree, in particular for medical science.
(11) Not including specialised teacher diplomas for basic school.
(12) Diplomas of Faculties, Fine Arts Academy, Higher Schools and for the 3rd cycle scientific institutions.

Table 20

DISTRIBUTION BY DISCIPLINES OF UNIVERSITY DEGREES (EXCLUDING POST-GRADUATE LEVEL)

Academic year beginning in : Percentage

	1965		1970		1975		1976		1977		1978		1979		1980	
	M	F	M (1973)	F	M	F	M	F	M	F	M	F	M	F	M	F
GERMANY																
Numbers (000)	27.4	15.2	38.3	21.8	42.8	28.7	47.4	30.4	46.8	29.8	46.0	31.1	44.8	30.0		
Humanities			18.5	53.2	21.1	53.7	26.6	52.5	26.5	53.9	25.2	53.9	23.3	50.0		
Social sciences			28.3	8.3	27.4	9.1	24.0	10.3	26.5	11.4	27.6	13.5	26.2	14.0		
Science			22.3	21.6	23.4	21.6	21.4	20.6	20.1	20.2	19.3	17.7	18.3	16.7		
Technology			12.7	0.9	13.2	0.7	13.2	0.7	13.0	1.1	15.0	1.5	15.0	1.7		
Medical science			14.7	7.3	12.4	4.9	11.7	5.3	8.8	4.0	7.6	3.5	12.8	7.7		
Law					Included in social sciences											
Other			3.4	8.7	2.5	10.1	3.2	10.6	5.1	9.4	5.3	9.8	4.5	10.0		
of which teacher diploma as % of total			31.1	72.9	36.0	78.0	39.0	75.0	38.0	71.5	34.8	68.5	29.9	62.0		
AUSTRALIA "Bachelor" University																
Numbers (000)	6.6	2.4	9.7	3.8	14.0	7.8	14.7	8.3	14.5	9.3	14.9	9.7	15.6	10.6	25.9	
Humanities					32.2		32.4		32.5		31.5		31.7		30.9	
Social sciences					16.4		16.3		17.5		17.7		17.6		17.8	
Education					3.7		4.3		4.5		4.7		5.0		5.5	
Science					22.2		20.9		19.9		20.6		19.8		20.5	
Technology					7.9		7.4		7.1		6.3		6.1		5.8	
Medical science					7.7		7.6		8.0		8.3		9.2		8.7	
Law					4.6		5.8		5.6		6.0		5.7		6.0	
Other					5.2		5.3		4.9		4.9		5.0		4.9	
Bachelor - CAE					(1974)											
Numbers (000)					1.9	0.6	3.4	1.4	4.3	2.3	5.2	3.5	5.9	4.7	6.3	5.6
Humanities					9.1		16.4		17.6		11.6	22.7	11.0	21.8	10.9	21.0
Social sciences					22.4		24.2		22.3		26.8	8.9	25.3	10.1	27.7	10.5
Education					8.5		8.0		12.5		13.9	29.5	15.0	28.4	15.6	28.7
Science																
Technology					40.2		32.9		26.1		31.8	6.6	30.7	7.3	27.5	9.9
Medical science					11.9		11.4		10.2		3.9	23.4	4.1	21.3	5.0	18.8
Other					7.9		7.1		11.4		11.9	8.9	13.9	11.1	13.3	11.1
AUSTRIA Diplomas and assimilated (1)																
Numbers (000)	2.5	0.9	3.1	1.0	3.1	1.3	2.9	1.3	3.5	1.6	3.3	1.7				
Humanities	13.8	27.3	14.9	30.9	22.7	42.5	27.3	51.6	15.5	34.5	24.0	46.1				
Social sciences	16.4	25.1	16.8	18.3	21.0	17.3	25.2	17.3	19.5	15.0	17.4	15.1				
Education																
Science			(3)		(3)		(3)		10.4	16.2	(3)					
Technology	36.4	4.3	37.5	6.3	31.6	5.0	34.2	4.9	28.5	5.2	29.2	5.2				
Medical science	2.0	10.9	1.9	11.3	2.0	7.6	1.7	5.8	1.0	3.4	1.5	5.7				
Law	22.0	11.6	21.4	10.2	11.6	4.9			15.1	8.1	17.0	9.8				
Other (2)	9.5	20.9	7.4	23.0	11.2	22.8	11.7	20.4	10.1	17.5	10.9	17.9				

./...

Table 20 (cont'd)

DISTRIBUTION BY DISCIPLINES OF UNIVERSITY DEGREES (EXCLUDING POST-GRADUATE LEVEL)

Academic year beginning in : Percentage

	1965		1970		1975		1976		1977		1978		1979		1980	
	M	F	M	F	M	F	M	F	M	F	M	F	M	F	M	F
CANADA Bachelor/ First professional																
Numbers (000)			41.5	25.5	44.7	38.5	45.7	41.6	46.0	43.3	44.3	42.8	43.6	42.8	42.1	42.8
Humanities			11.2	16.3	9.7	14.4	9.9	14.3	8.9	13.6	8.7	13.1	8.7	13.3	8.3	12.1
Social sciences			24.8	15.9	28.6	20.5	29.1	22.2	30.0	23.2	30.9	24.2	31.1	24.5	30.9	25.8
Education			17.5	31.9	16.6	31.6	16.1	29.9	14.8	29.4	13.6	28.5	12.1	27.1	11.9	26.7
Science			10.5	6.9	11.9	8.4	12.3	8.4	12.3	8.3	11.8	8.2	11.9	8.4	11.8	8.1
Technology			11.2	16.3	10.2	0.4	11.0	0.6	12.1	0.9	13.9	1.1	15.4	1.3	15.4	1.4
Medical science			4.7	7.2	5.7	7.6	5.5	7.7	5.3	7.5	5.4	7.9	5.4	8.0	5.6	8.1
Law			4.3	0.7	4.6	1.5	4.5	1.8	4.7	1.9	4.5	2.2	4.5	2.5	4.7	2.6
Other			15.8	4.8	12.7	15.6	11.6	15.1	11.9	15.2	11.2	14.8	10.9	14.9	11.4	15.2
1st cycle diplomas/ certificates																
Numbers (000)			2.6	3.1	5.0	5.3	4.3	4.9	5.6	6.6	5.2	6.9	4.9	6.4	5.9	8.0
Humanities			6.9	8.1	3.9	5.3	4.5	7.8	3.8	6.1	4.9	7.2	5.1	8.2	4.6	7.2
Social sciences			22.9	5.8	19.1	10.9	29.6	16.0	35.1	16.0	33.9	16.1	42.5	22.6	43.9	25.2
Education			44.5	46.3	48.5	54.6	43.0	48.8	42.8	53.9	43.3	60.5	34.6	48.1	33.3	54.5
Science			10.2	0.4	7.8	1.1	9.6	3.7	5.8	3.2	4.4	2.9	4.4	3.7	3.5	1.2
Technology			8.9	7.5	11.6	0.3	10.1	0.2	9.7	0.4	11.5	0.5	11.0	0.7	10.7	0.6
Medical science			1.5	29.8	2.7	22.7	3.2	23.5	2.8	20.4	2.0	12.8	2.4	16.7	1.7	7.9
Other			5.1	2.1	6.4	5.1									2.3	3.4
DENMARK Universities	(1966)															
Numbers (4)(000)	0.72	0.22	1.6	0.55	2.0	0.81	2.2	0.92	2.1	1.1	2.2	1.1	2.1	1.2		
Humanities	14.5	31.6	16.5	35.1	20.0		17.0	33.4	18.2	24.7	16.1	29.9	17.2	29.3		
Social sciences	36.0	28.9	33.3	26.2	31.5		23.4	24.2	26.6	40.0	23.1	27.9	23.4	28.1		
Education											2.7	3.5	4.8	3.8		
Science	17.2	20.9	17.2	12.9	5.8		12.5	4.8	11.2	4.7	12.7	5.1	12.4	6.1		
Technology					5.3		6.6	0.8	4.7	0.2	6.9	1.2	5.3	1.1		
Medical science	32.3	18.7	33.0	25.8	21.0		24.6	18.4	23.6	17.7	21.8	18.1	22.4	19.5		
Law					16.3		15.8	18.2	14.9	12.3	15.5	14.0	13.7	11.9		
Other							0.1	0.3	0.8	0.3	1.2	0.3	0.7	0.3		
Other Univ. Institutions (5)																
Numbers (000)	0.84	0.13	0.91	0.20	1.2	0.38	1.1	0.43	1.2	0.44	1.2	0.42	1.2	0.41		
Humanities																
Social sciences																
Education					12.1	24.4	11.8	25.1	10.0	22.7	9.1	22.0	7.8	19.3		
Science																
Technology	60.6	16.4	55.8	9.5	44.4	8.7	44.2	6.8	47.5	8.7	47.4	9.5	49.9	13.5		
Medical science	14.9	67.2	12.8	78.1	9.5	43.8	10.4	40.1	9.4	38.8	10.4	36.7	11.7	36.9		
Other	24.5	16.4	31.3	12.4	33.9	23.1	33.7	27.9	33.1	29.8	33.0	31.8	30.6	30.4		

./...

Table 20 (cont'd)

DISTRIBUTION BY DISCIPLINES OF UNIVERSITY DEGREES (EXCLUDING POST-GRADUATE LEVEL)

Academic year beginning in : Percentage

	1965		1970		1975		1976		1977		1978		1979		1980	
	M	F	M	F	M	F	M	F	M	F	M	F	M	F	M	F
SPAIN : Faculties, higher technical schools and higher artistics education)																
Numbers (000)	8.0		12.8		18.0	9.3	19.4	13.0	23.1	15.0	24.7	16.7	24.0	17.5	25.6	19.6
Humanities	13.2		17.7		17.9	41.0	21.3	48.1	20.7	45.8	21.2	42.4	19.3	40.8	20.3	39.0
Social sciences	6.3		7.6		13.8	6.7	13.9	5.6	15.1	6.3	14.7	8.5	15.5	10.2	15.6	8.9
Education																
Science	12.6		17.6		13.4	15.7	14.8	14.4	14.1	14.7	13.0	12.1	13.1	13.0	12.1	11.7
Technology	19.1		19.8		17.9	0.9	14.5	0.8	13.7	0.7	11.3	0.6	11.3	0.8	9.9	0.8
Medical science	28.3		25.0		23.5	23.8	20.0	18.1	22.1	20.7	24.0	23.0	25.9	24.3	25.6	25.3
Law	14.5		10.1		10.9	8.0	11.7	8.9	11.3	8.4	12.6	8.5	12.3	8.3	13.3	9.7
Other	6.1		2.3		2.6	4.0	3.8	4.2	3.0	3.4	3.2	4.8	2.6	2.6	3.2	4.6
UNITED STATES "Bachelor"	(1964)		(1969)													
Numbers (000)	279.8	213.2	453.6	344.5	508.5	425.9	499.1	429.1	491.1	439.1	481.4	449.9	477.7	460.5		
Humanities	11.4	19.7	11.5	21.0	10.8	17.1	10.2	16.0	9.5	15.0	11.5		8.3	13.4		
Social sciences	41.2	18.9	44.6	23.3	45.7	27.8	45.7	29.8	45.8	32.0	40.6		46.9	36.1		
Education	10.0	42.5	9.2	36.4	8.3	26.8	8.1	24.5	7.7	22.7	13.8		6.6	19.3		
Science	16.5	7.6	13.9	6.9	12.4	7.0	12.2	7.0	11.7	6.9	9.1		10.8	6.6		
Technology	12.4	0.0	9.8	0.1	8.9	0.4	9.5	0.5	10.7	0.9	6.7		13.1	1.4		
Medical science	0.3	5.1	1.1	5.0	2.3	10.1	2.4	10.7	2.4	11.0	6.8		2.4	11.5		
Law	0.1	-	0.1	0.0	0.1	0.0	0.1	0.0	0.1	0.0	0.0		0.0	0.0		
Other	8.0	6.1	9.8	7.4	11.6	10.8	11.9	11.4	12.1	11.5	11.5		11.8	11.7		
First professional(6)																
Numbers (000)	39.9	6.1	33.3	1.9	53.2	9.9	52.7	12.1	52.6	14.4	52.9	16.3	53.0	17.5		
Humanities	12.1	5.0	15.7	5.6	10.0	4.1	10.5	5.3	10.9	4.9	9.3		11.5	5.7		
Medical Science	36.8	20.0	37.5	44.4	38.3	28.9	37.3	27.5	38.0	30.0	36.9		38.9	29.1		
Law	28.6	6.7	42.6	44.4	49.3	63.9	50.3	64.2	48.8	62.2	51.3		47.2	61.7		
Other	22.6	68.3	4.2	5.6	2.5	3.1	1.9	5.0	2.3	2.8	2.5		2.3	3.4		
FRANCE - Licence, Diplôme d'Ingénieur, Doctorats in Medical science	(1972)										P					
Numbers (000)	39.6		34.5	24.6	34.7	26.1	37.8	27.9			35.1	28.2				
Humanities	33.5		19.9	55.7	15.0	44.8	12.9	41.1			16.3	43.1				
Sciences économiques	1.9		7.1	3.7	6.7	4.6	9.8	5.5			7.1	5.2				
Education																
Science	26.9		11.8	11.5	10.9	11.1	9.9	10.1			12.0	7.8				
Technology	19.9		26.2	2.1	27.0	3.4	23.4	3.3			27.9	4.6				
Medical science	12.4		22.1	16.5	27.9	23.2	28.1	23.0			23.1	22.1				
Law	5.4		13.0	10.5	11.5	11.7	14.5	15.1			11.9	14.8				
Other					1.0	1.2	1.4	1.8			1.7	2.4				

./...

Table 20 (cont'd)

DISTRIBUTION BY DISCIPLINES OF UNIVERSITY DEGREES (EXCLUDING POST-GRADUATE LEVEL)

Academic year beginning in : Percentage

	1965		1970		1975		1976		1977		1978		1979		1980		1981	
	M	F	M	F	M	F	M	F	M	F	M	F	M	F	M	F	M	F
FRANCE (cont'd)																		
1st cycle diplomas (2 years)																		
Numbers (000)					21.9	23.0	25.3	23.8										
Humanities					18.5	43.5	18.8	43.7										
Social sciences					13.0	6.9	12.8	6.7										
Education					-													
Science					20.6	12.9	20.0	12.2										
Technology					-													
Medical science					23.3	15.1	23.7	14.2										
Law					19.5	17.1	19.0	17.9										
Other					5.0	4.6	5.6	5.3										
GREECE																		
Numbers (000)	3.4	1.2	5.7	2.8	8.9	4.8	8.1	4.7	6.8	4.7								
Humanities	8.5	31.9	6.5	31.4	5.9	26.2	6.0	29.9	7.4	33.7								
Social sciences	44.2 (7)	33.0 (7)	36.0 (7)	33.6 (7)	44.0 (7)	44.6 (7)	42.3 (7)	39.8 (7)	32.3	26.5								
Education																		
Science	14.6	14.0	18.2	12.2	19.4	14.2	18.1	14.1	14.3	8.0								
Technologie	12.7	6.0	14.3	4.8	11.7	3.0	13.2	4.1	16.0	4.4								
Medical science	14.5	13.5	16.5	14.0	13.6	10.0	17.1	10.8	16.8	13.0								
Law									10.7	13.6								
Other	5.5	1.6	8.6	4.0	5.4	2.0	3.3	1.4	2.5	0.8								
ITALY "Laureati"											P							
Numbers (000)	18.0	10.1	33.9	25.6	39.8	30.1	41.4	31.8	41.2	31.0	41.0	31.2	39.8	30.3	39.2	30.8		
Humanities	9.5	58.9	17.2	67.4	13.5	56.9	12.5	53.5	9.8	49.3	9.5	45.6	9.0	42.7	8.3	40.0		
Social sciences	21.0	8.4	20.4	8.7	14.6	7.1	12.7	6.2	12.7	6.3	12.5	6.7	13.1	7.2	12.7	7.7		
Education	-																	
Science	14.8	19.9	15.2	14.8	13.1	20.3	12.7	20.9	12.3	22.8	11.0	23.1	10.2	22.2	10.8	22.2		
Technology	17.5	1.4	18.4	2.0	24.8	3.2	24.8	3.2	24.1	3.3	24.7	4.1	25.3	4.8	22.4	5.0		
Medical science	12.9	3.3	12.1	3.0	20.2	6.6	23.1	9.7	26.3	11.7	26.7	12.3	25.8	13.2	27.8	14.4		
Law	21.1	8.0	14.5	4.0	10.8	5.7	11.2	6.0	11.5	6.1	11.9	7.5	12.6	8.9	12.4	9.3		
Other	3.3	0.1	2.2	0.1	3.1	0.3	3.0	0.4	3.3	0.5	3.7	0.7	4.0	1.0	4.5	1.3		
% of non-course students																		
Humanities	70.7	77.4	56.6	62.3	65.4	67.1	65.2	72.0	68.7	69.1	77.0	77.9						
Social sciences	86.4	78.4	76.8	68.9	77.4	71.0	77.3	73.2	79.7	65.5	76.9	72.3						
Education																		
Science	66.9	61.8	57.4	47.7	64.4	49.5	67.1	53.8	70.1	54.7	78.4	65.8						
Technology	82.7	91.5	62.5	38.7	64.7	53.3	68.2	51.9	70.7	54.2	75.4	65.6						
Medical science	48.9	43.7	24.5	17.1	39.9	25.8	43.0	37.6	42.8	34.9	52.8	44.9						
Law	74.7	67.6	63.3	60.7	68.9	49.8	72.5	69.7	76.1	67.9	72.5	65.0						
Other	74.8	50.0	62.3	66.7	70.7	63.3	72.1	67.7	65.7	55.6	77.7	67.5						
Total	73.7	72.6	59.2	58.9	62.2	59.7	64.5	64.1	64.7	60.9	66.8	69.1						

./...

Table 20 (cont'd)

DISTRIBUTION BY DISCIPLINES OF UNIVERSITY DEGREES (EXCLUDING POST-GRADUATE LEVEL)

Academic year beginning in :

Percentage

	1965		1970		1975		1976		1977		1978		1979		1980		1981	
	M	F	M	F	M	F	M	F	M	F	M	F	M	F	M	F	M	F
JAPAN 1st degree (9)																		
Numbers (000)	136.1	26.3	192.2	48.8	245.5	67.5	252.0	79.1	259.3	80.5	270.9	86.1	283.2	91.7	285.0	93.7	290.5	95.5
Humanities	10.6	48.1	7.7	46.4	7.9	44.3	7.2	44.5	7.7	44.1	7.6	43.3	7.6	43.8	7.9	43.8	7.9	43.7
Social sciences	49.6	5.0	51.4	9.9	50.6	13.7	50.6	14.3	50.2	14.7	50.6	15.3	50.2	15.5	50.1	15.2	49.6	15.4
Education	5.6	23.5	4.7	20.3	4.1	20.5	3.9	20.1	4.0	20.4	4.0	20.6	4.2	20.2	4.5	20.3	4.6	19.2
Science	3.1	2.2	3.2	2.1	3.3	2.1	3.3	2.1	3.3	2.0	3.3	1.9	3.3	1.9	3.4	2.1	3.3	2.2
Technology	22.0	0.5	25.1	0.5	26.4	0.8	26.7	0.7	26.5	0.8	26.0	0.8	25.9	0.8	25.5	0.9	25.5	1.0
Medical science	3.6	9.2	3.1	8.4	3.1	7.8	3.3	7.7	3.5	7.7	3.7	7.7	4.0	7.6	4.0	7.6	4.2	7.9
Law	5.6	10.6	4.7	12.4	4.6	10.8	4.6	10.5	4.8	10.3	4.8	10.3	4.8	10.3	4.8	10.1	4.7	10.5
Other																		
NETHERLANDS																		
Numbers (000)	3.6	0.6	6.5	1.2	8.4	2.1	8.4	2.2	10.2		10.6		10.8					
Humanities	8.9	17.3	6.6	15.7	6.4	15.5	6.6	14.9	9.4		10.0		11.7					
Social sciences	19.6	18.2	22.6	18.8	24.5	30.2	24.8	31.4	28.2		29.1		29.5					
Education	5.5	18.2	6.2	18.6	4.7	10.1	4.6	8.9										
Science	13.8	10.3	13.6	9.2	11.5	7.7	11.8	8.6	12.3		12.3		11.2					
Technology	23.9	0.5	19.6	1.3	19.0	1.3	18.6	1.7	15.5		15.5		13.0					
Medical science	15.0	19.9	16.1	16.7	16.3	17.6	16.2	16.8	17.4		17.4		18.7					
Law	9.2	12.9	12.4	18.3	13.2	14.4	13.7	14.8	14.0		14.0		12.8					
Other	4.2	2.8	2.9	1.4	4.4	3.2	3.7	2.9	3.2		3.2		3.2					
UNITED KINGDOM																		
Universities (10)	(1968)		(1971)															
Numbers (000)	38.9	35.2	46.8	43.5	46.9	44.8	46.7	44.8	45.4	43.0	47.7	43.7						
Humanities	6.8	10.0	6.5	8.9	5.9	9.4	6.1	10.0	6.6	11.0	6.5	11.7						
Social sciences	16.9	8.7	17.4	8.5	18.3	10.7	19.1	11.8	21.4	13.4	21.8	14.4						
Education (9)	22.3	64.8	23.6	65.6	22.2	58.5	21.4	56.1	15.5	50.9	15.5	49.4						
Science	22.1	8.4	20.4	7.6	21.0	8.9	21.2	9.3	21.3	10.0	21.0	10.1						
Technology	17.8	0.2	17.3	0.3	16.4	0.6	15.6	0.6	17.0	0.8	17.2	0.9						
Medical science	6.3	2.8	6.2	2.5	7.2	4.1	7.5	4.5	8.4	5.2	8.1	5.0						
Other	7.9	5.0	8.6	6.5	9.0	7.7	9.1	7.7	9.9	8.6	9.9	8.5						
CNAA																		
Numbers (000)			2.9		8.6	3.1	12.9		17.2									
Humanities			2.1		1.6	6.3	2.7		2.4									
Social sciences			12.7		28.8	27.6	31.2		34.5									
Education					0.5	3.2	1.1		6.0									
Science			15.2		18.3	11.5	14.5		15.0									
Technology			27.0		28.5	0.9	19.2		16.8									
Medical science			3.1		2.6	4.0	3.0		2.2									
Other			39.9		19.8	46.4	28.3		23.1									

./...

Table 20 (cont'd)

DISTRIBUTION BY DISCIPLINES OF UNIVERSITY DEGREES (EXCLUDING POST-GRADUATE LEVEL)

Academic year beginning in : Percentage

	1965		1970		1975		1976		1977		1978		1979		1980	
	M	F	M	F	M	F	M	F	M	F	M	F	M	F	M	F
SWEDEN Before the reform																
Numbers(000)	5.0	2.7	11.6	8.1	8.4	5.5	8.2	5.8								
Humanities	14.2	35.8	9.2	31.7	7.2	17.9	6.9	16.6								
Social sciences	22.4	17.5	35.4	28.0	32.9	36.1	31.1	37.9								
Education	1.5	6.3	10.9	18.0	8.4	15.9	7.6	13.8								
	(11)	(11)														
Science	15.4	12.8	11.9	7.0	5.9	3.7	5.5	4.1								
Technology	19.1	1.7	14.3	1.6	19.0	3.2	21.3	3.3								
Medical science	20.0	23.9	13.1	11.7	18.6	18.9	19.1	19.6								
Law	4.6	1.6	3.8	1.5	6.2	3.1	6.8	3.2								
Other	2.7	0.4	1.3	0.5	1.8	1.1	1.7	1.5								
Afther the reform	Higher Education Total															
Numbers(000)(12)									27.7		29.4		30.0			
Technology									11.4		10.1		10.4			
Adm. écon. soc.									17.1		17.4		17.3			
Med. para medic.									30.8		31.6		32.7			
Education									36.1		36.3		35.3			
Communic., cult.									4.6		4.6		4.2			
YUGOSLAVIA (2nd cycle diplomas of Faculties, Fine Arts Academies, High School)																
Numbers (000)	9.3	3.7	9.3	4.9	13.3	8.7	13.8	10.3	14.8	11.4						
Humanities	5.7	23.5	7.1	19.1	7.2	20.3	7.7	22.6	6.5	19.4						
Social sciences	21.3	15.4	20.5	18.2	19.0	19.9	20.4	20.8	21.0	22.1						
Education	2.3	1.0	3.1	1.6	3.9	2.9	3.8	1.7	4.0	2.2						
Science	3.7	7.0	6.1	10.3	5.0	8.8	5.1	8.4	4.9	8.3						
Technology	29.3	16.3	31.0	14.9	34.9	13.4	33.0	12.7	33.2	11.8						
Medical science	11.6	19.7	10.4	20.2	9.4	16.4	8.3	14.4	8.0	15.5						
Law	12.3	10.1	11.3	10.4	10.7	12.5	12.0	13.6	13.2	15.3						
Other	13.8	7.0	10.6	5.3	10.0	5.9	9.7	5.8	9.2	5.3						
Proportion of non-course students among 2nd cycle graduates	17.0	8.2	19.8	12.0	16.2	10.7	18.3	12.3	18.1	12.6						
1st cycle diplomas																
Numbers (000)	4.2	1.5	1.2	0.7	1.6	0.9	1.8	1.0	1.8	1.1						
Humanities	4.4	17.3	2.6	4.2	0.0	-	0.3	4.2	0.3	5.7						
Social sciences	24.9	25.4	28.2	36.4	45.7	73.7	42.3	71.4	40.4	73.5						
Education	2.7	6.7	9.7	7.0	4.9	1.6	5.4	1.6	6.2	1.3						
Science	2.7	4.1	6.7	8.8	5.8	7.1	1.4	3.9	1.4	4.1						
Technology	39.3	16.8	18.2	5.6	38.3	9.7	44.5	9.2	43.1	6.6						
Medical science	0.8	4.3	0.1	0.3					0.0							
Law	15.3	13.5	26.6	20.7	1.3	0.8	3.2	4.3	3.8	4.6						
Other	9.7	12.0	8.1	17.1	4.0	7.2	2.9	5.2	4.7	4.2						
Proportion of non-course students among 1st cycle graduates	26.3	16.6	46.5	35.2	47.9	32.4	58.3	38.2	54.3	36.0						

./...

Table 20 (cont'd)

Notes :

(1) For certain disciplines the doctorate is the first degree, in particular before the reorganisation of university education.
(2) Including Fine Art Academies.
(3) Included in humanities.
(4) Not including the University of Copenhagen in the distribution by disciplines.
(5) As from 1975 types of education taken into account do not correspond exactly to those in previous years.
(6) Obtained after at least 6 years of study except in 1964 (5 years).
(7) Including Law.
(8) Including "diplomati", numbering 4,938 in 1977.
(9) Regular students only.
(10) Including teacher training graduates.
(11) Not including specialised teacher diplomas for basic school.
(12) Total of higher education, excluding graduates from separate courses (21 in 1979) or courses corresponding to the old system : 4,1 in 1977 ; 3,5 in 1978 and 3,0 in 1979.

Table 21

DISTRIBUTION BY DISCIPLINES OF HIGHER DEGREES

Academic year beginning in :

Percentage

	1965		1970		1975		1976		1977		1978		1979		1980	
	M	F	M	F	M	F	M	F	M	F	M	F	M	F	M	F
GERMANY - Doctorates			(1973)													
Numbers (000)	6.7	1.0	8.5	1.6	9.7	1.7	9.8	1.7	9.6	1.8	9.9	1.9	9.7	2.2		
Humanities			10.8	18.4	11.3	17.8	10.3	17.6	12.6	22.2	10.3	15.6	8.4	13.5		
Social sciences			13.5	4.3	12.3	5.9	12.4	5.9	12.6	5.6	12.4	5.2	11.5	4.5		
Education																
Science			22.7	6.1	24.7	11.8	25.8	11.8	26.3	16.7	23.8	15.6	25.1	13.5		
Technology			8.2	0.6	10.2	0.6	10.2	0.6	10.4	0.6	10.2	0.5	11.4	0.5		
Medical science			41.8	67.5	38.1	59.2	38.1	58.8	34.8	50.0	40.3	57.3	40.7	63.1		
Law				Included in social sciences												
Autres			3.0	3.1	3.3	4.7	3.2	5.3	3.2	5.0	3.0	5.7	3.0	5.0		
AUSTRALIA - Master																
Numbers (000)	0.49	0.08	0.75	0.14	1.3	0.25	1.5	0.3	1.6	0.37	1.6	0.45	1.6	0.51	0.9	
Humanities					13.5		10.9		10.5		10.7		15.5		11.5	
Social sciences					27.0		25.4		28.4		27.3		23.8		29.4	
Education					14.2		15.5		15.2		16.4		17.0		18.1	
Science					15.3		16.6		13.4		15.4		16.7		13.3	
Technology					17.2		15.0		12.5		12.4		11.1		11.0	
Medical science					1.9		3.1		4.1		3.9		2.4		3.9	
Law					2.4		3.2		4.3		3.8		3.7		2.7	
Other					8.5		10.3		11.6		10.1		9.7		10.1	
- Doctorates																
Numbers (000)			0.60	0.06	0.70	0.09	0.73	0.12	0.69	0.11	0.71	0.13	0.78	0.15	2.1	
Humanities					10.1		8.9		8.2		8.1		17.0		10.9	
Social sciences					8.3		10.7		11.0		12.4		9.9		10.7	
Education					1.5		1.9		2.6		3.6		2.9		4.7	
Science					49.0		44.9		42.8		41.2		36.3		43.7	
Technology					13.6		10.8		13.5		13.0		9.5		10.8	
Medical science					11.8		12.0		13.4		11.7		12.8		10.7	
Law					0.4		0.6		0.2		0.7		0.6		0.5	
Other					5.3		10.2		8.3		9.3		10.9		7.9	
-Post-graduate diploma and others																
Numbers (000)			1.1	1.3	1.8	2.3	1.9	2.3	2.0	2.1	1.9	2.1	1.7	1.9	3.0	
Humanities									0.4		0.2		1.7		1.1	
Social sciences					15.3		7.5		6.1		7.8		9.3		10.6	
Education					75.6		85.2		83.0		80.9		76.2		74.9	
Science					2.5		1.8		2.2		3.2		5.2		4.9	
Technology					1.0		0.9		0.6		0.4		0.6		0.6	
Medical science					2.1		2.8		2.6		3.3		2.4		3.9	
Law					1.0		0.0		1.8		1.9		1.9		2.7	
Other					2.5		1.8		3.3		2.3		2.6		1.2	

./...

Table 21 (cont'd)

DISTRIBUTION BY DISCIPLINES OF HIGHER DEGREES

Academic year beginning in :

Percentage

	1965		1970		1975		1976		1977		1978		1979		1980	
	M	F	M	F	M	F	M	F	M	F	M	F	M	F	M	F
AUSTRALIA (cont'd)																
Graduate diploma (CAE)					(1974)											
Numbers (000)					1.5	1.5	2.3	2.1	2.6	2.7	2.7	2.8	3.0	3.1	3.0	3.2
Humanities					7.9		8.5		11.5		8.7	22.4	11.1	26.0	15.8	30.9
Social sciences					9.4		7.9		12.7		25.7	6.2	28.3	8.9	33.5	10.7
Education					74.3		74.7		63.7		49.6	60.3	40.4	52.8	25.5	40.1
Science					[		[		[		[		[		[	
Technology					4.3		4.7		5.7		9.6	2.4	12.3	2.3	13.1	3.8
Medical science					1.7		1.9		1.7		0.9	3.8	1.3	4.7	2.5	4.4
Other					2.4		2.3		4.7		5.5	4.8	6.5	5.2	9.6	10.0
AUSTRIA (1)																
Numbers (000)	1.5	0.45	2.2	0.58	1.9	0.57	2.1	0.6	1.9	0.75	2.1	0.75				
Humanities (2)	22.7	43.2	24.7	42.2	25.3	40.9	24.6(2)	39.2(2)	12.3	30.4	23.6	34.9				
Social sciences	15.8	6.5	13.4	3.5	8.8	2.3	8.9	4.0	8.5	3.2	8.0	2.8				
Education																
Science									10.8	6.9						
Technology	6.6	0.4	8.2	0.3	8.6	1.0	7.7	0.7	7.8	0.8	7.8	1.4				
Medical science	21.5	28.7	24.5	29.2	38.4	43.0	34.8	39.3	35.4	40.0	36.7	40.6				
Law	32.0	19.8	28.5	23.8	16.2	9.6	21.1	14.8	20.6	13.7	21.4	16.6				
Other	1.4	1.3	0.7	1.0	2.8	3.1	2.9	2.0	4.6	5.0	2.5	3.8				
CANADA - Master																
Numbers (000)			7.5	2.1	8.0	3.5	8.5	3.9	8.5	4.2	7.9	4.4	7.8	4.7	7.9	5.1
Humanities			17.0	35.0	13.0	26.5	12.9	25.0	12.9	24.0	10.9	22.7	10.4	21.1	10.6	20.6
Social sciences			33.1	29.3	38.0	32.2	37.0	30.9	36.4	31.2	37.7	31.1	38.5	32.0	39.1	30.9
Education			13.8	18.7	18.5	24.6	18.6	26.1	20.3	26.7	19.8	28.4	19.6	27.9	20.3	30.4
Science			15.3	8.0	12.7	7.1	12.4	7.1	12.4	6.8	11.9	6.2	11.7	6.4	10.8	5.8
Technology			15.6	0.6	12.2	0.9	12.8	1.0	12.7	1.7	13.8	1.5	13.3	1.7	12.0	1.7
Medical science			2.3	4.0	2.1	3.8	1.7	5.7	2.1	5.9	2.4	6.4	2.2	7.1	2.8	6.7
Law			0.4	0.1	0.7	0.2	1.5	0.4	0.8	0.4	0.8	0.2	1.3	0.6	1.5	0.6
Other			2.5	4.3	2.8	4.7	3.1	3.8	2.4	3.3	2.7	3.5	3.0	3.2	2.9	3.3
CANADA - Doctorates																
Numbers (000)			1.5	0.2	1.4	0.3	1.4	0.3	1.5	0.3	1.4	0.4	1.3	0.4	1.4	0.4
Humanities			9.6	25.2	12.1	29.2	12.5	29.1	12.8	24.4	13.7	25.7	12.2	19.8	13.4	25.0
Social sciences			12.0	23.8	22.6	24.2	18.9	26.5	20.9	29.0	20.3	27.1	22.0	26.3	21.3	27.4
Education			4.9	3.3	8.1	14.5	9.4	13.7	7.9	11.8	9.6	15.2	9.3	20.3	9.3	17.0
Science			41.2	27.8	32.4	15.1	32.4	17.0	31.2	15.7	28.2	14.1	30.7	13.5	29.6	15.4
Technology			15.9		12.9	3.5	14.4	0.7	14.6	2.1	15.5	2.4	13.8	1.5	14.9	2.1
Medical science			5.7	6.0	6.1	6.6	5.6	8.8	6.5	8.5	6.3	11.7	6.9	11.3	5.8	7.6
Law			0.9	1.3	0.6	0.3	0.3	0.3	0.1	0.6	0.3	0.3	0.2		0.4	0.5
Other			9.8	12.6	5.2	6.6	6.5	3.9	6.0	7.9	6.1	3.5	4.9	7.3	5.3	5.0

./...

Table 21 (cont'd)

DISTRIBUTION BY DISCIPLINES OF HIGHER DEGREES

Academic year beginning in :

Percentage

	1965		1970		1975		1976		1977		1978		1979		1980	
	M	F	M	F	M	F	M	F	M	F	M	F	M	F	M	F
CANADA (cont'd)																
-Higher degrees and certificates																
Numbers (000)			0.7	0.2	0.9	0.5	0.8	0.5	1.2	0.6	1.0	0.5	1.0	0.6	0.8	0.6
Humanities			0.8	1.9	0.9	5.4	2.4	3.9	3.1	8.8	4.7	7.4	2.4	8.8	0.6	4.0
Social sciences			34.3	15.0	38.3	26.2	37.6	24.8	61.6	32.7	58.1	40.5	59.6	38.0	59.5	40.0
Education			38.2	57.2	34.4	49.2	32.6	50.1	16.2	39.8	19.1	36.1	14.8	34.0	13.9	38.1
Science			3.0	1.9	2.8	2.8	4.0	3.2	2.8	2.2	3.3	2.6	4.0	2.5	5.2	3.6
Technology			4.0	0.5	2.3		2.1		1.2	0.2	1.5		1.5	0.2	2.3	
Medical science			19.7	23.5	21.3	16.4	21.3	18.0	15.1	16.3	13.3	13.4	15.4	14.3	15.8	11.4
Other													2.3	2.2	2.7	2.9
UNITED STATES - Master	(1964)		(1969)													
Numbers (000)	76.2	36.0	126.1	83.2	167.7	145.3	168.2	150.0	161.7	151.1	153.8	148.3	151.2	147.9		
Humanities	9.8	16.1	9.9	20.1	8.6	14.0	8.4	13.4	7.9	12.8	9.7		7.4	11.4		
Social sciences	21.3	10.0	29.7	12.5	37.1	14.8	38.8	16.5	40.3	18.0	30.4		43.1	21.8		
Education	30.1	57.8	28.2	53.1	27.3	57.0	25.7	55.7	23.8	53.4	37.2		20.5	49.2		
Science	13.5	6.4	10.4	5.2	7.1	2.9	6.9	3.1	7.1	2.9	5.1		6.7	3.0		
Technology	15.7	0.3	12.4	0.2	9.4	0.4	9.2	0.5	9.6	0.6	5.1		10.0	0.7		
Medical science	1.8	3.1	1.8	2.8	2.6	5.7	2.5	5.9	2.6	6.7	5.2		2.9	7.7		
Law	0.9		0.6		0.7	0.1	0.8	0.1	0.9	0.2	0.5		1.0	0.2		
Other	7.0	6.2	7.1	6.2	7.1	5.0	7.6	4.9	7.8	5.3	6.7		8.5	6.0		
- Doctorates																
Numbers (000)	14.7	1.8	25.9	4.0	26.3	7.8	25.1	8.1	23.7	8.5	23.6	9.2	22.9	9.7		
Humanities	13.5	26.3	13.5	27.9	18.6	29.0	18.9	29.0	18.7	26.6	20.5		18.3	24.5		
Social sciences	15.5	13.7	15.4	14.7	18.3	16.1	17.1	14.6	17.4	15.1	16.0		16.2	14.2		
Education	14.9	29.8	18.1	30.1	19.8	33.3	20.7	34.2	19.5	34.9	23.6		19.2	36.4		
Science	33.8	23.4	30.9	20.1	25.1	14.4	25.9	14.3	25.4	14.6	22.6		26.2	14.8		
Technology	14.2	0.6	14.2	0.6	10.3	0.8	10.0	0.9	9.8	0.7	7.6		10.5	1.0		
Medical science	1.4	0.9	1.4	1.5	1.5	2.1	1.2	2.1	1.7	3.0	2.1		1.7	3.6		
Law	0.0	0.1	0.0	0.0	0.3	0.0	0.2	0.1	0.2	0.0	0.0		0.0	0.0		
Other	6.7	5.2	6.6	5.1	6.1	4.3	6.0	4.7	7.2	5.1	7.5		7.9	5.5		
FRANCE - Master											P					
Numbers (000)			7.6	6.7	18.5		28.2				14.6	13.9				
Humanities			47.2	73.8	39.2	68.8	23.0	44.5			25.1	46.3				
Social sciences																
Education					8.3	2.6	18.3	9.7			17.1	9.4				
Science			52.8	26.2	49.2	27.6	30.1	19.3			32.5	18.3				
Technology					3.3	1.0	0.9	0.4								
Medical science																
Law							27.0	25.3			23.4	24.0				
Other							0.7	0.9			2.0	1.9				
- Doctorates											P					
Numbers (000)	2.3		4.6	1.1	4.2	1.1	4.5	1.3			3.0(5)	1.2(5)				
Humanities	16.4		19.1	33.3	19.1	30.8	23.2	39.2			29.0	41.4				
Social sciences	3.7		6.4	1.8	8.4	3.4	9.1	4.9			12.5	5.1				
Science	60.8		58.8	59.1	55.2	57.3	50.4	46.9			48.5	47.7				
Technology	9.2		8.5	2.1	10.6	3.5	9.4	3.2								
Law	9.8		7.2	3.7	6.7	4.9	7.9	5.8			10.0	5.8				

./...

Table 21 (cont'd)

DISTRIBUTION BY DISCIPLINES OF HIGHER DEGREES

Academic year beginning in :

Percentage

	1965		1970		1975		1976		1977		1978		1979		1980	
	M	F	M	F	M	F	M	F	M	F	M	F	M	F	M	F
JAPAN - Master	(1964)															
Numbers (000)	4.8		9.4		13.5		13.3		13.6	1.3	14.4	1.3	15.8			
Humanities									13.0		11.6					
Education									3.2		3.2					
Social sciences									11.5		11.3					
Science									10.7		10.3					
Technology									46.5		48.6					
Medical science									3.5		3.3					
Law																
Other									11.5		11.6					
- Doctorates																
Numbers (000)	2.1		3.2		2.9		3.1		3.1	0.2	3.0	0.2	3.4			
Humanities									14.1		15.4					
Education									3.5		3.1					
Social sciences									13.2		13.6					
Science									17.4		15.7					
Technology									20.2		18.0					
Medical science									24.3		25.2					
Law																
Other									7.2		8.9					
UNITED KINGDOM	(1968)		(1971)													
Higher degrees (universities only for distribution by disciplines)																
Numbers (000)	11.6	4.5	15.5	6.7	18.7	9.3	19.5	9.5	19.5	9.4	20.1	9.8				
Humanities	5.9	19.8	6.0	19.9	5.9	16.2	5.5	14.8	5.0	13.9	5.3	12.3				
Education	3.4	7.8	3.7	5.5	7.4	11.7	7.2	11.3	7.2	11.7	8.1	12.5				
Social sciences	15.7	19.0	19.0	22.4	20.0	24.5	21.1	23.2	22.1	26.1	21.4	25.7				
Science	36.5	30.8	31.9	26.8	26.5	18.6	27.7	20.6	27.2	20.3	26.9	21.6				
Technology	23.0	2.4	23.6	3.7	23.2	4.2	22.1	4.1	22.0	4.5	22.9	5.2				
Medical science	5.6	10.0	6.1	8.9	5.2	10.0	5.3	10.7	5.3	8.9	5.3	9.4				
Law																
Other	10.0	10.2	9.6	12.9	11.7	14.9	11.0	15.4	11.1	14.6	10.1	13.3				
Higher diplomas/certificates																
Numbers (000)	6.4	3.8	7.0	4.8	6.4	5.0	6.5	5.1	6.2	5.1	6.1	4.9				
Humanities	1.8	1.8	1.1	1.6	1.5	1.8	1.8	2.0	1.7	1.9	1.6	1.9				
Education	46.8	73.6	49.6	74.7	57.1	71.7	58.9	69.6	57.8	68.8	58.3	69.9				
Social sciences	12.3	14.6	14.1	15.1	17.4	16.9	17.3	17.2	16.5	17.7	16.5	17.1				
Science	6.4	1.1	5.9	1.6	6.2	2.3	3.3	1.1	4.2	1.2	5.4	1.5				
Technology	8.4	0.2	9.4	0.1	4.6	0.4	5.5	0.7	5.3	0.7	6.8	0.8				
Medical science	18.4	4.0	12.8	2.8	6.2	2.8	5.9	2.9	5.9	3.0	6.0	3.4				
Law																
Other	5.9	4.8	7.2	4.0	7.0	4.0	7.4	6.5	8.6	6.7	5.4	5.4				

./...

Table 21 (cont'd)

DISTRIBUTION BY DISCIPLINES OF HIGHER DEGREES

Academic year beginning in :

Percentage

	1965		1970		1975		1976		1977		1978		1979		1980	
	M	F	M	F	M	F	M	F	M	F	M	F	M	F	M	F
SWEDEN - Doctorates (Before the reform)																
Numbers (000)	0.64	0.08	1.2	0.28	0.80	0.41	0.68	0.22	0.68	0.21						
Humanities			13.9	27.1	7.5	5.1	11.3	12.3	8.8	16.5						
Education																
Social sciences (6)			15.4	23.1	32.1	77.4	21.4	50.7	22.2	51.9						
Science			32.2	31.4	16.6	7.5	22.4	17.8	23.1	13.6						
Technology			20.3	4.0	17.2	1.9	15.2	1.8	18.9	2.4						
Medical science			14.3	13.0	22.7	7.3	26.5	16.4	24.9	14.1						
Law			0.6	0.7	0.8		0.3	0.9	0.6							
Other			3.4	0.7	3.1	0.7	2.8		1.6	1.5						
YUGOSLAVIA																
3rd cycle diplomas (7)																
Numbers (000)	0.26	0.10	0.55	0.18	1.2	0.34	1.2	0.36	1.4	0.49						
Humanities	11.1	25.7	6.5	13.9	8.3	13.0	7.6	14.0	8.8	15.8						
Education			1.5	0.6	1.5	2.7	2.5	1.4	0.7	0.2						
Social sciences	22.2	5.9	26.5	7.2	27.0	23.9	27.2	29.5	28.5	20.7						
Science	16.1	23.8	17.1	33.9	8.6	14.7	8.1	13.5	6.9	14.8						
Technology	12.6	9.9	17.6	13.9	27.6	15.3	25.4	12.9	28.5	22.8						
Medical science	8.4	19.8	7.3	13.3	6.0	15.0	8.2	15.2	7.5	12.9						
Law	5.0		2.9	2.8	3.4	1.8	5.1	3.6	3.7	2.3						
Other	24.5	14.8	20.6	14.4	17.7	13.6	15.9	9.9	15.4	10.4						
Doctorates																
Numbers (000)	0.11	0.03	0.25	0.06	0.48	0.13	0.59	0.12	0.55	0.14						
Humanities	13.8	33.3	16.7	11.1	15.7	20.0	10.8	12.8	9.5	10.1						
Education			0.4		0.4		1.4		0.7							
Social sciences	13.8		9.5	7.9	10.3	6.9	11.4	2.4	11.5	7.2						
Science	22.0	22.2	21.4	41.3	14.9	25.4	11.5	15.2	15.9	29.5						
Technology	12.8		13.1	3.2	16.5	7.7	14.4	6.4	21.0	12.9						
Medical science	19.3	33.3	22.2	23.8	27.6	32.3	32.2	52.0	25.9	26.6						
Law	3.7	3.7	4.4	1.6	2.5	1.5	3.6	2.4	4.0	4.3						
Other	14.7	7.4	12.3	11.1	12.1	6.2	14.7	8.8	11.4	8.6						

(1) For certain disciplines the doctorate is the first degree, in particular before the reorganisation of higher education.
(2) Including science.
(3) Including agriculture.
(4) Included in Social sciences.
(5) Not including "Doctorats d'Etat" in humanities and science and engineering doctorates.
(6) Including psychologist's diploma.
(7) Diplomas of Faculties, Fine Arts Academies, Colleges of higher education and scientific institutions.

Table 22

DISTRIBUTION BY DISCIPLINES OF NON-UNIVERSITY DIPLOMAS

Academic year beginning in :

Percentage

	1965		1970		1975		1976		1977		1978		1979		1980	
	M	F	M	F	M	F	M	F	M	F	M	F	M	F	M	F
GERMANY			(1973)													
Numbers (000)	16.4	0.2	25.4	3.8	25.3	6.6	22.4	6.9	25.0	8.3	23.5	7.3	25.3	8.8		
Humanities			0.8	10.8	0.4	6.0	0.4	5.9	1.2	7.3	2.1	9.6	0.8	6.9		
Social sciences			21.7	53.8	29.3	67.4	30.9	68.2	30.3	64.2	25.8	57.5	32.5	66.3		
Science			0.7	0.5	2.0	1.2	1.2	0.6	1.0	0.6	1.3	1.4	2.6	1.7		
Technology			69.0	16.1	60.5	12.0	61.7	13.4	61.5	17.0	64.8	19.2	58.2	13.7		
Other			7.8	18.9	7.8	13.5	5.8	11.9	6.0	10.9	5.9	12.3	6.0	11.5		
AUSTRALIA Diploma (CAE)					(1974)											
Numbers (000)					5.2	7.9	6.3	11.6	5.8	12.0	5.9	11.3	4.9	10.2	4.5	9.2
Humanities					1.7		1.4		3.9		2.9	2.1	4.2	2.9	5.3	3.4
Social sciences					7.7		5.9		6.8		10.8	2.1	10.2	3.2	8.0	2.5
Education					72.3		76.6		70.9		58.6	82.7	55.3	78.4	60.3	78.3
Technology					8.0		5.6		5.1		10.7	1.9	11.2	2.1	6.3	1.5
Medical science					2.2		2.6		3.5		2.3	4.5	2.7	6.0	4.8	7.0
Other					8.1		7.9		9.8		14.7	6.7	16.4	7.4	15.4	7.4
Associate diploma (CAE)					(1974)											
Numbers (000)					1.0	0.77	0.95	0.73	0.94	0.71	0.82	0.87	0.95	1.1	1.2	1.3
Humanities					3.5		7.1		15.5		15.9	26.1	12.5	31.8	13.1	32.1
Social sciences					17.3		15.1		17.0		25.6	14.6	24.0	14.2	25.4	11.7
Education					24.9		29.2		25.4		0.5	0.1	0.6	0.4	0.5	0.5
Technology					18.0		7.9		6.2		21.3	8.0	24.8	6.1	26.8	7.8
Medical science					22.9		26.0		24.0		12.2	41.1	11.6	37.1	9.8	31.2
Other					13.4		14.7		11.9		24.5	10.1	26.4	10.4	24.4	16.6
CANADA																
Numbers (000)					25.1	31.6	26.7	34.0	29.0	35.9	29.9	37.9	29.2	37.2	29.3	38.2
Humanities					5.3	5.6	5.1	5.9	5.1	5.9	5.6	7.2	5.9	7.8	6.0	8.0
Social sciences					19.6	29.2	18.9	29.3	18.5	31.9	18.8	33.0	20.6	36.1	22.9	38.5
Education					0.1	0.4	0.2	0.4	0.1	0.4	0.1	0.3	0.1	0.3	0.1	0.3
Technol. and related					29.7	2.5	29.4	3.0	30.8	3.6	31.4	4.1	33.2	4.2	35.5	4.6
Medical science					3.6	34.4	3.7	31.4	3.4	27.1	3.5	24.6	3.3	23.6	3.4	24.1
Other diplomas leading to a career					1.1	0.4	0.9	0.3	0.9	0.4	0.9	0.3	1.1	0.4	1.0	0.4
General					39.2	26.8	41.3	29.3	40.9	30.3	39.6	30.5	35.7	27.6	31.1	24.1
Unknown					1.4	0.7	0.5	0.4	0.3	0.3						
DENMARK (1)	(1966)															
Numbers (000)	2.5	2.2	3.1	3.0 //	3.7	3.9	3.8	4.2	3.7	4.2	3.4	3.9	3.8	5.4		
Humanities			1.2	1.3 //	1.7	4.0	2.2	5.5	2.3	5.0	2.4	5.6	1.9	4.1		
Social sciences	4.9	18.2	12.8	16.4 //	36.0	34.1	35.6	38.9	35.9	36.9	37.5	40.2	34.2	28.8		
Education	52.5	72.4	50.9	71.5 //	42.7	52.8	43.8	47.0	43.6	47.1	40.9	43.7	43.9	60.6		
Technology	42.5	0.0	34.9	0.3 //	17.0	0.1	16.1	0.3	15.6	0.4	15.6	0.3	17.4	0.2		
Medical science	0.1	9.4	0.1	10.5 //	0.3	7.3	0.4	6.5	0.8	8.9	1.1	8.8	0.6	5.1		
Other					2.2	1.8	1.9	1.8	1.7	1.8	2.6	1.5	1.9	1.2		

./...

Table 22 (cont'd)

DISTRIBUTION BY DISCIPLINES OF NON-UNIVERSITY DIPLOMAS

Academic year beginning in :

Percentage

	1965		1970		1975		1976		1977		1978		1979		1980		1981	
	M	F	M	F	M	F	M	F	M	F	M	F	M	F	M	F	M	F
SPAIN																		
Numbers (000)			17.6		21.2		22.6		26.9		13.9	20.0	13.9	17.9				
Social sciences			2.1		4.2		5.4		5.1		8.6	2.5	9.5	3.5				
Education			62.6		67.3		70.6		73.2		53.2	75.0	57.0	88.5				
Technology			35.4		28.5		23.9		21.7		33.1	1.5	31.1	1.7				
Medical science											5.0	21.0	2.4	6.3				
FRANCE - IUT, BTS, "capacité en droit"																		
Numbers (000)	5.3		15.8	9.2	19.0	12.6	20.1	13.3			37.2							
Primary/secondary sectors	54.3		60.5	16.1	69.6	19.6	68.6	18.7			55.9							
Tertiary sector	45.7		39.5	83.9	30.4	80.4	31.4	81.3			44.1							
GREECE																		
Numbers (000)			1.7	1.4	2.8	2.0	3.6	2.5										
Technology			48.4	62.5	49.7	74.4	59.1	82.6										
Education			51.6	37.5	50.3	25.6	40.9	17.4										
ITALY - Diplomi																		
Numbers (000)	1.0	0.5	1.1	0.6	1.1	1.0	1.3	1.4	2.5	2.5	1.8	2.1	1.6	2.2	1.9	2.1		
JAPAN-Junior Colleges																		
Numbers (000)	13.3	42.4	15.3	99.5	15.9	125.1	15.8	135.1	15.8	144.2	15.2	147.4	14.6	156.2	14.7	155.2	13.9	152.9
Humanities	9.5	28.3	7.4	29.2	6.8	32.5	7.0	32.4	7.1	31.7	7.5	30.9	9.1	31.3	8.4	31.6	8.5	32.1
Social sciences	48.3	4.1	39.3	5.4	34.5	6.6	38.0	6.6	35.4	6.5	33.8	6.6	32.8	6.4	32.0	6.5	31.2	6.4
Education	0.2	10.3	0.7	19.3	0.7	23.8	0.6	25.0	0.9	26.0	2.4	27.5	1.1	27.5	1.8	26.8	1.7	26.8
Sciences		0.2	0.1	0.1	0.1	0.0	0.0	0.1	0.0	0.1	0.0	0.0	0.1	0.1	0.1	0.0	0.1	0.0
Technology	37.3	0.3	41.5	0.3	47.4	0.2	43.6	0.2	45.1	0.3	43.9	0.3	43.5	0.4	44.1	0.4	43.4	0.4
Medical science		0.3	1.7	2.0	1.4	2.2	1.6	2.2	1.5	2.6	2.0	3.0	2.7	3.0	2.6	3.3	4.0	3.4
Other	4.7	56.5	9.4	43.8	9.2	34.5	9.3	33.4	9.9	32.8	10.3	31.7	10.7	31.4	11.1	31.4	11.1	30.9
NETHERLANDS																		
Numbers (000) FT	3.3	1.7	9.2	4.9	12.1	9.0	12.6	10.1	13.2	10.6	14.1	11.0	14.0	10.9	14.2	11.4		
Social sciences	2.1	1.9	5.7	2.6	7.6	3.5	7.3	4.3	7.7	6.0	7.2	5.5	7.7	6.7	9.0	2.2		
Education	28.9	63.4	40.9	76.7	43.1	80.2	45.4	79.5	44.1	78.8	49.3	81.9	45.8	79.0	43.2	83.3		
Technology	38.9	15.2	25.8	10.9	28.4	9.1	28.9	8.7	29.6	7.8	27.5	7.2	29.4	8.0	31.9	7.6		
Other	30.0	19.5	27.5	9.7	20.9	7.2	18.5	7.4	18.7	7.4	16.0	5.5	17.1	6.2	15.8	6.8		
Numbers (000) PT			1.8	1.3	4.9	2.9	5.0	2.1	4.9	2.5	5.1	2.5	5.0	3.0	5.7	7.9		
Social sciences											0.2	6.5	0.6	4.0				
Education											80.2	87.3	76.6	90.8	80.4	97.6		
Technology											15.9	3.4	18.8	2.5	16.6	1.0		
Other											3.7	2.7	4.0	2.7	3.0	1.4		

./...

Table 22 (cont'd)

DISTRIBUTION BY DISCIPLINES OF NON-UNIVERSITY DIPLOMAS

Academic year beginning in :

Percentage

	1965		1970		1975		1976		1977		1978		1979		1980		1981	
	M	F	M	F	M	F	M	F	M	F	M	F	M	F	M	F	M	F
UNITED KINGDOM (First diploma/certificate, HND/HNC)	(1968)		(1971)															
Numbers (000)	19.4		21.1		25.9		28.3		29.9		32.3							
Science and Technol	84.0		76.2		56.3		56.2		52.6		51.7							
Commerce and administ	8.8		20.0		41.8		42.1		45.8		46.7							
Other	7.2		3.8		1.9		1.7		1.6		1.6							
YUGOSLAVIA Higher Schools																		
Numbers (000)	6.6	2.7	9.0	6.8	9.9	9.5	9.3	9.3	9.7	9.5								
Social sciences	41.1	32.7	32.0	22.1	35.4	27.4	37.6	28.3	37.9	29.6								
Education	29.5	55.2	38.1	64.0	26.7	57.1	25.2	54.0	24.8	53.6								
Technology	21.5	4.3	23.8	5.0	32.9	6.9	32.3	6.5	32.0	7.4								
Medical science	2.1	7.5	2.3	8.2	1.9	8.0	2.1	10.7	2.7	0.5								
Other	5.9	0.4	3.8	0.8	3.1	0.6	2.9	0.6	2.6	0.5								
Proportion of non-course students	36.7	35.6	45.9	41.6	50.7	54.3	50.9	56.2	52.6	55.9								

// Change of classification.

(1) As from 1975 types of education taken into account do not correspond exactly to those in previous years and pre-primary teacher training is included only for 1979.

Table 23

PARTICIPATION IN VARIOUS TYPES OF ADULT EDUCATION

Thousands

	1965	1970	1975	1976	1977	1978	1979	1980
GERMANY (1)								
Volkshochschule (2)	1695.7	2227.3	3761.0	3770.5	3757.5	4144.1	4411.6	
Vocational training given under the Act of training for work								
Redeployment		117.2	216.4	117.4	100.5	128.9	149.8	176.5
Retraining		23.4	36.6	19.1	20.0	25.8	30.9	37.9
Adaptation		29.6	17.9	15.1	15.4	20.5	28.8	32.6
CANADA - Participation in continuing education								
Courses with credits								
Primary/secondary level		222.6	174.3	182.3	182.3			
Community colleges			134.3	131.9				
Universities		279.4	334.2	347.4	386.3			
Particip. rate (3) °/°°						Survey on adult education discontinued		
Primary/secondary level		16.9	11.8	12.3	12.0			
Community colleges			9.1	8.9				
Universities		21.2	22.7	23.4	25.4			
Total			43.6	44.6				
Courses without credits								
Primary/secondary level		318.8	521.3	559.5	709.8			
Community colleges			293.7	326.0	372.9			
Universities		117.7	206.0	218.3	235.9			
Particip. rate (3)°/°°								
Primary/secondary level		24.2	35.3	37.6	40.2			
Community colleges			19.9	21.9	24.6			
Universities		8.9	14.0	14.7	15.5			
			70.2	74.2	80.3			
- Vocational training								
Vocational training courses at trade level								
Registered Apprentices		55.5	74.1	77.5	82.5	99.0	104.1	113.2
Pre-employment courses		[201.0	106.4	92.2				
Refresher courses			13.7	24.3				
Pre-vocational training courses			78.1	75.4				
Training in industry		59.2	57.0	60.8	69.6			
Training in enterprises (Ontario)		14.0	74.3	76.5	85.2			
Rehabilit. of disabled persons		2.8	4.7					
Total all levels		446.7	596.7	603.6				
Particip. rate °/°°°		33.9	40.4	40.6				

DENMARK - Training for the labour market	1965 M	1970 F	1975 M	1975 F	1976 M	1976 F	1977 M	1977 F	1978 M	1978 F
Semi-skilled training			37.9	8.7	33.8	9.1	35.5	10.1	37.6	11.1
Redeployment			0.2	0.1	0.1	0.2	0.2	0.2	0.1	0.4
Refresher courses for skilled workers			17.2	3.1	18.8	3.5	20.7	3.8	24.2	5.6
Preparatory training			-	-	-	-	-	-	7.5	2.2
Total			55.4	11.8	52.7	12.8	57.2	14.2	69.4	19.2

./...

Table 23 (cont'd)

PARTICIPATION IN VARIOUS TYPES OF ADULT EDUCATION

Thousands

	1965		1970		1975		1976		1977		1978		1979		1980	
	M	F	M	F	M	F	M	F	M	F	M	F	M	F	M	F
UNITED STATES			(1969)													
Adult education			13041.0		17059.0						16843.0					
Vocational education classes																
Secondary (4)			5114.5		9510.9		8980.5		9770.8		10960.7					
Post-secondary (4)			1013.4		1897.9		2231.1		2397.7		2110.5					
Adult			2666.1		4077.0		4134.2		4295.6		4527.4					
Total			8794.0		15485.8		15345.9		16464.2		17598.6					
FINLAND																
Schools for workers	35.0	77.5	86.0	187.4	131.8	322.7	138.5	328.8	143.0	348.4	148.4	371.4				
Popular sec. schools			3.4	3.7	7.8	14.7	9.5	15.6	9.4	15.2	9.5	15.9				
Study circles					174.1		192.9									
Study centers					27.2		72.0									
FRANCE																
Actions financed by State agencies			722.0		883.0		805.0		894.0		993.0		1041.0			
Adult vocational training			73.0		100.0		102.0		105.0		104.0		106.0			
National employment Fund			20.0		16.0		16.0		14.0		10.0		12.0			
Employment-train. contrats					6.0		23.0		42.0		69.0		91.0			
Conservatoire national des arts et métiers			22.0		30.0		33.0		33.0		34.0		38.0			
Distance learning centre			91.0		101.0		117.0		115.0		121.0		124.0			
Voc. training fund			516.0		630.0		514.0		585.0		655.0		670.0			
Actions financed by enterprises (1% contribution)					1840.0		1814.0		1774.0		1735.0		1686.0			
% of personnel in train.											17.6		17.2			
In-service training of State employees (5)									98.1		102.3		125.5			
% of personnel in training									10.2		11.6		13.9			
ITALY																
General education																
Middle ed. for workers			74.1	56.5	70.2		84.8		84.7							
Popular school					24.9	24.4	25.5	26.5	23.3	26.2						
Secondary education			16.2	4.2	28.3	10.3	30.6	12.7	27.7	12.1						
Musical education			29.2	8.7	33.8	16.3	33.9	17.7	29.3	15.4						
Fixed reading centres					82.5	55.3	78.2	56.6	72.0	54.9						
Continuing educ. centres					47.7	33.0	49.7	36.6	43.8	33.0						
Cultural refres. centres							6.8	5.7	7.1	6.9						
Other courses			106.2	70.7	22.9	20.0	76.4		..							
Vocational training			337.6		145.3	105.9	126.3	103.8	119.5	103.2						
Para-university courses			..		..		1.3	6.1	1.7	5.9						
JAPAN - Number of participants in social education classes organised by local education authorities					(1974)											
Total			3135.1		2701.1				2617.8						1880.8	
for adults			1889.3		1602.5				2122.5						1613.2	
-of which for women only			960.5		642.6				704.9						731.7	
for young people			448.2		399.6				495.3						262.6	
for parents			797.6		699.0											

./...

Table 23 (cont'd)

PARTICIPATION IN VARIOUS TYPES OF ADULT EDUCATION

Thousands

	1965		1970		1975		1976		1977		1978		1979		1980	
	M	F	M	F	M	F	M	F	M	F	M	F	M	F	M	F
NETHERLANDS																
Secondary general			9.1	3.3	17.6	15.0	17.7	21.5	18.3	30.7	20.1	45.9	23.4	62.4	28.5	18.8
Vocational, lower			123.6	34.9	85.9	85.0	84.5	33.7	89.8	36.7	95.3	38.0	100.9	40.1	95.1	40.7
" middle			27.2	13.3	14.0	13.8	74.9	14.5	14.6	14.8	15.2	15.7	16.6	16.6	17.6	19.1
" higher			35.3	16.5	36.2	20.5	35.5	22.1	33.5	25.8	34.6	30.1	35.7	36.1	36.3	43.2
UNITED KINGDOM (England and Wales)	(1967)		(1971)													
Adult education centres																
Advanced level	0.06	0.07	0.08	0.08	0.11	0.14	0.10	0.35	0.22	0.39	0.09	0.17				
Non advanced level	484.0	935.6	498.9	1020.2	624.3	1357.1	569.0	1227.8	537.9	1169.8	620.6	1384.4				
Courses for adults offered by universities and other responsibles bodies			115.4	155.8	118.2	167.7	121.4	165.8	117.1	155.9						
SWEDEN			(1971)													
Popular secondary school																
Courses of at least 30 weeks			6.2	8.2	5.0	7.4	5.2	7.7	5.3	7.9	5.5	7.8	5.4	7.4	5.3	7.6
Municipal adult education																
Basic school			14.4	23.1	10.7	23.8	11.2	27.4	12.9	31.1	12.1	30.7	12.0	29.6	11.5	28.4
Gym. 3/4-yr. courses (6)			18.5	26.0	17.3	31.5	17.2	31.6	19.8	33.7	18.8	34.8	18.1	32.4	17.4	20.9
" 2 yr. courses (7)			3.0	2.0	6.4	9.1	14.9	30.0	19.3	36.6	18.2	37.7	19.4	39.9	20.0	39.3
Special courses (8)			26.7	52.3	14.5	37.5	5.9	15.6	5.0	9.2	4.3	7.1	4.4	6.4	4.8	7.8
State schools for adults (11)			2.0		5.6	5.0	7.9	7.7	10.2	9.2	12.2	10.9	10.9	9.7	10.8 (9)	9.6 (10)
Training for the labour market (11)			16.4	17.7					33.5	28.2						

(1) According to a microcensus in April 1978, 1414.0 persons, i.e. 5.2 per cent of employees (6.0 per cent men, 4.0 per cent women) had benefited from vocational training leave since 1976.
(2) Not including attendance at lectures or other specific events.
(3) In relation to the population aged 15 and over, not in full-time education.
(4) Although a large number of participants are regular pupils in secondary or post-secondary education, they are presented here for reasons of convenience and to avoid double counting in the tables on school enrolments.
(5) Ministry of Education, Ministry of the Universities and dependent institutions only.
(6) Gymnasium for 1968 and 1970.
(7) "Fackskola" (further ed.) for 1968 and 1970.
(8) Including the former part-time vocational schools.
(9) Of which 7.8 men following correspondence courses only.
(10) Of which 7.2 women following correspondence courses only.
(11) Number of participants as at 15th September (includes training in the enterprises).

Table 24

PROPORTION OF GIRLS IN THE DIFFERENT TYPES OF SECONDARY EDUCATION AND IN TOTAL NON-COMPULSORY SECONDARY (NC)

School year beginning in — Percentage

	1965	1970	1975	1976	1977	1978	1979	1980	1981
GERMANY									
Comprehensive			48.3	48.3	48.4	48.3	48.4		
Middle "Realschule"	51.5	52.9	52.5	54.2	54.1	53.9	53.7		
Gymnasium 1st cycle	42.2	44.7	48.4	49.1	49.5	49.9	50.1		
" 2nd cycle	37.8	41.4	46.4	46.3	46.8	47.8	48.9		
Techn./vocational FT	63.3	51.6	55.2	56.2	57.1	56.8	55.4		
Vocational PT	44.1	41.9	40.0	40.0	39.9	40.4	40.3		
Total NC	44.3	43.6	45.6	45.9	46.2	46.6	46.6		
AUSTRALIA									
2nd cycle secondary	45.3	46.3	48.7	49.1	49.8	50.1	50.5	50.7	50.9
AUSTRIA									
Upper primary		51.2	50.3			49.7	49.0		
Secondary 1st cycle		43.5	45.3			47.3	47.4		
Secondary 2nd cycle		47.7	51.8			51.7	52.4		
Polytechnic year		42.9	39.4			39.9	38.0		
Comprehensive						48.3	48.4		
Technical short		73.1	55.5			54.2	48.5		
Technical long		30.7	34.6			40.8	41.9		
Vocational PT		33.3	31.4			31.2	32.3		
Total NC		42.8	41.4			41.8	41.5		
CANADA									
10th year of study and beyond	48.2	48.7	49.1	49.2	49.2	49.1	49.1	48.9	49.1
DENMARK									
2nd cycle general	45.9	48.4	52.1	53.7	54.9	55.5			
Technical		21.9	27.5	26.7	24.4	31.1			
Commercial and other	36.9		61.2	66.1	67.5	69.3			
Apprenticeship, technical		5.4	4.8	5.4	6.3	7.1			
Apprenticeship, commercial	61.1	60.6	56.6	57.7	58.6	60.5			
Total NC			38.3	40.7	42.5	43.6			
SPAIN									
2nd cycle general/teacher ed.	40.3	43.2	48.8	50.0	50.8	52.3	52.9	53.5	
Technical and other	29.5	33.5	60.3	60.3	61.7	63.5	62.5	64.0	
Vocational training	3.3	5.1	28.9	32.2	34.3	35.4	36.8	37.9	
Total NC	27.3	37.5	46.4	47.5	48.1	49.1	50.1	49.8	
FINLAND									
General-gymnasium	56.1	57.5	59.3	60.3	60.9	61.1	61.0	61.0	
Vocational			46.7	46.3	46.4	46.4	47.2	47.1	
Apprenticehip			37.2	39.4	47.0	47.8	46.6	46.0	
Total NC			53.1	53.3	53.7	53.8	54.1	54.1	

./...

Table 24 (cont'd)

PROPORTION OF GIRLS IN THE DIFFERENT TYPES OF SECONDARY EDUCATION AND IN TOTAL NON-COMPULSORY SECONDARY (NC)

School year beginning in

Percentage

	1965	1970	1975	1976	1977	1978	1979	1980	1981
FRANCE									
2nd cycle general	50.9	53.8	55.7(1)	56.0(1)	56.5(1)	57.0(1)			
Vocational short	54.7	49.4	47.5	47.1	47.0	46.8			
Technical	35.6	47.8							
Apprenticeship		21.2	21.4	21.8	22.2	23.1			
Total NC		47.7	49.5	49.4	49.5	49.7			
GREECE									
2nd cycle general	44.7	46.3	49.2	49.0	48.9				
Technical/vocational	16.2	19.0	21.0	23.4	27.2				
Total NC	38.0	41.2	43.1	43.5	44.4				
ITALY									
2nd cycle general	38.6	43.2	47.2	47.8	48.5	49.3	50.1		
Vocational	37.0	41.4	45.2	45.4	45.4	45.9	45.7		
Technical/artistic	23.8	25.9	32.8	34.1	35.6	36.8	37.9		
Teacher education	86.7	89.2	92.3	93.1	93.6	93.9	93.7		
Total NC	39.4	41.6	44.3	45.0	45.9	46.9	47.8		
JAPAN									
2nd cycle general	52.2	52.9	51.5	51.7	51.0	51.0	51.1	51.2	51.3
Vocational training	40.3	43.0	45.4	45.7	45.7	45.5	45.3	45.2	45.1
Total NC	40.8	48.8	49.2	49.2	49.2	49.2	49.2	49.3	49.9
NETHERLANDS									
1st cycle general FT		49.1	51.0	51.3	51.6	52.1	51.4	52.9	
1st cycle vocat. FT		40.6	43.8	42.7	42.3	41.8	41.2	40.6	
1st cycle general PT		30.3	48.7	59.2	68.0	74.8	77.0	70.6	
1st cycle vocat. PT		43.8	48.7	50.8	46.5	42.4	38.3	26.2	
2nd cycle general FT		41.7	45.4	46.1	46.6	47.4	48.5	49.5	
2nd cycle tech/vocat FT		46.4	41.0	40.6	42.7	43.8	43.3	43.6	
2nd cycle general PT		23.0	41.3	45.9	49.5	55.2	61.7	65.0	
2nd cycle tech/vocat. PT		32.0	49.5	49.3	50.4	50.8	50.6	52.0	
Apprenticeship		6.2	15.8	16.8	17.9	18.0	18.6	21.1	
Young worker education		56.6	54.8	56.1	58.1	58.7	59.9	58.1	
Total NC		37.6	41.5	40.5	46.2	46.8	47.2	48.0	

./...

Table 24 (cont'd)

PROPORTION OF GIRLS IN THE DIFFERENT TYPES OF SECONDARY EDUCATION AND IN TOTAL NON-COMPULSORY SECONDARY (NC)

School year beginning in — Percentage

	1965	1970	1975	1976	1977	1978	1979	1980	1981
UNITED KINGDOM (2)									
Secondary		46.6	48.1	48.4	48.6				
Further ed. non-adv. FT		42.7	51.9	52.8	53.4				
Further ed. non-adv. PT(3)		31.8(4)	36.7(4)	37.1	37.9				
Total NC		37.5	43.1	43.9	44.5				
SWEDEN		(1971)							
3/4-yr. courses		42.3	41.4	41.9	42.4	42.8	44.2	45.6	
Humanities, Soc. sc., Econo.		61.6	62.2	62.5	63.1	63.8	65.1	67.1	
Science		37.6	38.2	39.8	41.0	41.7	43.1	43.9	
Technical		5.1	5.9	7.1	9.0	10.1	11.9	12.3	
2-yr. courses		47.4	51.8	51.3	51.9	52.5	52.1	51.4	
Humanities, Soc.sc., Econo.		72.7	81.5	81.1	81.2	80.5	79.6	79.2	
Technical		4.0	7.5	7.5	7.7	7.6	7.5	8.1	
Special courses (5)		46.8	58.3	60.5	61.2	61.8	62.9	62.0	
Humanities, Soc. sc., Econo.		83.1	84.9	85.9	86.1	87.0	86.8	85.4	
Technical		8.1	11.4	12.2	11.7	11.9	11.7	14.9	
Total NC		45.0	48.9	49.5	49.9	50.4	50.8	50.7	
YUGOSLAVIA									
General	53.4	55.8	52.8	52.3	52.1	52.6			
Teacher education	62.0	64.2	74.7	71.6	74.1	73.8			
Skilled worker training	20.8	28.1	29.6	27.9	26.8	26.6			
Other technical/Vocational	52.8	54.6	52.3	54.0	53.8	54.1			
Common core			47.5	46.5	45.7	45.7			
Total NC	43.0	44.4	45.4	45.5	45.6	45.4			

FT = Full-time - PT = Part-time

(1) Including technical.
(2) Pupils aged 16 and over although in 1971 compulsory schooling stopped at 15.
(3) Including evening classes and not including pupils aged over 20.
(4) Including advanced level courses representing about 3 % of total students considered.
(5) Courses of variable duration - a few weeks to 1 year or more - preparing for specific trades.

Table 25

PROPORTION OF GIRLS AMONG GRADUATES IN DIFFERENT TYPES OF 2nd CYCLE SECONDARY EDUCATION

Percentage

	1965	1970	1975	1976	1977	1978	1979	1980
GERMANY	(1967)							
General	36.6	39.7	45.7	47.0	46.9	47.2	45.6	48.1
Technical		35.3		28.3	31.7	36.4	37.2	38.3
Vocational PT						40.2	41.8	42.0
DENMARK								
General	46.2	47.2	51.1					
Vocational	42.0	41.7	56.5	59.8				
Apprenticeship	58.7 (1)	61.7 (1)	23.6	27.1	29.3			
UNITED STATES								
High School	50.3	50.5	50.7	51.0	51.0	51.1	51.0	
FINLAND								
General	56.7	58.5	59.7	61.0	60.6	61.8	63.2	
Technical	44.8	46.8	45.6					
FRANCE								
General	51.6		56.7	56.5	57.1	57.3		
Vocational, short	42.5	43.2	43.3	44.0	43.0	43.7		
Technical		49.0	55.0	56.0	57.1	56.5		
GREECE								
General		52.2	52.9	53.3				
Vocational	24.8	28.6	26.1	27.4				
ITALY								
General								
Scientific "Maturity"	21.9	32.3	40.8	40.7	41.0	42.6		
Classical "Maturity"	42.7	47.4	55.9	54.0	54.3	52.9		
Pre-primary teacher	100.0	100.0	100.0	100.0	100.0	100.0		
Primary teacher	85.7	84.3	87.1	84.2	85.2	84.2		
Technical "Maturity"	27.4	19.8	27.3	27.8	32.2	32.5		
Vocational/artistic "Maturity"	63.2	63.2	47.9	45.8	48.9	48.5		
Vocational qualification	41.9	42.6	46.7	47.8	48.4			
NETHERLANDS	(1967)							
General, short	87.0	58.0	50.7	52.0	52.8	50.2	50.2	51.6
General, long	25.7	30.2	40.9	42.7	42.1	42.7	42.7	43.1
Vocational, 2nd cycle FT		72.5	67.0	63.3	52.8	54.7	56.9	56.1
" " PT		40.7	60.0	59.1	61.4	60.2	56.4	56.7
UNITED KINGDOM	(1967)							
GCE A Level/SCE H Grade	43.4	45.8	46.3	46.2	46.6			
GCE O Level/CSE/SCE O Gr.	51.0	52.0	52.4	52.4	52.7			
No Higher Grade	48.5	48.1	46.7	47.1	46.3			
SWEDEN		(1972)						
3/4-yr. courses		37.1	36.5	36.7	37.5	37.8	39.1	40.1
2-yr. courses		45.0	51.3	51.2	51.5	52.4	52.9	51.2
Special courses		64.4	68.5	69.4	70.7	70.0	71.2	70.6

(1) Not including apprenticeship in technical fields.

FT = Full-time - PT = Part-time

Table 26

PROPORTION OF WOMEN AMONG NEW ENTRANTS INTO HIGHER EDUCATION
UNIVERSITY-TYPE (U) AND NON-UNIVERSITY-TYPE (NU)

Academic year beginning in :

Percentage

	1965	1970	1975	1976	1977	1978	1979	1980	1981
GERMANY									
U	32.4	37.8	41.1	38.5	42.8	42.9	41.6	43.4	45.2
NU		15.0	24.0	24.5	28.1	30.8	32.2	31.8	32.4
AUSTRALIA FT and PT									
Universities		38.7(1)	40.9	41.4	42.2	43.4	44.5	46.1	46.7
CAE (Bachelor)		24.7(2)	26.8	31.0	36.6	38.7	43.0	43.2	44.4
CAE (diploma, associate diploma)			58.5	59.6	61.3	63.2	63.7	61.5	57.4
AUSTRIA (Regular Austrian Students)		(1972)	(1974)						
U		37.8	44.0			47.0	46.2		
BELGIUM									
Total							38.8	41.5	42.3
CANADA									
U						47.2	47.3	47.9	48.4
NU							50.4	50.9	51.4
DENMARK	(1966)								
U	28.5	31.5	36.4	39.4	38.8	39.4	40.5	40.7	
NU				58.4	49.8(3)	49.0(3)	47.1(3)	55.0	
SPAIN									
U	24.2	28.1	37.7	39.0	39.9	38.5	42.7	46.4	
NU			35.4	38.6	40.1	42.8	46.5	47.3	
UNITED STATES	(1966)								
U	44.0	45.9	48.6	49.6	50.5	50.8	51.2	51.4	
NU	40.7	42.2	46.1	50.8	52.9	53.7	54.5	54.4	
FINLAND									
U	50.8	47.1	51.6	51.6	51.5	51.1	50.8	52.3	
NU	56.3	62.0	65.8						
GREECE									
U	34.7	31.4	39.2	39.6					
NU			36.4	34.8					
ITALY									
U		36.5	40.6	41.5	42.7	44.3	44.6	44.8	45.4
NETHERLANDS									
U	19.0	21.6	30.4	31.2	32.1	33.3	34.4	35.4	

./...

Table 26

PROPORTION OF WOMEN AMONG NEW ENTRANTS INTO HIGHER EDUCATION
UNIVERSITY-TYPE (U) AND NON-UNIVERSITY-TYPE (NU)

Academic year beginning in :

Percentage

	1965	1970	1975	1976	1977	1978	1979	1980	1981
UNITED KINGDOM	(1968)								
Universities	29.8	31.9	35.2	36.2	37.7	39.5	39.5		
SWEDEN									
U before the reform		41.4	46.9	47.9					
Total Higher educ. after the reform					57.0	59.0	59.0		
YUGOSLAVIA		(1969)							
U	35.9	38.5	40.0	39.0	38.4	38.4			
NU	35.6	42.5	38.3	37.7	37.4	38.7			

FT = Full-time - PT = Part-time

(1) 1973.
(2) 1971.
(3) Not including pre-primary teacher training.

Table 27

ENROLMENTS IN UNIVERSITY-TYPE EDUCATION (U) ACCORDING TO DEGREE OR DIPLOMA PREPARED AND IN NON-UNIVERSITY-TYPE EDUCATION (NU) AND PROPORTION OF WOMEN

Thousands

	1965	1970	1975	1976	1977	1978	1979	1980	1981
GERMANY									
U Enrolments	308.4	421.0	695.5	720.2	747.9	773.1	801.2	842.2	879.0
% women	28.9	34.6	36.0	35.8	36.6	37.3	37.8	38.4	41.4
NU Enrolments	70.0	89.5	145.2	157.1	165.4	172.8	182.4	202.0	224.7
% women		11.8	22.8	23.2	24.5	26.3	28.1	29.5	30.0
AUSTRALIA									
Universities FT and PT									
1st degree Enrolments		101.7	120.1	124.6	127.3	128.9	129.2	130.7	132.4
% women		32.3	37.7	39.2	40.4	41.5	42.5	43.6	44.6
Master Enrolments			11.7	12.3	13.0	13.4	14.0	14.4	15.4
% women			23.1	24.4	26.2	27.6	28.6	29.8	31.3
Doctorate Enrolments			5.0	5.3	5.5	5.8	5.9	6.2	6.4
% women			18.3	20.2	20.6	21.8	23.2	24.0	24.3
Non-degree course Enrolments		9.6	10.5	11.8	12.6	12.0	11.7	11.9	12.4
% women		41.8	46.1	44.1	46.0	45.8	45.4	46.1	46.5
Total FT Enrolments		73.6	97.1	100.6	102.9	101.4	99.1	99.0	99.9
% women		31.8	37.3	38.2	39.0	39.4	39.9	40.5	41.2
Total PT Enrolments		43.1	51.2	53.4	55.5	58.7	61.7	64.2	66.7
% women		26.9	35.2	36.7	38.6	40.5	42.3	43.9	45.0
CAE FT et PT									
1st degree Enrolments			37.7	46.2	57.1	67.2	75.3	82.5	87.9
% women			25.2	28.3	33.3	36.2	39.3	40.9	41.9
Master Enrolments			0.3	0.4	0.5	0.7	0.9	1.0	1.1
% women			20.5	17.7	16.9	23.8	22.5	22.7	21.3
Post-graduate diploma Enrolments			8.4	9.9	11.7	13.9	16.2	18.4	20.5
% women			39.5	39.1	41.9	42.4	43.8	46.2	47.8
Diploma/Associate Diploma Enrolments			76.1	78.1	71.0	68.2	63.3	57.6	53.2
% women									59.5
Total FT Enrolments			74.8	82.6	84.9	84.3	82.1	78.2	76.7
% women			54.0	55.2	55.2	55.6	56.0	56.0	55.8
Total PT Enrolments			47.8	52.0	55.4	65.6	73.6	81.2	88.4
% women			29.3	31.9	35.2	38.4	40.5	41.7	41.7
AUSTRIA									
U Enrolments	52.2	57.3	89.6	97.4	105.0	113.8 //	97.8	105.1	113.2
% women	24.5	25.7	34.0	35.4	37.0	38.0 //	39.8	40.7	41.2
NU Enrolments							12.6	12.7	13.1
% women							74.6	75.6	75.6
BELGIUM									
Enrolments		(1972) 78.3	83.4	86.8	89.3	89.6	92.5	95.2	95.9
% women							35.9	36.9	37.6

./...

Table 27 (cont'd)

ENROLMENTS IN UNIVERSITY-TYPE EDUCATION (U) ACCORDING TO DEGREE OR DIPLOMA PREPARED AND IN NON-UNIVERSITY-TYPE EDUCATION (NU) AND PROPORTION OF WOMEN

Thousands

	1965	1970	1975	1976	1977	1978	1979	1980	1981	1982
CANADA Universities										
1st degree FT Enrolments	187.0	276.3	330.5	335.9	333.2	326.8	329.6	337.9	354.5	
% women	32.7	36.7	42.4	43.7	44.4	44.9	45.5	46.0	46.7	
1st degree PT Enrolments	65.3	142.2	158.3	163.3	183.1	186.7	199.3	213.0	219.5	
% women	41.2	42.4	54.3	56.5	58.0	58.5	59.5	60.1	59.9	
Post-graduate FT Enrol.		33.2	39.9	40.6	41.0	41.2	41.8	44.7	47.2	
% women		22.3	29.2	30.5	31.8	33.2	35.3	36.1	37.3	
Post-graduate PT Enrol.		14.4	27.0	27.7	28.6	29.7	30.6	32.1	32.4	
% women		23.7	30.0	32.5	34.8	36.1	37.0	38.7	40.7	
NU Enrolments	69.4	166.1	221.6	226.2	241.7	249.8	252.1	260.8	273.4	
% women	58.8	46.9	49.6	50.4	50.6	50.5	50.8	51.1	51.5	
DENMARK										
Universities Enrolments	24.5	34.6	// 51.0	53.5	52.7	51.6	48.8	48.4		
% women	34.3	35.8	//	39.3	39.7	40.1	40.8	41.3		
Other U institutions Enrol.	7.6	9.4	// 11.3	12.1	12.8	13.0	13.0	13.7		
% women	17.1	19.1	//	26.4	27.3	27.7	29.2	29.9		
NU Enrolments	18.3	20.7	// 42.4	35.4	34.2	32.4	32.5	38.6		
% women	45.9	45.4	//	46.6	47.4	48.5	47.1	53.6		
SPAIN										
Universities and assimilated U. Enrolments	125.9	213.1	393.6	415.4	477.4	449.9	460.5	470.1		
% women	21.2	26.4	37.2	38.5	39.0	39.3	41.0	42.8		
University schools (1) and other NU Enrolments	65.5	112.9	140.8	160.4	179.5	176.4	178.8	179.0		
% women			37.6	41.1	42.1	44.3	45.7	47.2		
UNITED STATES										
4-yr. institutions U FT Enrolments	3439.6	4696.6	5134.3	5110.1	5209.7	5180.7	5281.4	5425.4	5433.0	P 5398.0
% women	38.6	40.5	43.2	44.7	45.7	46.5	47.2	47.6	47.4	47.2
4-yr. institutions U PT Enrolments	1351.0	1725.6	2154.5	2094.7	2126.4	2146.4	2175.8	2253.0	2308.0	2258.0
% women	40.4	44.2	48.9	50.4	51.3	52.3	53.3	54.4	54.0	53.8
2-yr. institutions NU FT Enrolments	497.7	1168.9	1788.6	1692.9	1686.1	1589.9	1620.0	1779.4	1748.0	1805.0
% women	35.3	37.4	41.4	45.9	48.6	49.7	50.7	50.0	51.1	51.1
2-yr. institutions NU PT Enrolments	679.2	1058.3	2213.3	2223.7	2393.8	2474.9	2629.9	2776.8	2882.0	2897.0
% women	39.1	44.6	48.9	51.5	53.4	55.5	56.8	57.9	58.3	58.3
FINLAND										
U Enrolments	41.2	57.9	75.8	77.9	80.5	81.1	81.8	82.9		
% women			49.0	49.0	49.4	49.4	49.3	49.6		
NU Enrolments				41.4	41.9	41.7	41.0	40.2		
% women				43.6	43.0	42.9	43.8	45.3		

./...

Table 27 (cont'd)

ENROLMENTS IN UNIVERSITY-TYPE EDUCATION (U) ACCORDING TO DEGREE OR DIPLOMA PREPARED AND IN NON-UNIVERSITY-TYPE EDUCATION (NU) AND PROPORTION OF WOMEN

Thousands

	1965	1970	1975	1976	1977	1978	1979	1980	1981	1982
FRANCE		(1971)								
Universities 1st and 2nd cycles Enrolments	331.0	566.9	599.2	608.0	621.4	633.7	[	805.3	829.7	
3rd cycle Enrolments	41.9	75.4	147.6	148.5	148.1	150.2	799.4			
% women Total Univers.	42.6	47.2	48.6	48.7	48.9			49.8		
Grandes Ecoles (2) U Enrolments	60.8	77.5	142.1	133.1	136.7					
NU Enrolments	86.3	132.4	173.4	174.1	190.9	191.6	188.1	194.0	212.6	
GREECE										
U Enrolments	54.3	72.3	95.4	95.0	96.6					
% women	30.4	31.0	37.4	38.6	38.7					
NU Enrolments	9.9	13.9	21.9	27.8	22.8					
% women		33.1	35.2	34.9						
ITALY										
U Enrolments regul.stud	297.8	560.6	736.3	762.0	762.8	777.8	767.7	764.0	724.5	
% women	35.5	37.6	39.6	40.2	41.3	42.5	43.5	244.1	226.4	
NU Enrolments "Non-course" students	107.2	121.2	199.5	219.3	233.3	254.8	268.2			
% women	28.3	37.7	38.3	39.4	39.6	39.7	40.4			
JAPAN (3)										
Universities Enrolments	924.0	1385.3	1700.5	1754.1	1800.3	1822.6	1807.6	1795.5	1781.4	
% women	16.1	17.9	21.2	21.6	22.0	22.0	22.1	22.1	22.1	
1st degree Enrolments	895.5	1344.4	1652.0	1702.2	1747.1	1769.3	1754.3	1741.5	1725.8	
Master Enrolments	16.8	27.7	33.6	36.2	36.9	36.2	35.4	35.8	37.2	
Doctorate Enrolments	11.7	13.2	14.9	15.7	16.4	17.1	17.9	18.2	18.4	
Junior College NU Enrol.	145.5	259.7	348.9	360.0	369.4	375.7	369.4	366.2	367.5	
% women	74.7	82.8	86.4	87.0	87.8	88.1	88.5	89.1	89.6	
Techni. College NU Enrolment	3.0	14.6	18.1	17.5	18.0	17.7	17.2	17.2		
% women		1.7	1.3	1.4	1.6	1.8	1.6	1.7		
NETHERLANDS		(1971)	(1974)							
Universities Enrolments	64.4	112.9	113.8	127.7	135.8	141.6	151.1	149.5 P	152.1 P	
% women	18.0	20.8	23.3	26.2	27.4	28.5	29.4	30.9 P	32.2 P	
NU FT Enrolments		72.1	111.2	118.4	123.8	126.9	129.6	131.8	134.0	
% women		36.6	39.2	39.7	40.3	40.9	41.0	41.5	42.1	
NU PT Enrolments		51.8	56.6	57.6	59.3	64.7	71.8	78.7		
% women		31.9	36.2	38.4	43.5	46.5	50.3	53.6		

./...

Table 27 (cont'd)

ENROLMENTS IN UNIVERSITY-TYPE EDUCATION (U) ACCORDING TO DEGREE OR DIPLOMA PREPARED AND IN NON-UNIVERSITY-TYPE EDUCATION (NU) AND PROPORTION OF WOMEN

Thousands

	1965	1970	1975	1976	1977	1978	1979	1980	1981	1981
UNITED KINGDOM	(1968)	(1971)								
Universities FT										
1st degree Enrolments	179.0	192.5	218.1	228.2	238.5	245.9	252.0			
% women	29.0	30.4	35.4	35.8	36.2	37.0	38.1			
Post-graduate Enrolments	38.4	45.3	50.7	51.0	49.6	50.0	48.5			
% women	21.9	22.7	26.4	27.3	27.8	28.6	28.9			
"Further education" FT (4) Enrolments	201.9	233.4	257.4	245.9	233.5	223.7				
% women	52.6	51.2	51.0	48.4	46.2	44.3				
Universities PT										
1st degree Enrolments	45.0	3.7	3.8	3.8	4.2	4.1	4.4			
% women	40.0	37.8	47.4	50.0	50.0	50.2	49.3			
Post-graduate Enrolments	16.8	19.8	22.5	23.5	24.6	25.5	27.0			
% women	14.9	18.7	23.1	23.8	26.0	26.7	28.5			
"Further Education" PT (5) Enrolments	122.4	118.1	136.6	139.7	151.1	164.2				
% women	8.3	10.3	15.6	16.8	20.5	22.5				
Open University Enrol.		19.6	49.4	51.0	55.1	58.8	60.6			
% women		27.0	37.7	39.0	40.5	41.3	42.4			
SWEDEN Before the reform										
Universities Enrolments	66.4	120.2	110.0	113.8						
% women	37.0	38.1	39.7	41.2						
of which Post-graduate Enrol	7.1	12.3	14.5	15.2						
% women			23.4	23.7						
After the reform										
Total Higher Enrolments							201.0			
% women							45.4			
1st degree							41.2			
Post-graduate							26.5			
NU							70.5			
YUGOSLAVIA		(1969)								
U Regular students Enrol.	90.3	132.3	197.9	206.6	220.9	234.2				
% women	34.6	39.2	42.3	42.0	41.6	41.7				
U Non regular students Enrolments	25.9	29.5	75.1	79.8	84.0	90.9				
% women	25.5	31.9	34.8	35.0	34.3	34.4				
NU Regular students Enrol.	31.6	38.7	43.1	49.9	51.1	51.2				
% women	34.2	43.4	40.4	39.3	39.7	40.4				
NU Non-regular students Enrolments	37.1	39.2	77.8	69.3	68.5	63.5				
% women	35.8	43.4	38.7	38.2	37.8	37.6				

./...

Table 27 (cont'd)

ENROLMENTS IN UNIVERSITY-TYPE EDUCATION (U) ACCORDING TO DEGREE OR DIPLOMA PREPARED AND IN NON-UNIVERSITY-TYPE EDUCATION (NU) AND PROPORTION OF WOMEN

// Change of classification or reform.

P Provisional

FT Full-time - PT Part-time.

(1) Including as from 1970 teacher training schools and as from 1975 management schools integrated into non-university higher education.

(2) As the number of schools taken into account may vary from year to year data are not really comparable.

(3) Students enrolled in regular courses only. The total number of students is

	1980	1981	1982
Universities	1835.3	1822.1	1817.6
Junior Colleges	371.1	372.4	374.3
Technical Colleges	17.2	17.2	17.5

(4) Advanced level full-time or "sandwich" course.

(5) Advanced level part-time day and evening courses.

Table 28

PROPORTION OF WOMEN AMONG HIGHER EDUCATION GRADUATES

Academic year beginning in :

Percentage

	1965	1970	1975	1976	1977	1978	1979	1980	1981
GERMANY									
Diplomas and equivalent	35.7	30.0	40.1	39.1	38.9	40.3	40.1		
- of which teacher training	67.3	47.3	59.3	55.2	54.5	57.1	58.1		
Doctorates	13.0	15.0	15.0	14.8	15.8	16.1	18.5		
Non-univ.	12.0	10.1	20.7	23.5	24.9	23.7	25.8		
AUSTRALIA/Univ.									
Bachelor	26.7	30.4	35.8	36.2	39.1	39.5	40.5		
Master	13.5	16.3	16.2	16.7	19.1	21.5	23.8		
Doctorate	7.0	10.2	11.7	13.6	14.1	15.3	16.2		
Post-graduate diploma	46.2	48.8	55.9	54.7	51.7	52.3	52.8		
CAE									
Bachelor		27.0	24.6	29.5	35.0	41.2	44.2	46.7	47.7
Master			0.0	27.8	19.5	21.3	19.7	25.0	22.3
Graduate dipl.			50.4	48.1	51.5	50.9	50.6	51.2	52.6
Diploma/associate diploma			52.0	62.8	65.4	64.3	65.9	65.0	64.2
AUSTRIA									
Diplom	25.7	23.8	29.4	31.9	32.0	33.9			
Doctorate	22.9	20.8	22.8	22.4	25.7	26.6			
CANADA									
Bachelor/first professional	32.6	38.0	46.3	47.7	48.5	49.2	49.6	50.4	
Master	18.2	22.0	30.5	31.3	32.8	36.0	37.4	39.2	
Doctorate	11.0	9.3	18.8	18.0	18.2	20.5	23.0	24.0	
Diploma/Certif. 1st cycle		54.5	51.6	53.1	54.0	56.9	56.4	57.4	
Diploma/Certif. 2nd and 3rd cyc		22.3	35.8	36.8	31.5	34.6	36.6	40.6	
NU		58.7	55.7	56.0	55.3	55.9	56.0	56.6	
DENMARK									
Dip. Univers.	22.2	25.6	28.7	29.8	35.4	33.9	36.6		
Dip. other U institutions(1)	13.4	18.0	24.0	27.2	26.8	28.0	25.9		
Dip. NU (1)	46.8	49.2	51.3	52.5	53.5	53.4	58.9		

./...

Table 28 (cont'd)

PROPORTION OF WOMEN AMONG HIGHER EDUCATION GRADUATES

Academic year beginning in :

Percentage

	1965	1970	1975	1976	1977	1978	1979	1980	1981
SPAIN									
Dip.Faculties higher techni. artist. schools			34.1	40.1	39.4	40.3	45.0		
Dip. Univers. Schools			45.2	49.9	51.4	58.6	56.2		
UNITED STATES									
Bachelor	42.6	43.5	45.6	46.2	47.2	48.3	49.2		
First profes-sional (2)	14.5	6.5	15.6	18.7	21.5	23.6	24.9		
Master	33.8	40.1	46.4	47.1	48.3	49.1	49.5		
Doctorate	11.6	14.3	22.9	24.3	26.4	28.1	29.7		
FRANCE		(1972)				P			
Diploma 1st cycle (2 yrs)			51.3	51.1		58.8			
Licence/dip. ing./Doct.Med.		39.9	42.9	42.5	44.5				
Master		52.1	50.7	49.0	48.9				
Doctorate		19.3	21.2	21.7	27.7(3)				
NU(IUT,BTS, capac. droit)		36.8	39.9	39.7					
GREECE									
1st degree	25.5	32.9	35.2	36.6	41.1				
Post-graduate			9.3	10.2	14.8				
Doctorate	15.4	12.8	18.5	19.4	20.7				
NU		46.4	41.2	40.9					
ITALY									
"Laureati"	35.9	43.1	43.1	43.4	42.9	42.9	43.2	44.0	
"Diplomati"(NU)	49.6	48.6	49.2	52.0	50.9	54.3	57.0	52.4	
JAPAN (4)									
1st degree	16.2	20.2	21.6	22.7	23.7	24.1	24.5	24.7	24.7
Master	7.8	8.2	8.2	8.8	8.8	8.5	9.6	10.7	11.2
Doctorate	5.6	5.5	5.8	6.6	5.9	6.2	6.6	7.6	7.1
Junior Col.	76.1	86.7	88.7	89.5	90.1	90.7	91.4	91.3	91.7
Colleges tech.		1.7	1.8	1.2	1.5	1.5	1.9	1.9	1.6
NETHERLANDS									
Dipl. U		14.2	19.1	20.3	22.8	23.0	24.9		
NU FT		40.9	44.0	42.5	44.1	43.7	44.0	44.5	
NU PT		43.0	30.2	29.3	33.4	32.5	36.9	58.1	

./...

Table 28 (cont'd)

PROPORTION OF WOMEN AMONG HIGHER EDUCATION GRADUATES

Academic year beginning in :

Percentage

	1965	1970	1975	1976	1977	1978	1979	1980	1981
UNITED KINGDOM	(1967)								
First degrees									
Universities	29.1	30.6	34.1	35.4	35.9	35.9			
CNAA			26.2						
London Univ.					36.4				
Open Univ.		20.6(5)	33.4	36.4		43.5			
Higher degrees									
Universities	11.2	13.3	18.9	19.1	20.3	21.1			
CNAA			18.1	14.0					
London Univ.					12.4				
Teacher training graduate	72.5	72.9	71.6	71.6	75.9	74.8			
Teacher training post-grad	53.7	55.0	55.9	53.0	54.2	54.8			
First diplomas/ Certificates	40.7	35.2	32.9	42.2	40.3	44.1			
Higher diplomas/ Certificates	36.9	40.6	43.7	44.3	45.0	44.7			
SWEDEN Before the reform									
1st degrees	34.8	41.4	39.8	41.3					
Higher degrees	11.1	19.0	34.0	24.3					
After the reform									
1st degree							48.6		
Post-graduate							23.8		
NU							58.4		
YUGOSLAVIA									
Dip. 2nd cycle	28.2	34.5	39.6	42.7	43.5				
Dip. 3rd cycle	28.0	24.7	22.4	23.2	25.6				
Doctorates	19.9	20.0	21.4	17.5	20.2				
Dip.1st cycle	25.7	35.9	35.4	35.0	37.5				
Higher schools	29.3	43.0	49.1	50.0	49.4				

P = Provisional

(1) As from 1975 types of education taken into account do not correspond exactly to those in previous years.
(2) Obtained after at least 6 years of study except in 1964 (5 years).
(3) Not including Doctorats d'Etat in humanities and science and engineering doctorates.
(4) Students enrolled in regular courses only.
(5) 1971-1972.

Table 29

DISTRIBUTION OF PUPILS BY SOCIO-ECONOMIC ORIGIN AT DIFFERENT STAGES OF THEIR EDUCATION

A - GERMANY

	Self-employed workers	Civil servants	Clerical	Manual	Others	Total (000)=100
1966 Universities (1)	30.9	28.6	31.8	6.5	2.2	40.7
Higher Tech. shools (1)	25.3	20.4	33.3	17.5	3.5	21.9
1972 Pupils under 10 years (2)						
Primary	15.1	9.2	24.2	47.5	4.0	3800.0
Pupils aged 10-15 years						
Primary/upper primary	14.2	5.2	14.7	59.5	6.5	3137.0
Middle school	19.7	9.4	23.4	43.5	3.8	709.0
Gymnasium	23.7	16.6	38.4	18.4	2.8	829.0
Pupils over 15 years						
Middle school	20.6	11.1	26.8	36.0	5.4	369.0
Gymnasium	23.7	18.4	34.7	15.9	7.3	674.0
1970 Universities (1)	26.5	25.2	34.0	12.0	2.3	66.1
1976 Pupils aged 6-10 yrs						
Primary	13.1	9.6	27.3	43.4	6.4	3062.0
Pupils aged 10-15 yrs						
Primary/upper primary	12.8	5.8	18.3	53.7	9.5	3053.0
Middle school	15.5	8.4	28.8	41.2	6.0	985.0
Gymnasium	18.4	17.8	41.6	17.4	4.4	982.0
Pupils aged 15-18 yrs						
Upper primary	11.6	3.9	14.4	55.6	13.7	466.0
Middle school	15.8	8.4	27.2	39.4	8.1	467.0
Gymnasium	19.1	16.5	38.0	19.7	6.6	618.0
Vocational school	14.6	5.5	20.5	44.3	11.9	219.0
1975 Universities (1)	22.8	22.6	36.7	15.0	2.9	91.5
Higher tech. schools (1)	21.8	14.4	32.8	27.6	3.4	32.1
1977 Universities (1)	21.3	21.8	37.1	14.8	5.0	95.2
Higher tech. schools (1)	21.5	14.3	33.5	26.7	4.0	35.4
1979 Universities (1)	22.1	21.7	38.9	14.8	2.6	97.5
Higher tech. schools (1)	21.3	15.0	34.4	25.3	4.0	37.9

(1) 1st semester of study. German students.
(2) Including a certain number of pupils aged over 15.

./...

Table 29 (cont'd)

B - AUSTRALIA

Percentage

	Professional, technical, administrative workers	Clerical, commercial workers	Other workers	Out of the the labour force	Other categories
1974 Universities					
Full-time students	43.0	10.0	31.0	13.0	3.0
Part-time students	28.0	11.0	25.0	33.0	3.0
CAE					
Full-time students	32.0	10.0	42.0	12.0	4.0
Part-time students	22.0	10.0	30.0	34.0	4.0
Male population 45-54 yrs	18.0	12.0	59.0	6.0	5.0
1975 TAFE Technical and Further Education	14.0	13.0	64.0	1.0	8.0

1979 Father's occupation	Professional	Employer and senior managerial	Middle managerial	Clerical workers	Manual workers	Agricult.	Unknown
Universities	32	28	8	4	19	6	3
CAE	19	26	10	5	26	10	4

C - CANADA

PARENTS EDUCATIONAL ATTAINMENT OF FULL-TIME POST-SECONDARY STUDENTS BY LEVEL

Percentage

	Community college				University under-graduate				University Post-graduate			
	1968-69		1974-75		1968-69		1974-75		1968-69		1974-75	
	Father	Mother	Father	Mother	Father	Mother	Father	Mother	Father	Mother	Father	Mother
Elementary	32.0	28.2	29.1	27.5	19.4	18.3	18.5	16.3	21.0	20.4	21.7	19.3
Some high school	25.2	30.9	26.0	29.7	23.9	27.5	24.4	24.4	21.2	23.9	21.8	26.0
Completed high school	10.8	16.4	14.5	19.2	13.9	21.7	15.1	21.2	17.2	24.1	14.4	20.3
Some University	4.4	3.8	7.6	11.3	7.4	7.6	9.1	18.3	6.9	6.8	8.3	15.8
University degree	8.4	2.5	11.2	2.7	17.5	6.8	22.5	8.0	18.6	7.8	23.9	9.3
Other education or training	19.2	18.2	11.6	9.6	17.9	18.1	10.4	11.8	15.1	17.0	9.9	9.3

./...

Table 29 (cont'd)

D - DENMARK

Percentage

Year		Managerial and clerical workers	Self-employed	Skilled manual workers	Unskilled manual workers	Other
1978	1st year secondary 2nd cycle	44.7	29.0	10.5	5.6	9.9
1977	Male labour force	35.9	19.3	18.6	26.2	-

RATE OF PARTICIPATION IN 2ND CYCLE GENERAL SECONDARY EDUCATION BY SOCIO-ECONOMIC CATEGORY

Year	Professional and senior managerial	Middle managerial & assimilated	Clerical workers, small business	Skilled manual & assimilated	Unskilled manual
1965	56	23	11	7	2
1971	65	53	26	16	9

E - SPAIN

Percentage

Year		Professional and senior managerial	Middle managerial	Business Heads	Clerical, manual workers	Out of labour force	Unknown
1975	Universities	32.9	18.5	21.4	14.4	6.4	6.4
1976	Universities	30.6	18.6	21.1	15.2	7.0	7.5
	Higher techn. sch.	36.2	20.5	20.6	12.7	4.9	5.1
1977	Universities	28.4	18.9	22.1	16.6	5.9	8.1
	Higher techn. sch.	34.7	19.9	21.3	13.1	3.9	7.3
1978	Universities	29.4	19.7	21.8	16.3	5.5	7.3
	Higher techn. sch.	36.3	22.4	20.5	12.1	3.7	5.0
1979	Universities	28.3	19.2	21.6	16.8	6.5	7.6
	Higher techn. sch.	35.0	21.5	21.1	12.9	3.5	6.0
1980	Universities	27.8	19.2	21.8	16.7	6.9	7.6
	Higher techn. sch.	35.9	22.0	20.8	12.4	3.7	5.2

./...

Table 29 (cont'd)

F - UNITED STATES

DISTRIBUTION ACCORDING TO FAMILY INCOME, OF YOUNG PEOPLE AGED 3-17 YEARS ENROLLED OR NOT ENROLLED IN AN EDUCATIONAL INSTITUTION (1)

Percentage

	Under $5,000		$5,000-9,999		$10,000 14,999		$15,000 19,999		$20,000 24,999		$25,000 and over		Unknown	
	M	F	M	F	M	F	M	F	M	F	M	F	M	F
1978 Pre-primary	9.6	10.5	14.9	17.3	21.3	18.9	16.3	18.5	14.8	13.9	14.8	14.2	8.4	6.7
Primary	9.1	9.6	16.9	16.8	19.9	20.0	17.0	16.7	13.0	13.7	16.0	14.8	8.1	8.3
Secondary	7.1	6.6	14.8	14.4	16.3	16.5	16.0	17.0	14.0	14.6	22.9	21.3	9.0	9.6
Not enrolled (14-17 yrs)	13.5	23.5	24.8	22.8	25.1	17.4	12.1	11.2	8.4	5.7	6.3	7.9	9.8	11.6
% of non-graduates (2)	90.9	93.0	91.7	88.3	84.4	74.1	84.7	60.0	78.0	64.3	66.7	51.3	87.5	80.7

(1) Excluding pupils enrolled in higher education.
(2) Without high school level diploma.

RATE OF PARTICIPATION IN HIGHER EDUCATION OF DEPENDENT YOUNG PEOPLE AGED 18-24 YEARS ACCORDING TO FAMILY INCOME (IN 1967 $) AND RACE

	Under $ 5,000	$5,000-9,999	$10,000-14,999	$15,000 and over	All incomes	Whites	Blacks
1967	20.0	37.9	51.9	68.3	39.1	26.9	13.0
1970	20.8	36.6	48.4	61.7	39.1	27.1	15.5
1974	20.3	31.7	41.4	57.5	36.2	25.2	17.9
1976	22.4	36.3	47.5	58.2	38.8	27.1	22.6
1977	22.6	34.3	46.9	59.8	37.8	26.5	21.3
1978						25.7	20.1

./...

Table 29 (cont'd)

G - FRANCE

Percentage

	Professional, senior managerial	Middle managerial	Business heads	Clerical	Farmers	Workers, agricultural workers, service personnel	Other
1968 Popul. 16 years and under	6.8	7.4	9.1	8.1	11.4	46.6	10.5
1967 "4e" (8th year)	7.9	9.8	9.5	10.4	7.4	45.5	9.6
4e pratique and CPPN (1)	1.6	4.2	6.0	7.4	6.1	63.1	11.5
2e humanities/science	20.3	17.0	12.4	11.7	6.9	23.5	7.9
2e technical	7.6	12.8	12.1	12.1	7.4	39.0	9.1
1968 Universities	28.5	15.9	14.0	8.9	7.1	13.9	11.7
1973 "4e"	6.2	8.6	8.8	12.0	7.3	47.2	9.9
4e pratique and CPPN	0.6	2.6	5.4	9.0	6.8	61.8	13.8
2e humanities/science	21.5	17.6	11.6	12.7	6.1	22.6	7.9
2e technical	7.6	12.8	11.3	13.9	7.6	38.8	8.1
Universities	32.6	16.2	11.9	9.4	6.1	13.9	9.9
1975 Popul. 16 years and under	8.3	8.5	8.7	8.7	9.5	45.2	11.2
1976 "4e"	6.9	8.8	8.3	11.4	6.3	47.4	9.6
4e pratique and CPPN	0.6	2.2	5.4	8.6	6.0	61.5	15.6
2e humanities/science	24.6	17.9	10.8	11.6	5.1	21.9	8.0
2e technical	7.7	12.9	10.2	14.4	5.1	40.0	9.7
"Bacheliers" Total	19.8	17.5	11.1	12.0	7.7	20.4	11.5
" serie C (2)	30.6	20.7	10.3	9.8	6.6	12.3	9.7
Universities	33.6	17.1	11.2	9.3	5.5	13.9	9.4
1978 Universities							
1st cyc. incl. IUT(3)	29.1	18.7	10.4	9.7	5.8	17.5	8.8
2nd cycle	38.0	17.2	10.8	8.4	5.2	11.9	8.4
3rd cycle	40.8	14.9	11.4	7.5	4.6	8.7	12.0
1980 4e Public	11.4	14.4	10.8	9.6	5.5	40.2	8.8
CPPN "	0.6	2.6	5.7	5.2	4.4	62.5	19.0
2e human. "	16.2	18.0	11.7	10.5	3.7	30.1	9.9
2e econ. "	10.7	15.6	11.2	10.6	5.4	36.5	10.0
2e scient. "	29.9	20.2	9.8	8.6	4.3	20.4	6.8
2e techn. "	10.8	16.4	9.9	10.4	4.8	38.6	9.1
Total 2e Public	17.7	17.5	10.6	9.9	4.7	30.8	8.8
Universities - French students							
New entrants							
1st cycle + IUT	27.3	19.2	9.9	9.9	5.9	18.8	9.1
IUT only	15.7	18.9	11.1	10.3	9.3	27.3	7.4
Total students							
1st cycle + IUT	27.0	17.8	9.3	9.1	5.2	16.6	15.0
2nd cycle	35.7	16.1	9.4	7.5	4.6	11.0	15.7
3rd cycle	35.3	13.4	9.0	6.3	3.9	7.6	24.5
Total	31.0	16.6	9.3	8.2	4.8	13.4	16.5

(1) CPPN = Classes pré-professionnelles de niveau. (Pre-vocational courses).
(2) Série C : Maths and Physics.
(3) IUT : Institut universitaire de technologie : 2 years of study.

./...

Table 29 (cont'd)

G - FRANCE (cont'd)

PROGRESS OF 100 PUPILS IN THE COHORT ENROLLED IN "6e" IN 1973-1974

Percentage

Situation in :	General education		Pre-vocational or short vocational and other education	Obtained Baccalaureat (1980 session)	of which entering		Not in education
	behind	normal age			University (1)	Non university (2)	
1975-1976							
Professional & senior managerial	11.2	85.2	1.8				1.9
Middle managerial	16.5	75.9	6.5				1.1
Manual	16.3	49.6	32.0				2.1
1977-1978							
Professional & senior managerial	24.6	64.9	5.2				5.3
Middle managerial	28.3	47.4	16.8				7.4
Manual	15.5	19.0	36.7				28.8
1979-1980							
Professional & senior managerial	29.0	46.1	9.0	37.2			15.9
Middle managerial	24.2	30.8	17.8	23.0			27.2
Manual	9.4	11.6	15.2	8.2			63.8
1980-1981							
Professional & senior managerial					27.9	3.5	
Middle managerial					14.6	4.9	
Manual					3.4	2.4	

(1) University and Preparatory classes for the "Grandes Ecoles".
(2) IUT et BTS (Higher technical certificate).

./...

Table 29 (cont'd)

H - NETHERLANDS

SCHOOL ORIENTATION AT THE END OF PRIMARY EDUCATION ACCORDING TO LEVEL OF SCHOOL PERFORMANCE (1) AND SOCIAL ORIGIN

	Senior managerial		Middle managerial		Clerical workers		Self-employed with employ.		Self-employed without employ.		Manual workers		Other	
	M	F	M	F	M	F	M	F	M	F	M	F	M	F
1977														
Level 2	100	100	100	100	100	100	100	100	100	100	100	100	100	100
General secondary, long	8	7	4	4	4	4	1	2	1	2	1	2	1	2
" " short	49	65	48	48	40	45	37	49	37	37	22	36	23	32
Vocational	30	16	35	35	47	42	51	42	53	55	65	54	65	59
Others	14	13	14	12	10	10	10	8	10	6	12	9	11	8
Level 3	100	100	100	100	100	100	100	100	100	100	100	100	100	100
General secondary, long	32	36	24	26	19	22	15	22	11	14	11	12	15	15
" " short	57	54	56	61	56	61	53	63	46	64	52	65	50	61
Vocational	7	5	15	9	17	13	23	8	34	14	33	20	28	18
Others	4	5	6	4	9	5	9	6	9	7	6	4	7	6
Level 4	100	100	100	100	100	100	100	100	100	100	100	100	100	100
General secondary, long	76	75	70	69	61	59	56	63	49	52	46	51	50	53
" " short	21	23	27	28	34	37	76	34	36	43	44	42	38	42
Vocational	1	0	1	0	1	1	6	2	11	4	8	4	9	2
Others	2	2	2	3	4	3	2	2	4	2	2	3	4	3
Distribution by level of school performance (Percentage)														
Level 1	3.0	2.3	5.4	5.3	8.0	7.2	8.9	7.9	12.7	9.9	17.2	15.4	22.4	20.9
Level 2	16.5	13.1	18.6	19.7	23.8	24.8	25.5	24.8	27.1	30.7	35.2	32.2	31.8	32.2
Level 3	30.0	33.2	34.3	33.0	34.2	34.8	32.3	35.1	33.6	32.9	27.5	31.0	26.1	27.1
Level 4	37.0	37.9	31.4	31.2	26.8	27.0	27.2	25.8	23.1	22.4	17.4	18.1	15.9	16.5
Level 5	13.6	13.6	10.3	10.8	7.3	6.1	6.1	6.3	3.4	4.0	2.7	3.3	3.7	3.3

(1) Levels run from 1 (the lowest) to 5.

DISTRIBUTION OF STUDENTS ENROLLED IN 1st YEAR OF UNIVERSITY STUDIES

	Upper Class		Middle Class		Lower Class	
	M	F	M	F	M	F
1964	35	54	52	41	13	4
1970	33	48	51	44	15	8
1974	30	40	49	47	20	13

./...

Table 29 (cont'd)

I - SWEDEN

PROPORTION OF PUPILS LEAVING BASIC SCHOOL IN 1971 WHO ENTERED GYMNASIUM AND THEN HIGHER EDUCATION WITHIN 4 YEARS BY SEX AND SOCIAL CLASS

	University graduates		Other senior managerial		Middle managerial, Clerical workers		Skilled workers, farmers		Unskilled workers		Unknown		Total	
	M	F	M	F	M	F	M	F	M	F	M	F	M	F
Basic school completed	100	100	100	100	100	100	100	100	100	100	100	100	100	100
Options followed in 9th years														
English normal, maths norm	2	4	13	10	26	19	38	31	47	41	45	41	33	28
" " " adv.	3	1	5	3	10	4	14	5	15	5	10	3	11	4
" adv., maths normal	4	13	8	19	11	26	8	20	9	22	7	24	9	22
" " , " adv.	90	82	73	67	53	51	40	44	29	33	39	31	47	46
Entered gymnasium 2nd cycl	86	86	82	80	68	74	63	70	55	59	61	47	64	67
3- and 4-yr. courses	75	59	49	42	29	26	19	16	12	11	18	11	25	20
theoretical courses	6	18	10	17	14	22	9	22	8	13	12	12	10	17
2-yr. vocational courses	2	6	15	13	19	16	30	18	27	22	24	19	23	18
special courses (1)	4	3	8	8	6	10	6	14	8	13	6	5	7	11
Entered university	71	66	33	38	21	26	11	21	6	11	-	-	17	22
of wh. prestige courses(2)	30	12	11	2	7	2	3	1	1	1	-	-	6	2

PROPORTION OF PUPILS ENTERING UNIVERSITY ACCORDING TO COURSE FOLLOWED AT GYMNASIUM

	University graduates	Other senior managerial	Middle managerial, Clerical workers	Skilled workers, farmers	Unskilled workers	Unknown	Total
3- and 4-year courses	85	61	56	56	41		59
2-yr. theoretical courses	34	18	19	16	14		17
2-yr. vocational courses	23	10	12	8	6		8
special courses	24	4	7	4	3		5

DISTRIBUTION ACCORDING TO SOCIAL ORIGIN OF STUDENTS ENROLLED FOR THE FIRST TIME IN HIGHER EDUCATION

1966	17.9	31.2	24.5	26.5
1970	13.8	27.9	25.8	32.5
1974	14.8	30.1	23.0	32.1
1976	14.8	30.6	23.4	31.2

(1) Courses of a few weeks to a year or more.
(2) Long courses with numerus clausus .

Table 30

DISTRIBUTION BY LEVEL OF QUALIFICATION OF PUPILS LEAVING THE EDUCATION SYSTEM (1)

Percentage

	1965		1970		1975		1976		1977		1978		1979		1980		1981	
	M	F	M	F	M	F	M	F	M	F	M	F	M	F	M	F	M	F
AUSTRALIA																		
As % of enrolments in year of study			(1972)															
7th year of study			0.6	0.6			-	0.2		0.2								
8th			5.6	5.2			3.4	2.5	2.8	2.2	2.7	1.9	2.2	1.2	1.4	0.6		
9th			12.0	12.9			9.3	8.4	8.4	7.8	9.0	7.3	8.1	6.5	7.7	6.3		
10th			40.4	42.5			50.8	37.3	41.4	36.8	42.9	37.6	42.6	36.6	42.3	35.5		
11th			30.5	32.4			34.0	30.7	34.3	31.5	36.5	33.3	36.7	33.2	37.1	33.9		
AUSTRALIA																		
Numbers : aged 15 to 24 yrs. (000)					123.1	115.3			118.1	108.9			157.7	130.7			154.4	133.8
Secondary school					81.7	78.5			74.6	63.6			70.6	66.8			65.6	62.4
University					7.7	4.3							14.2	8.4			10.4	7.2
CAE					5.9	7.7			25.3	36.3			7.2	8.8			8.6	9.0
Technical college					4.2	6.5							8.0	9.9			11.1	12.6
Others					0.6	2.9							-	6.0			4.2	8.7
% unemployed					9.8	14.5			14.3	14.7			16.6	23.6			12.8	18.6
CANADA - Persons leaving full-time education and likely to enter the labour market																		
	(1966)		(1971)				P		P		P		P		P		P	
Numbers (000)	186.9	173.6	270.9	247.2	287.7	254.9	306.1	273.5	324.5	290.8	318.1	287.2	310.8	281.2	308.2	281.8	303.1	280.3
Secondary not completed	54.6	50.5	53.8	48.0	48.1	41.5	46.9	39.4	49.7	40.6	47.4	38.5	46.6	37.6	46.1	37.2	45.4	37.3
Secondary completed	26.1	31.9	14.8	25.7	15.5	24.7	16.7	25.3	16.4	25.1	17.2	25.3	17.6	25.1	17.8	25.0	18.0	25.0
Post-secondary not complet	7.1	4.5	16.2	10.8	20.3	15.5	21.1	16.7	19.3	15.4	20.8	16.7	20.8	16.7	21.0	16.9	20.9	16.5
Certificat/diploma NU	3.5	8.3	4.5	8.4	5.1	8.6	5.1	8.8	5.0	8.9	5.1	9.2	5.5	9.9	5.7	10.1	5.8	10.0
University first degree	7.4	4.5	8.7	6.4	9.2	8.8	8.5	8.9	8.1	9.0	7.9	9.3	7.9	9.6	7.8	9.7	8.2	10.0
Master and assimilated	1.0	0.3	1.8	0.7	1.5	0.9	1.5	1.0	1.4	0.9	1.4	1.0	1.4	1.0	1.5	1.0	1.5	1.1
Doctorate	0.2	0.0	0.3	0.0	0.3	0.1	0.2	0.1	0.2	0.1	0.2	0.1	0.2	0.1	0.2	0.1	0.2	0.1
FRANCE (2)			(1973)															
Numbers (000)			776.2		761.2		761.3		782.1		773.4							
Level VI			15.4	(8)	15.1		14.7		14.7		13.1	(4)						
" V bis			17.9	(18)	16.8		15.9		15.6		12.9	(10)						
" V			33.3	(41)	33.7		35.5		37.0		37.8	(49)						
" IV			16.3	(16)	16.4		15.6		14.2		15.5	(16)						
" III			7.7		7.8		8.9		9.3		10.6							
" II and I			9.4		10.2		9.5		9.2		10.1							
ITALY																		
Percentage of pupils/students interrupting their studies without completing the study cycle																		
Primary and middle					2.1		2.4											
2nd cycle secondary					8.1		8.1											
University					13.7		13.2											
of which 1st year					27.9		28.0											

./...

Table 30 (cont'd)

DISTRIBUTION BY LEVEL OF QUALIFICATION OF PUPILS LEAVING THE EDUCATION SYSTEM (1)

Percentage

	1965		1970		1975		1976		1977		1978		1979		1980		1981	
	M	F	M	F	M	F	M	F	M	F	M	F	M	F	M	F	M	F
JAPAN																		
Numbers (000)	903.5	865.6	902.8	812.8	776.6	629.0	652.4	573.1	673.8	598.0	670.1	598.6	671.9	604.4	671.2	605.7	673.3	610.8
1st cycle secondary	37.7	40.6	17.4	17.4	9.4	8.0	5.8	5.3	5.2	4.4	5.1	4.2	4.9	3.8	5.1	3.7	5.1	3.6
2nd " "	46.3	51.7	59.4	64.7	56.4	64.1	52.8	58.9	53.2	58.6	51.3	57.4	49.8	55.8	49.5	55.9	49.0	56.5
Technical secondary	0.0	-	0.7	0.0	1.0	0.0	1.2	0.0	1.1	0.0	1.1	0.0	1.1	0.0	1.1	0.0	1.1	0.0
Junior College	1.2	4.7	1.5	11.9	1.8	17.9	2.1	22.9	2.0	23.6	2.0	24.0	1.9	25.3	1.9	25.0	1.8	24.4
University 1st degree	14.3	2.9	20.0	5.9	29.8	19.7	36.3	12.7	36.3	13.2	38.3	14.1	40.0	14.8	40.3	15.1	40.9	15.3
Higher degree	0.5	0.0	1.0	0.1	1.6	0.2	1.8	0.2	2.0	0.2	2.2	0.2	2.2	0.2	2.1	0.3	2.2	0.3
NETHERLANDS	(1967)																	
Numbers (000)	103.3	102.1	101.8	101.7	103.3	86.0	113.5	104.2	123.9	107.3	132.2	114.4	133.0	118.9				
1st cy. sec. without dip(4)	33.7	35.7	24.9	31.3	16.8	17.4	17.6	17.0	18.3	18.5	17.3	16.6	18.0	15.4				
of whith general (4)	18.3	17.3	11.0	13.0	8.7	10.4	8.1	8.4	7.7	9.2	7.3	8.2	7.6	8.4				
vocational	15.4	18.4	13.9	18.3	8.1	7.0	9.5	8.6	10.6	9.3	11.0	8.4	10.4	7.0				
1st cycle secondary with diploma	35.9	33.5	37.4	29.8	26.2	17.4	29.0	29.1	29.4	29.5	29.3	28.3	28.8	26.5				
- of which general	7.5	12.6	7.2	13.4	5.3	13.6	4.4	10.6	3.7	10.5	3.7	9.5	3.3	8.8				
vocational	28.3	20.9	30.2	16.4	20.9	3.8	24.6	18.5	25.7	19.0	25.6	18.7	25.5	17.7				
2nd cycle secondary without diploma	4.2	5.0	6.9	6.6	11.7	12.0	10.7	9.5	11.3	11.6	11.9	12.7	12.2	14.3				
- of which general	1.5	1.3	3.3	2.5	4.6	4.5	4.1	3.8	4.0	4.1	4.6	4.5	5.0	5.6				
vocational	2.7	3.7	3.6	4.1	7.1	7.5	6.7	5.6	7.2	7.6	7.3	8.2	7.2	8.7				
2nd cycle secondary with diploma	10.0	18.3	12.6	23.8	18.8	37.7	17.1	30.2	15.6	24.5	16.1	26.3	15.8	27.6				
- of which general	4.8	5.4	5.8	7.9	8.8	12.6	9.7	11.0	6.7	11.3	6.8	11.8	6.1	11.2				
vocational	5.3	12.9	6.9	16.0	9.9	25.1	9.4	19.2	8.9	13.2	9.3	14.5	9.8	16.4				
Non-university without diploma	2.8	1.4	3.3	1.6	6.2	2.8	5.6	2.8	6.4	3.8	6.3	3.9	6.4	3.9				
Non-university with diploma	8.0	4.7	7.9	5.4	9.4	9.3	9.8	8.3	9.5	8.9	9.3	8.7	9.7	8.6				
University without diploma	1.7	0.7	1.3	0.6	3.3	1.4	3.1	1.3	3.0	1.4	2.9	1.5	2.9	1.4				
University with diploma	3.8	0.6	5.5	0.9	7.7	2.0	7.1	1.8	6.5	1.9	6.0	2.0	6.2	2.1				
% of total entering apprenticeship/ PT education	37.6	10.2	35.8	10.0	20.4	13.2	29.4	24.1	28.6	23.6	26.2	21.1	28.0	23.0				

./...

Table 30 (cont'd)

DISTRIBUTION BY LEVEL OF QUALIFICATION OF PUPILS LEAVING THE EDUCATION SYSTEM (1)

Percentage

	1965		1970		1975		1976		1977		1978		1979		1980		1981	
	M	F	M	F	M	F	M	F	M	F	M	F	M	F	M	F	M	F
UNITED KINGDOM (5)																		
Numbers (000)	315.4	266.4	279.7	236.4	324.5	269.1	346.2	286.8	338.4	276.7	346.6	284.1						
without qualification					20.0	20.2	18.1	18.4	16.6	16.6	15.1	14.5						
1 to 4 grades lower	64.3	71.6	61.7	67.0														
than GCE					35.8	35.6	35.6	35.9	37.4	36.0	37.6	37.4						
GCE or equivalent																		
1 to 4 O levels	14.4	14.0	18.2	18.4	23.1	25.5	23.9	26.2	23.1	26.8	24.3	27.2						
5 or more O levels or 1 A level	11.9	10.6	8.0	8.9	8.0	9.8	9.0	10.5	9.1	10.6	9.0	10.9						
2 or more A levels	3.0	1.8	3.3	2.7	4.1	4.2	4.3	4.1	4.1	4.6	4.2	4.2						
1st University degree	5.3	1.9	6.9	2.6	7.1	4.1	7.3	4.3	7.9	4.8	8.1	5.1						
Higher degree	1.1	0.2	1.8	0.3	1.9	0.6	1.8	0.6	1.8	0.7	1.8	0.7						
% of pupils leaving secondary education and continuing studies	11.2	16.7	19.1	23.2	19.1	25.8	18.0	25.7	17.8	25.8	17.2	25.8						

(1) Whatever their destination : permanent or temporary employment, unemployment, out of labour force, or unknown.

(2) Apprenticeship is not taken into account, i.e. young people leaving education for apprenticeship are counted as exits. Figures in brackets indicate the distribution if apprenticeship is considered as forming part of initial training.

Level VI :	Exit penultimate year 1st cycle secondary general or pre-vocational classes.
" V bis :	Exit end 1st cycle secondary general or short vocational not completed.
" V :	Exit end short vocational, or 2nd cycle secondary not completed.
" IV :	Exit end 2nd cycle secondary and drop-outs before level III.
" III :	End non-university-type higher or 1st cycle university.
" II et I :	End 2nd or 3rd cycle university or Grandes écoles.

(3) Including persons in vocational training.

(4) Including pupils leaving before 1st cycle.

(5) Below university 1st degree : England and Wales for 1965-76, England for subsequent years. Further education is not included.

P = Provisional

Table 31

LEVEL OF EDUCATIONAL QUALIFICATION OF UNEMPLOYED YOUNG PEOPLE

Percentage

	1970		1975		1976		1977		1978		1979		1980		1981		1982	
	M	F	M	F	M	F	M	F	M	F	M	F	M	F	M	F	M	F
GERMANY - 15-19 yrs																		
Numbers (000) = 100				115.8		102.6		105.9		92.0		68.6		81.1				
Voc. train. not completed				67.4		62.6		67.6		71.0		72.5		74.1				
of which without dipl.																		
Basic education						26.3		27.9		28.1		29.1		30.6				
- with dip. basic ed.						27.1		26.4		28.0		28.2		28.3				
- with higher diploma						7.4		11.6		13.1		12.8		12.6				
- qualification unknown						1.8		1.7		1.8		2.2		2.6				
Voc. train. completed				32.6		37.4		32.5		29.0		27.5		25.8				
AUSTRALIA - Unemployed aged 15-19 = 100																		
Sec. school not completed												65.0		65.6		63.1		
Sec. school completed												17.0		14.6		15.9		
NU level												6.7		7.9		7.8		
U level												0.0		0.0		0.0		
Still in education												11.2		11.9		13.2		
CANADA - Unemployment rate for 15-24 year-olds in labour force																		
0-8 yrs of study				21.1		20.9		24.3		24.1		23.0		22.5		22.2		31.9
Secondaire (1)				12.9		13.6		15.3		15.4		13.7		14.1		14.2		20.0
Some years post-secondary				9.3		9.6		11.6		11.5		9.4		9.4		10.1		14.6
NU diploma				6.6		8.4		9.1		9.1		8.7		8.8		8.0		12.5
U Degree				6.2		7.7		8.3		8.6		7.1		7.1		7.4		10.3
DENMARK - Unemployment rate for 15-24 year-olds not in education																		
7th-8th year of study									19.6	31.2								
9th-10th " "									17.5	24.3								
Dip. 1st cycle second.									14.3	16.6								
Dip. 2nd cycle second.									15.8	14.9								
Apprenticeship									9.7	11.6								
Voc. training completed									1.1	9.3								
UNITED STATES - Unemployment rate for 16-24 year-olds not in education																		
Under 8 yrs of study	11.9	18.7	19.0	25.7	12.1	20.9	12.4	18.7	15.4	12.9	10.1	16.7	15.8	28.3	18.4	18.8		
8 yrs of study	15.4	14.8	20.9	31.3	26.8	34.3	16.6	33.6	21.4	19.8	22.7	27.6	26.5	31.7	24.3	32.0		
1 to 3 yrs sec. school	16.7	20.8	22.8	31.0	22.2	30.2	17.4	27.6	16.4	23.2	15.7	25.2	24.1	28.3	25.7	32.5		
4 yrs secondary school	9.7	10.1	13.6	13.6	11.3	13.0	8.9	12.2	7.1	10.4	8.0	11.8	13.5	11.4	13.5	14.2		
1 to 3 yrs higher educ.	8.7	7.0	10.1	10.9	8.0	11.8	8.0	7.3	5.1	6.1	5.8	7.1	9.9	7.9	8.1	9.0		
4 yrs or more high educ.	8.2	5.1	9.8	7.0	6.3	7.9	5.9	9.7	6.7	6.0	5.3	4.7	6.4	5.4	6.9	4.1		

./...

Table 31 (cont'd)

LEVEL OF EDUCATIONAL QUALIFICATION OF UNEMPLOYED YOUNG PEOPLE

Percentage

	1970		1975		1976		1977		1978		1979		1980		1981	
	M	F	M	F	M	F	M	F	M	F	M	F	M	F	M	F
UNITED STATES - Percentage of unemployed and out-of-labour-force among secondary school leavers with or without high school diploma (3)																
Unemployed																
Dipl. High School	11.3	16.2	17.5	15.1	15.3	15.0	13.0	13.8	10.2	13.8	12.9	15.6	17.1	15.1	16.9	19.0
No diploma	22.4	7.6	28.3	14.5	21.9	16.1	20.0	15.9	19.2	18.3	15.0	19.4	22.2	17.5	21.5	24.6
Out of labour force																
Dipl. High School	12.6	31.2	8.5	27.4	8.7	23.2	9.2	19.1	8.2	18.7	8.0	17.8	10.3	19.9	13.1	19.0
No diploma	21.1	60.5	17.6	56.6	22.4	55.9	19.0	45.8	19.8	46.7	21.0	46.8	27.3	47.4	25.9	47.4
FRANCE - Unemployment rate at exit from education system (apprentices included in labour force)			(1973)													
No diplôma			8	13			19	38			21	51				
Dipl. 1st cycle sec.			5	15			19	38			28	45				
" short vocational			6	10			17	26			14	45				
" 2nd cycle sec.			9	10			15	22			27	37				
" higher short (NU)			3	4			7	9			9	11				
" higher long (U)			10	12			14	14			11	19				
Total			7	12			17	24			19	38				
JAPAN - Proportion of young people without employment (4) on exit from education system																
1st cycle sec.	27.3		48.5		18.2		18.2	20.7	18.7	22.1	19.0	23.5	17.6	24.0	16.9	22.8
2nd " "	23.9		33.0		19.0		24.6	11.7	20.6	10.7	18.7	9.9	16.4	9.3	14.1	8.9
Technical colleges	0.9		4.5		6.5		5.8	2.5	4.5	5.2	3.4	4.2	2.5	4.9	1.9	6.4
Junior College	21.4		18.5		22.0		9.6	20.4	12.0	21.7	10.0	20.9	10.3	17.0	9.7	15.4
University 1st degree	8.7		10.4		12.3		7.9	23.8	8.1	24.3	7.9	23.6	6.7	20.5	6.8	19.9
" higher degree	15.1		14.5		20.1		15.3	38.0	15.2	37.8	13.8	38.5	13.2	37.2	13.4	34.5
UNITED KINGDOM - Percentage of new university graduates (5) assumed to be unemployed																
1st degree	9.2	7.4	6.1	6.1	5.8	5.4	4.7	4.7	4.8	5.0	8.8	7.8				
Higher degree	1.7	4.2	1.7	3.1	1.8	3.4	1.2	2.2	1.4	2.4	1.7	3.2				
GREAT BRITAIN - Educational qualifications of new entrants to the Youth Opportunities Programme (6) for young unemployed aged 16-18 years																
No qualification									49		45		35			
CSE (below grade 1)									25		30		35			
Other qualifications									26		25		30			
Total (000) = 100									162.0		216.0		360.0			

(1) Persons having completed a few years of secondary education or the total of it, but with no higher education.
(2) Young people leaving high school before end of studies.
(3) Situation in October of a given year of high school graduates and drop-outs of the preceding year. Not including persons simultaneously in education and the labour force.
(4) Unemployed and out of labour force.
(5) Whose destination is known.
(6) Training and work experience scheme.

Table 32

GROWTH RATE OF PUPIL AND TEACHER NUMBERS IN PRIMARY AND SECONDARY EDUCATION

School year beginning in :

	1965	1965-70	1970-75	1975-76	1976-77	1977-78	1978-79	1979-80	1975-LY	1980-81
	(000)									
GERMANY										
Primary and upper primary										
Pupils	5564.7	2.7	0.2	-2.3	-4.1	-4.9	-6.4	-5.8	-4.4	
Teachers	168.1	3.7	3.0	1.7	-0.6	-0.5	-0.5		0.0	
Middle (Realschulen)										
Pupils	570.9	8.6	6.4	5.8	5.4	2.6	1.1	-1.0	3.7	
Teachers	24.3	9.2	6.5	5.2	6.2	4.1	2.3		4.4	
Gymnasium 1st and 2nd cycle second.										
Pupils	957.9	7.6	6.2	2.7	3.0	2.1	3.8	1.9	2.9	
Teachers	53.8	7.5	5.0	4.7	5.2	4.0	4.6		4.6	
Vocational education										
Pupils	2146.4	0.6	1.6	-1.0	2.9	6.5	5.3		3.4	
Teachers	44.2	2.8	4.9	2.8	4.2	5.4	4.8		4.3	
AUSTRALIA	(1973)		(1973-75)		(1975-77)		(1977-79)			
Primary										
Pupils	1811.0		0.1		1.5		0.0	0.0	0.2	-0.7
Teachers	70.1		5.7		4.7		2.8	0.7	2.1	0.1
Second. 1st and 2nd cycl.										
Pupils	1042.4		2.8		0.9		-0.9	-0.2	0.3	1.4
Teachers	65.2		7.0		4.8		2.1	1.0	2.3	1.2
AUSTRIA	(1970)		(1970-74)		(1974-77)		(1977-79)			
Primary										
Pupils	595.9		-3.2		3.8		-4.6		-4.2	
Teachers	24.8		0.5		4.0		-3.7		0.1	
Upper primary										
Pupils	308.9		6.3		-2.6		-3.2		-2.9	
Teachers	16.0		8.9		8.7		2.7		5.7	
Secondary 1st and 2nd cycles										
Pupils	141.2		4.5		1.0		2.6		1.8	
Teachers	9.5		5.1		4.8		5.0		4.9	
CANADA										
Primary (Kindergarten to 8th year)										
Pupils	3909.5	1.3	-1.4	-2.1	-2.5	-3.0	-2.3	-1.0	-0.2	-1.8
Teachers	147.5	3.4	0.8	1.6	-0.2	-2.1	-1.2	-1.2	0.7	-0.4
Secondary (9th and over)										
Pupils	1250.0	5.9	0.5	0.1	-0.4	-0.3	-1.4	-2.5	-4.0	-1.4
Teachers	61.6	9.5	0.2	1.0	0.0	-1.0	-1.3	-0.7	-0.2	-0.4
DENMARK			(1970-76)				(1977-79)			
Basic school										
Pupils	758.5	-1.4	1.2		-0.8	-1.8			-1.2	
Teachers	36.3	3.5	4.7		2.8		4.2		3.5	

./...

Table 32 (cont'd)

GROWTH RATE OF PUPIL AND TEACHER NUMBERS IN PRIMARY AND SECONDARY EDUCATION

School year beginning in :

	1965	1965-70	1970-75	1975-76	1976-77	1977-78	1978-79	1979-80	1975-LY	1980-81
	(000)									
SPAIN										
Pre-primary and primary										
Pupils	3942.9	3.8	6.1	1.7	1.3	1.2	1.5	1.4	1.4	
Teachers	113.5	5.0	9.0	0.6	3.0	2.6	1.0	1.8	1.8	
Secondary										
Pupils	1006.2	11.0	-7.8	7.0	6.8	13.2	7.9	8.1	5.6	
Teachers	43.9	12.4	-0.6	0.1	4.0	13.3	7.9	7.2	6.5	
UNITED STATES										
Primary, (1st-8th year)										
Pupils	35463.0	0.7	-1.4	-1.0	-2.1	-3.2	-1.5	-0.7	-1.7	
Teachers	1112.0	2.8	1.1	-0.2	1.9	0	0	-0.9	0.2	
Secondary										
Pupils	13010.1	2.4	1.3	0.3	-0.4	0	-3.1	-2.5	-1.1	
Teachers	822.0	4.1	1.8	0.5	0.7	-0.9	-1.9	-0.5	-0.4	
FRANCE	(1970)									
Primary										
Pupils	4799.1		-0.8	-0.7	-0.4	-0.3	-0.9		-0.2	
Teachers	187.0		0.0	1.8	0.3	1.5	1.4		1.2	
1st cycle secondary										
Pupils	2910.2		1.7	0.9	-0.8	-0.6	-0.4		-0.2	
Teachers	78.1		7.2	5.8	10.7	2.8	2.0		5.3	
2nd cycle secondary long										
Pupils	848.4		2.5	3.7	2.7	6.6	1.1		3.5	
Teachers	59.2		2.2	-6.4	-4.7	0.5	0.8		-2.5	
Voc. education short										
Pupils	645.9		2.9	0.7	0.5	1.0	0.0		0.5	
Teachers	23.1		6.1	5.5	1.5	1.8	5.6		3.6	
GREECE										
Primary										
Pupils	975.9	-1.3	0.5	0.2	-0.5	-1.2			-0.5	
Teachers	27.4	1.4	1.1	5.5	6.1	2.9			4.8	
Secondary, 1st and 2nd cycles										
Pupils	374.6	3.2	4.5	2.9	3.0	0.9			2.3	
Teachers	11.2	2.9	7.7	16.6	11.5	10.7			12.9	
ITALY										
Primary										
Pupils	4520.5	1.4	0.0	-2.1	-1.8				-2.0	
Teachers	202.9	1.9	3.3	3.9	0.1				2.0	
Middle										
Pupils	1801.2	3.8	5.1	3.3	2.4				2.9	
Teachers	131.1	8.5	4.8	-0.8	3.8				1.5	
Secondary, 2nd cycle.										
Pupils	828.7	5.3	14.3	4.7	3.3				4.0	
Teachers	105.2	7.1	6.1	8.3	4.3				6.3	

./...

Table 32 (cont'd)

GROWTH RATE OF PUPIL AND TEACHER NUMBERS IN PRIMARY AND SECONDARY EDUCATION

School year beginning in :

	1965	1965-70	1970-75	1975-76	1976-77	1977-78	1978-79	1979-80	1975-LY	1980-81
	(000)									
JAPAN										
Primary										
Pupils	9775.5	-0.6	1.8	2.4	2.0	3.0	4.3	1.7	2.7	
Teachers	345.1	1.3	2.5	2.2	2.1	2.9	3.1	1.8	2.4	
Secondary, 1st cycle										
Pupils	5966.6	-4.5	0.2	1.5	3.0	1.4	1.6	2.6	2.0	
Teachers	237.7	1.1	0.9	1.2	2.3	1.9	-0.6	2.1	1.4	
Secondary, 2nd cycle.										
Pupils	5065.6	-3.5	0-5	1.2	-0.1	0.8	1.6	3.1	1.3	
Teachers	193.6	0.9	1.9	1.7	1.7	1.4	1.6	2.5	1.8	
NETHERLANDS	(1971)		(1971-74)	(1974-76)						
Primary										
Pupils	1464.4		-0.4	-0.1	-0.9	-1.5	-2.4	-3.4	-1.7	
Teachers	50.2		2.3	1.5	2.5	0.0	1.4	-1.1	0.9	
Secondary, 1st and 2nd cyc										
Pupils	1231.8		1.3	4.1	0.3	2.3	6.0		3.2	
Teachers	38.9		4.2	5.0	3.3	2.5	0.9		2.9	
UNITED KINGDOM	(1967)	(1967-70)								
Primary										
Pupils	5654.3	2.8	0.4	-1.6	-2.5	-6.4			-3.5	
Teachers	195.4	3.8	2.8	-1.2	-1.8	-0.3			-1.1	
Secondary										
Pupils	3580.1	3.0	4.3	2.4	1.1	-4.0			-0.2	
Teachers	191.7	3.0	5.5	2.8	1.6	1.6			2.0	
SWEDEN										
Basic school, special and 2nd cycle secondary					(1975-77)					
Pupils	958.9	4.3	1.0		0.7				0.7	
Teachers	85.0	2.6	3.2		6.3				6.3	
YUGOSLAVIA		(1965-71)	(1971-75)							
Primary										
Pupils	2945.5	-0.7	0.2	-0.2	-0.7	0.4	-0.6		-0.3	
Teachers	102.1	2.9	1.9	0.4	0.0	-0.2	-0.8		-0.1	
Secondary, 1st and 2nd cyc										
Pupils	647.8	2.9	3.9	5.9	2.2	2.9	6.7		4.4	
Teachers	28.3	8.2	3.0	7.8	2.2	3.6	4.3		4.5	

LY : Last year available.

Table 33

TRENDS IN THE PERCENTAGE OF GDP ALLOCATED TO PUBLIC EDUCATIONAL EXPENDITURE (1)

Percentage

	1965	1970	1975	1976	1977	1978	1979	1980
GERMANY	3.0(2)	3.7	5.1	4.8	4.7	4.7	4.6	
AUSTRALIA	3.5	3.5	6.2	6.2	6.4	6.1	5.9	
AUSTRIA	3.6	4.6	5.7	5.7	5.5	5.7	5.5	5.5
CANADA	5.3	8.1	7.2	7.3	7.6	7.3	7.0	7.0
DENMARK	5.8	6.9	7.8		6.6	6.1	6.1	
SPAIN		1.8	1.8	2.0	2.1	2.3	2.7	2.6
UNITED STATES	5.3	6.5	6.5	6.5	6.3	6.6	6.4	
FINLAND						6.3	5.6	5.6
FRANCE	3.4	3.7	3.1		3.5		3.7	
GREECE		2.1	1.9	1.8	2.1	2.4		
ITALY	4.7	4.0	4.5	4.7		4.6	5.1	
JAPAN	4.1	3.8	5.3	5.3	5.4	5.7	5.8	5.9
NETHERLANDS	5.7	6.7	8.2	8.0	8.0	8.1	8.1	
UNITED KINGDOM	5.1	5.2	6.3	6.1	5.6	5.4	5.5	
SWEDEN	5.9	7.7	7.1	7.4	8.3	8.7	9.0	9.1
YUGOSLAVIA	4.0	4.6	5.0	5.1	5.2	5.5	5.3	

(1) Total public educational expenditure (including subsidies to private education)

(2) 1967.

Table 34

ANNUAL GROWTH RATE OF EXPENDITURE PER PUPIL/STUDENT IN DIFFERENT LEVELS OF EDUCATION AND, FOR THE LAST YEAR AVAILABLE, COMPARISON WITH EXPENDITURE PER PRIMARY PUPIL (=100)

Percentage

	1965-70	1970-75	1975-76	1976-77	1977-78	1978-79	1979-80	1975 LY	In relation to primary
GERMANY									
Primary/upper primary	5.0	12.2	3.8	5.7	-1.9	12.9	15.6	7.0	100
Middle (Realschulen)	5.4	11.7	-3.7	0.4	5.1	6.1	11.5	3.8	91
Gym. 1st and 2nd cycl.sec.	5.1	6.7	1.4	1.7	5.6	3.7	9.2	4.3	135
Sec. techn. and voc.	8.2	12.3	8.2	3.8	6.3	5.4	10.3	6.8	74
Higher	5.2	3.8	-3.0	-2.2	2.9	4.1		0.3	437
CANADA (1)									
Elementary/secondary	13.5	12.5	23.9	19.4	7.9	12.8	12.7	15.3	100
Non-univers.	11.6	12.0	12.8	10.5	13.9	6.1	9.3	10.5	206
University	13.3	8.2	11.0	13.1	10.0	8.2	9.8	10.3	349
DENMARK									
Pre-primary			-8.1	8.8					45
1st year basic school			17.2	10.7					100
5th " " "			6.4	12.0					135
9th " " "			7.3	8.5					154
Gymnase 1st year			5.3	3.8					199
3rd year			-2.2	3.4					233
Vocational training basic year									
Metal working industries			-3.8	3.6					313
Clerical workers			2.1	-13.8					151
Universities									
Social sciences			-5.2	8.7					120
Humanities			-5.4	11.3					142
Natural sciences			-3.3	6.0					554
Technology			6.5	-4.0					872
Primary teacher training			3.5	8.2					270
SPAIN		(1971-75)				(1975-79)			
Pre-primary									81
Primairy, 1st cycle sec.		20.5				23.5		23.5	100
2nd cyc. sec. general		31.0				9.8		9.8	172
2nd cyc. sec. vocational									242
UNITED STATES									
Elementary et secondaire(2)		10.8	10.2	8.9	11.3	10.9	12.6	10.8	100
Higher, public (3)		6.4	1.6	12.3	6.5	11.8	10.0	8.4	160
" private (3)		7.0	4.5	9.5	6.1	8.7	11.3	8.0	302
FRANCE									
Pre-primary				22.8	8.1				71
Primary				17.8	7.2				100
Secondary, 1st cycle				14.9	6.3				229
" 2nd " long				13.2	2.6				376
" 2nd " short				13.2	3.6				331
Post baccalaureat (4)				12.5	-0.3				460
Special primary				6.2	10.3				257
" secondary				11.7	-1.7				349

./...

Table 34 (cont'd)

ANNUAL GROWTH RATE OF EXPENDITURE PER PUPIL/STUDENT IN DIFFERENT LEVELS OF EDUCATION AND, FOR THE LAST YEAR AVAILABLE, COMPARISON WITH EXPENDITURE PER PRIMARY PUPIL (=100)

Percentage

	1965-70	1970-75	1975-76	1976-77	1977-78	1978-79	1979-80	1975 LY	In relation to primary
JAPAN									
Pre-primary	20.2	20.9	3.4	11.7	10.7	6.8	9.0	8.3	64
Primary	17.5	21.4	8.0	11.0	9.7	3.3	5.7	7.5	100
Secondary, 1st cycle	19.1	23.1	7.9	8.7	10.6	8.8	5.9	8.4	122
" 2nd "	18.6	21.3	8.4	9.9	10.8	6.0	4.6	8.0	138
Higher	6.9	15.8	9.8	11.9	9.4	8.4	7.0	9.3	639
Special	18.1	25.7	10.4	15.8	21.2	-11.7	9.9	9.1	927
NETHERLANDS	(1966-70)								
Pre-primary	9.4	20.2	14.0	15.0	15.8	10.9		14.9	93
Primary	10.3	15.6	11.9	9.9	8.9	8.3		10.2	100
Secondary general	10.5	9.8	10.4	4.0	6.9	10.3		7.1	161
Vocational/technical	7.6	11.6	11.1	8.5	10.7			10.1	244
Teacher training	15.9	10.2	16.4	6.8	14.4	13.3		2.1	171
University	5.5	14.3	5.9	-0.6	1.0	4.8		3.0	972
of which Social sciences/humanities		17.1	4.8	1.4	2.7			3.0	
Pure science/technology		14.5	7.6	1.1	0.4			3.0	
Special	10.6	15.7	13.7	12.1	9.3	12.0		11.7	317
ENGLAND AND WALES (5)	(1968-73)	(1973-75)			P				
Primary	3.1	5.4	2.3	1.4	4.5			2.7	100
Secondary, 1st cycle (6)	3.4	0.7	0.0	0.4	2.6			1.0	138
" 2nd " (7)	3.0	1.7	0.1	-3.5	1.5			-0.7	240
Further education (8)									
Non-advanced level	-1.8	0.9	0.0	4.3	-3.3			0.3	316
Advanced level	-1.8	0.8	0.0	4.4	-3.2			0.4	492
Polytechnics									
Non-advanced level		-0.6	-10.7	-4.7	-0.7			-5.4	384
Advanced level		-0.7	-10.8	-4.3	-0.9			-5.3	595
Teacher training	0.3	10.0							
Universities (9)	-1.9	-0.5	-1.8	-0.9	-2.8			-1.8	696
Special	3.1	8.0	5.4	1.9	-4.2			1.0	472
Adult	0.5	5.7	-6.2	-2.2	4.5			-1.4	62
SWEDEN		(1970-74)	(1974-76)						
Basic school	13.3	5.9	34.2						100
2nd cycle secondary	23.0	3.5	17.5						119
Popular secondary school	9.8	7.2	22.3						121
Pre-primary teach. train.	14.6	6.2	14.0						97
Special		-1.5	31.2						652

./...

Table 34 (cont'd)

Percentage

LY : Last year available.

(1) Operating expenditure only.
(2) Dollars adjusted to 1977-78 purchasing power.
(3) Dollars at constant prices 1976-77.
(4) Education provided in lycées.
(5) At 1979 prices.
(6) Pupils of compulsory school age.
(7) Pupils over compulsory school age.
(8) Without polytechnics.
(9) Great-Britain.

OECD SALES AGENTS
DÉPOSITAIRES DES PUBLICATIONS DE L'OCDE

ARGENTINA – ARGENTINE
Carlos Hirsch S.R.L., Florida 165, 4° Piso (Galería Guemes)
1333 BUENOS AIRES, Tel. 33.1787.2391 y 30.7122

AUSTRALIA – AUSTRALIE
Australia and New Zealand Book Company Pty, Ltd.,
10 Aquatic Drive, Frenchs Forest, N.S.W. 2086
P.O. Box 459, BROOKVALE, N.S.W. 2100. Tel. (02) 452.44.11

AUSTRIA – AUTRICHE
OECD Publications and Information Center
4 Simrockstrasse 5300 Bonn (Germany). Tel. (0228) 21.60.45
Local Agent/Agent local :
Gerold and Co., Graben 31, WIEN 1. Tel. 52.22.35

BELGIUM – BELGIQUE
Jean De Lannoy, Service Publications OCDE
avenue du Roi 202, B-1060 BRUXELLES. Tel. 02/538.51.69

BRAZIL – BRÉSIL
Mestre Jou S.A., Rua Guaipa 518,
Caixa Postal 24090, 05089 SAO PAULO 10. Tel. 261.1920
Rua Senador Dantas 19 s/205-6, RIO DE JANEIRO GB.
Tel. 232.07.32

CANADA
Renouf Publishing Company Limited,
Central Distribution Centre,
61 Sparks Street (Mall),
P.O.B. 1008 - Station B,
OTTAWA, Ont. KIP 5R1.
Tel. (613)238.8985-6
Toll Free: 1-800.267.4164
2182 ouest, rue Ste-Catherine,
MONTRÉAL, Qué. H3H 1M7. Tel. (514)937.3519

DENMARK – DANEMARK
Munksgaard Export and Subscription Service
35, Nørre Søgade
DK 1370 KØBENHAVN K. Tel. +45.1.12.85.70

FINLAND – FINLANDE
Akateeminen Kirjakauppa
Keskuskatu 1, 00100 HELSINKI 10. Tel. 65.11.22

FRANCE
Bureau des Publications de l'OCDE,
2 rue André-Pascal, 75775 PARIS CEDEX 16. Tel. (1) 524.81.67
Principal correspondant :
13602 AIX-EN-PROVENCE : Librairie de l'Université.
Tel. 26.18.08

GERMANY – ALLEMAGNE
OECD Publications and Information Center
4 Simrockstrasse 5300 BONN Tel. (0228) 21.60.45

GREECE – GRÈCE
Librairie Kauffmann, 28 rue du Stade,
ATHÈNES 132. Tel. 322.21.60

HONG-KONG
Government Information Services,
Publications/Sales Section, Baskerville House,
2nd Floor, 22 Ice House Street

ICELAND – ISLANDE
Snaebjörn Jönsson and Co., h.f.,
Hafnarstraeti 4 and 9, P.O.B. 1131, REYKJAVIK.
Tel. 13133/14281/11936

INDIA – INDE
Oxford Book and Stationery Co. :
NEW DELHI-1, Scindia House. Tel. 45896
CALCUTTA 700016, 17 Park Street. Tel. 240832

INDONESIA – INDONÉSIE
PDIN-LIPI, P.O. Box 3065/JKT., JAKARTA, Tel. 583467

IRELAND – IRLANDE
TDC Publishers – Library Suppliers
12 North Frederick Street, DUBLIN 1 Tel. 744835-749677

ITALY – ITALIE
Libreria Commissionaria Sansoni :
Via Lamarmora 45, 50121 FIRENZE. Tel. 579751/584468
Via Bartolini 29, 20155 MILANO. Tel. 365083
Sub-depositari :
Ugo Tassi
Via A. Farnese 28, 00192 ROMA. Tel. 310590
Editrice e Libreria Herder,
Piazza Montecitorio 120, 00186 ROMA. Tel. 6794628
Costantino Ercolano, Via Generale Orsini 46, 80132 NAPOLI. Tel. 405210
Libreria Hoepli, Via Hoepli 5, 20121 MILANO. Tel. 865446
Libreria Scientifica, Dott. Lucio de Biasio "Aeiou"
Via Meravigli 16, 20123 MILANO Tel. 807679
Libreria Zanichelli
Piazza Galvani 1/A, 40124 Bologna Tel. 237389
Libreria Lattes, Via Garibaldi 3, 10122 TORINO. Tel. 519274
La diffusione delle edizioni OCSE è inoltre assicurata dalle migliori librerie nelle città più importanti.

JAPAN – JAPON
OECD Publications and Information Center,
Landic Akasaka Bldg., 2-3-4 Akasaka,
Minato-ku, TOKYO 107 Tel. 586.2016

KOREA – CORÉE
Pan Korea Book Corporation,
P.O. Box n° 101 Kwangwhamun, SÉOUL. Tel. 72.7369

LEBANON – LIBAN
Documenta Scientifica/Redico,
Edison Building, Bliss Street, P.O. Box 5641, BEIRUT.
Tel. 354429 – 344425

MALAYSIA – MALAISIE
University of Malaya Co-operative Bookshop Ltd.
P.O. Box 1127, Jalan Pantai Baru
KUALA LUMPUR. Tel. 51425, 54058, 54361

THE NETHERLANDS – PAYS-BAS
Staatsuitgeverij, Verzendboekhandel,
Chr. Plantijnstraat 1 Postbus 20014
2500 EA S-GRAVENHAGE. Tel. nr. 070.789911
Voor bestellingen: Tel. 070.789208

NEW ZEALAND – NOUVELLE-ZÉLANDE
Publications Section,
Government Printing Office Bookshops:
AUCKLAND: Retail Bookshop: 25 Rutland Street,
Mail Orders: 85 Beach Road, Private Bag C.P.O.
HAMILTON: Retail: Ward Street,
Mail Orders, P.O. Box 857
WELLINGTON: Retail: Mulgrave Street (Head Office),
Cubacade World Trade Centre
Mail Orders: Private Bag
CHRISTCHURCH: Retail: 159 Hereford Street,
Mail Orders: Private Bag
DUNEDIN: Retail: Princes Street
Mail Order: P.O. Box 1104

NORWAY – NORVÈGE
J.G. TANUM A/S
P.O. Box 1177 Sentrum OSLO 1. Tel. (02) 80.12.60

PAKISTAN
Mirza Book Agency, 65 Shahrah Quaid-E-Azam, LAHORE 3.
Tel. 66839

PORTUGAL
Livraria Portugal, Rua do Carmo 70-74,
1117 LISBOA CODEX. Tel. 360582/3

SINGAPORE – SINGAPOUR
Information Publications Pte Ltd,
Pei-Fu Industrial Building,
24 New Industrial Road N° 02-06
SINGAPORE 1953, Tel. 2831786, 2831798

SPAIN – ESPAGNE
Mundi-Prensa Libros, S.A.
Castelló 37, Apartado 1223, MADRID-1. Tel. 275.46.55
Libreria Bosch, Ronda Universidad 11, BARCELONA 7.
Tel. 317.53.08, 317.53.58

SWEDEN – SUÈDE
AB CE Fritzes Kungl Hovbokhandel,
Box 16 356, S 103 27 STH, Regeringsgatan 12,
DS STOCKHOLM. Tel. 08/23.89.00
Subscription Agency/Abonnements:
Wennergren-Williams AB,
Box 13004, S104 25 STOCKHOLM.
Tel. 08/54.12.00

SWITZERLAND – SUISSE
OECD Publications and Information Center
4 Simrockstrasse 5300 BONN (Germany). Tel. (0228) 21.60.45
Local Agents/Agents locaux
Librairie Payot, 6 rue Grenus, 1211 GENÈVE 11. Tel. 022.31.89.50

TAIWAN – FORMOSE
Good Faith Worldwide Int'l Co., Ltd.
9th floor, No. 118, Sec. 2,
Chung Hsiao E. Road
TAIPEI. Tel. 391.7396/391.7397

THAILAND – THAILANDE
Suksit Siam Co., Ltd., 1715 Rama IV Rd,
Samyan, BANGKOK 5. Tel. 2511630

TURKEY – TURQUIE
Kültur Yayinlari Is-Türk Ltd. Sti.
Atatürk Bulvari No : 191/Kat. 21
Kavaklidere/ANKARA. Tel. 17 02 66
Dolmabahce Cad. No : 29
BESIKTAS/ISTANBUL. Tel. 60 71 88

UNITED KINGDOM – ROYAUME-UNI
H.M. Stationery Office,
P.O.B. 276, LONDON SW8 5DT.
(postal orders only)
Telephone orders: (01) 622.3316, or
49 High Holborn, LONDON WC1V 6 HB (personal callers)
Branches at: EDINBURGH, BIRMINGHAM, BRISTOL,
MANCHESTER, BELFAST.

UNITED STATES OF AMERICA – ÉTATS-UNIS
OECD Publications and Information Center, Suite 1207,
1750 Pennsylvania Ave., N.W. WASHINGTON, D.C.20006 – 4582
Tel. (202) 724.1857

VENEZUELA
Libreria del Este, Avda. F. Miranda 52, Edificio Galipan,
CARACAS 106. Tel. 32.23.01/33.26.04/31.58.38

YUGOSLAVIA – YOUGOSLAVIE
Jugoslovenska Knjiga, Knez Mihajlova 2, P.O.B. 36, BEOGRAD.
Tel. 621.992

Les commandes provenant de pays où l'OCDE n'a pas encore désigné de dépositaire peuvent être adressées à :
OCDE, Bureau des Publications, 2, rue André-Pascal, 75775 PARIS CEDEX 16.

Orders and inquiries from countries where sales agents have not yet been appointed may be sent to:
OECD, Publications Office, 2, rue André-Pascal, 75775 PARIS CEDEX 16.

68045-10-1984

OECD PUBLICATIONS, 2, rue André-Pascal, 75775 PARIS CEDEX 16 - No. 43085 1984
PRINTED IN FRANCE
(91 84 02 1) ISBN 92-64-12630-9